HAMLET'S CHOICE

HAMLET'S CHOICE

Religion and Resistance in Shakespeare's Revenge Tragedies

PETER LAKE

YALE UNIVERSITY PRESS
NEW HAVEN AND LONDON

Published with assistance from the foundation established in memory of Oliver Baty Cunningham of the Class of 1917, Yale College.

For information about this and other Yale University Press publications, please contact:
U.S. Office: sales.press@yale.edu   yalebooks.com
Europe Office: sales@yaleup.co.uk   yalebooks.co.uk

Set in Fournier MT by IDSUK (DataConnection) Ltd
Printed in Great Britain by Gomer Press Ltd, Llandysul, Ceredigion, Wales

Library of Congress Control Number: 2020935711

ISBN 978-0-300-24781-7

A catalogue record for this book is available from the British Library.

10 9 8 7 6 5 4 3 2 1

Contents

Plates

1. *Henry III of France Murdered by Jacques Clement*, by Frans Hogenberg (active 1568–88).
2. *An Allegory of the Tudor Succession: The Family of Henry VIII*, unknown artist, *c.* 1590. Yale Center for British Art, Paul Mellon Collection.
3. *Elizabeth I*, by Marcus Gheeraerts the Younger, *c.* 1595. Photo 12 / Alamy.
4. *The Funeral Procession of Queen Elizabeth I to Westminster*, early seventeenth century. © British Library Board. All Rights Reserved / Bridgeman Images.
5. *King James Riding to Parliament with Three Noblemen* (f. 149v), from the friendship album of Michael van Meer, *c.* 1614–15. © The University of Edinburgh / CC BY-NC-ND 4.0.
6. The title page of William Shakespeare, *The Most Lamentable Romaine Tragedie of Titus Andronicus* (London: [Iohn Danter], 1594). Call #: STC 22328. Used by permission of the Folger Shakespeare Library.
7. The quarto title page for Q2 of *Titus Andronicus* (London: [I.R.], 1600).
8. Henry Peacham's illustration of lines from *Titus Andronicus* (1595).
9. Plate 33 from *Ecclesiæ anglicanæ trophæa* (ex officina Bartholomæi Grassi, 1584), by Niccolò Circignani (Il Pomarancio), sixteenth century.
10. Page 83 of Richard Verstegan, *Theatrum crudelitatum haereticorum nostri temporis* (1592).
11. Page 85 of Richard Verstegan, *Theatrum crudelitatum haereticorum nostri temporis* (1588). University of Glasgow Library / CC BY-NC-SA 2.0.
12. Robert Southwell. © National Portrait Gallery, London.
13. The title page of the first quarto of William Shakespeare, *Hamlet* (London: [N.L. and John Trundell], 1603).

14. 'Hamlet, Horatio, Marcellus and the Ghost (Shakespeare, Hamlet, Act 1, Scene 4)', by Robert Thew, from Boydell's *Illustrations of the Dramatic Works of Shakespeare* (first published 1796; reissued 1852).

15. The title page of Robert Burton, *The Anatomy of Melancholy* (Oxford: Henry Cripps, 1628).

16. *Young Man among Roses*, by Nicholas Hilliard, *c.* 1587. © Victoria and Albert Museum, London.

17. Portrait of a young man standing under a tree, probably Sir Robert Sidney, possibly Sir Thomas Knollys, *c.* 1584–88.

18. Page 25 of *Ecclesiæ anglicanæ trophæa* (ex officina Bartholomæi Grassi, 1584), by Niccolò Circignani (Il Pomarancio), sixteenth century.

Acknowledgements

In many ways I have to thank the same cast of characters here as I did in *How Shakespeare Put Politics on the Stage*. I first wrote up the material that comprises this book in the early 2000s, thinking about this topic even while working on that other book. Over time, it became clear that what I was in fact producing was a comparative study of Shakespeare's two revenge tragedies, organized around their relation to resistance and religion. In 2005–06, I remember giving the *Hamlet* material to Bill Bullman, Rupa Mishra and some other Princeton graduate students, when they still felt obliged to read things that I suggested to them (and also when they had much better things to be doing). I should also thank Nick Moskovachis, whom I first met shortly after we both arrived at Princeton – he as a graduate student and I as a faculty member. Nick was always very clear that historians ought to read literary texts, and it was at his suggestion – I might even say insistence – that I first read *Titus* with real attention. I delivered a preliminary version of the *Titus* material at the early modern English history seminar at the Huntington Library, and then slightly later at Oxford. I also inflicted a paper on *Hamlet* on the Tudor and Stuart seminar at the Institute of Historical Research.

When you are working at the edge of your competence (as I was during the writing of much of this book), other people's responses provide a very necessary reality check, and I should like to thank the participants in those seminars for their forbearance and their comments, all of which were extremely useful. In particular, I should like to thank Heather James and Rebecca Lemon of the University of Southern California, who were both very kind about this material during my period at the Huntington. They read stuff, and Heather commented in detail on my take on texts that she knew – and knows – infinitely better than I do. I should also thank Roy Ritchie and his wife Louise for making my time at the Huntington as enjoyable and fruitful as it was. This book is something like a final return on my time there.

ACKNOWLEDGEMENTS

Among historians, I should like to thank many of the usual suspects – Ann Hughes, Richard Cust, Tom Cogswell, Ken Fincham, Alex Gajda, Paul Hammer – all of whom have listened to me on this topic and made any number of sensible remarks, some of which I have even managed to act upon.

At Vanderbilt University, my colleagues and friends in history (particularly Joel Harrington, Helmut Smith and Jim Epstein) and in English (particularly Lynn Enterline, Bridget Orr and Jonathan Lamb) have all helped to make Vanderbilt a wonderful place to work and write. I should also thank Bill Jordan for doing the same at Princeton. Nick Zeppos, chancellor emeritus at Vanderbilt, helped to recruit me and has done a great deal to make my time there both productive and pleasurable. Michael Neill was a wonderfully tactful and patient editor. I found my piece for his *Oxford Handbook of Shakespearean Tragedy* really hard to write, and my procrastination and incompetence must at times have made me the contributor from hell. But, in fact, what seemed at the time to be a commitment I just should not have taken on, became the thing that finally gave what follows whatever claims to coherence and shape it currently possesses, and Michael's forbearance and advice had a great deal to do with that.

I also owe a particular debt to the two anonymous readers of this book – in particular to reader 2 – whose comments, late in the day, proved absolutely invaluable. Shakespeare world is a big place. It contains many mansions, the contents of which are constantly shifting. Look away and you have missed something important. Superficial tourism is not to be encouraged, and casual visitors are not always welcome. I have made a good-faith effort to familiarize myself with the contents of that world: an effort that I am keenly aware cannot but remain inadequate. This effort would have been even less successful than it was, had at least some of the denizens of that world not been prepared to offer me guidance as I tried to navigate my way around it. Such generosity cannot be taken for granted and I am very grateful.

At Yale, I owe a great debt to Robert Baldock, and latterly to Heather McCallum. My books for Yale have not been the most conventional pieces of academic writing, and I am intensely grateful that a major academic press has been prepared to commit the necessary time and resources to getting them into print. Robert's patience and advice have been crucial throughout.

Finally, I should like to thank my wife Sandy Solomon, who, despite the prose, always thought there was something here. Her encouragement – and at times insistence – has kept me going. If nothing else, she likes going to plays, which may be some compensation for having had to live so long both with me and with my obsessions.

Introduction

In *How Shakespeare Put Politics on the Stage*, I attempted to use the history play, and in particular Shakespeare's history plays, to think about the politics and political culture, the ways in which the Elizabethans of the *fin de siècle* thought about politics. The governing idea there was that since we know that contemporaries used history to think about their current political circumstances, and sought continually to draw parallels between the politics of the past and the present in order to extract from the study of the past moral and prudential rules and apophthegms that could be applied to the interpretation of the present, the history play itself could be viewed as an attempt to do just that, for popular audiences in London and throughout the kingdom. The method was to read the plays against other polemical and historical texts of the day, as well as against each other and against the political and polemical moments in which the plays themselves were written and performed, and to which, I was arguing, they were in some sense addressed. The aim was historical and particularizing, not general and universalising. I was concerned with what attached the plays to their times, rather than with what, down the ages, has made them seem applicable to radically different times, places and concerns.

The contention of that book was not that this was the best – still less the only – way to analyse these plays. Indeed, I would be the first to admit that this was not even an adequate mode of analysis, if the plays' abiding qualities were to be fully understood. My claim was that the plays lent themselves to this mode of analysis, and that such an approach was likely to yield insights into the politics and political culture of the late-Elizabethan period, and perhaps into aspects of the plays themselves. In the process, I constructed a notional narrative not only of Shakespeare's dramatic, but also of his political development throughout the 1590s, as he continually returned to certain themes and concerns, examining them again and again from different angles and in different texts, in light of his own experience of the times, and indeed the work of other dramatists.

The aim was most definitely not to reconstruct what Shakespeare believed. Nonetheless, it was probably inevitable that some sort of story about how his attitude towards those central topics changed over time would emerge. And so it did, despite the fact that the production of such an account was not the main point of the book. Precisely because the only evidence we have for what Shakespeare believed is provided by his plays, and because his plays are so notoriously polyvalent – not merely allowing, but positively eliciting very different takes on the central issues around which they are so precisely organized – definitive answers to the question of what Shakespeare thought on any given subject are simply unavailable. Consequently, anybody who hangs his or her hat on a claim to have provided such answers is asking for trouble.

So, my purpose in writing a book about 'power and succession in the history plays' was to use them to see precisely those topics of power and succession being staged and discussed in a series of plays performed before 'popular' – that is to say, both ideologically and socially mixed – audiences throughout the 1590s. Here the central problematic was provided by a series of linked questions: the nature of monarchical legitimacy; how it could be lost, and, once lost, how it could be regained; and the capacity of individual political agents to control events and impose, or re-impose, 'order' on a political scene from which all moral and political legitimacy had been stripped, either by a contested succession, usurpation, dynastic civil war, or the dialectics of tyranny and resistance. Also at stake was the relation of the efforts of such human political agents both to 'the times' and to the workings of divine providence.

The result was a distinctly political take on these plays, which I tried to read in terms of what I took to be the dominant political concerns, the sometimes unspoken, but always present (indeed prevalent) anxieties of the day – anxieties prompted by the prospect of the queen's now looming death, with the succession still unsettled, and in the midst of a confessionally inflected war with the greatest (Catholic) power in Europe. As I said, that political reading was proffered not as the best (still less, the only) way to work out what these plays mean, but merely as a fairly obvious and thus unobjectionable way to use the plays for broader historical purposes. The pursuit of those purposes involved a certain amount of rudimentary literary analysis, and the book itself drew heavily, indeed at times shamelessly, on the existing corpus of literary criticism, mixing and matching insights and arguments culled from a broad range of methodologically distinct – indeed, in extreme cases, virtually mutually exclusive – schools of literary criticism. But the book itself was not a work of literary criticism. It was an attempt at historical analysis using literary means to achieve its largely historical ends.

INTRODUCTION

I was recently foolish enough to agree to give a talk to a room full of aspiring theatre directors. Asked what my stake in this subject was, I replied that I was interested in the 1590s. This statement, which seemed obvious to me, came as something of a shock to my audience, and (I fear) quite rightly confirmed them in their already evident suspicions that anything I had to say about the plays would be completely irrelevant to their resolutely presentist and (highly politicized) concerns. There was a certain irony in the fact that a version of the plays as determinedly political as mine merely served to render them even more irrelevant to a set of actual and aspirant directors, all determined to make political drama out of Shakespeare, or indeed anything else that came to hand. On the one hand, I took some solace from this rather unsatisfactory engagement with the here and now, since it confirmed me in the purity of my historicizing practices and purposes. On the other, the exchange reminded me of the extremely partial nature of my (historicizing, and purely political) enterprise. I already knew it, of course; but nothing could have been better calculated to remind me of how much that was central to the plays themselves and to their meaning for generations of theatrical producers and consumers was (quite deliberately) omitted from my book.

The present enterprise is an attempt to redress that balance a little. In the course of writing about Shakespeare's history plays, I considerably expanded the genre to include plays conventionally regarded as tragedies and/or Roman plays. I did so using the argument that *Julius Caesar, Hamlet* and *Troilus and Cressida* were all based on what contemporaries regarded as history, and were thus available for the same processes of application to current political thought and practice as the plays about English history. In the case of *Titus Andronicus*, I argued that that play represented a simulacrum of the history play so exact that it could have performed precisely the same functions for its first audiences as any 'genuine' history play.

In the process of working my way through those texts, I realized that in some of them – *Titus, Julius Caesar* and *Hamlet* – other things were going on: discussions of the relationship to Christianity of paganism and pagan classical culture; issues of confessional identity and religious conflict; and theological questions about the relation between divine providence and grace and human agency, not merely in shaping events, but in determining the fate in the next life of human agents, and in particular of politicians and princes. Here were questions of predestination, of election and reprobation, of conversion; and here was religious melancholy and despair being played out on the public stage.

Some of that material was relevant to the argument of *How Shakespeare Put Politics on the Stage*, but a good deal of it was not. Since that book was already too long, I excised much of that discussion. In so doing, I regretfully parted company with one of the organizing principles of that book – one that goes some way to explaining its otherwise rather extreme heft. That was to conduct the argument through the explication of whole plays, arranged in the chronological order in which they were written and first performed, insofar as that chronology could be reconstructed. But in the instances of *Titus* and *Hamlet*, I pushed the argument through thoroughly attenuated accounts of the plays – accounts tailored to the organizing themes of the whole, rather than to the demands of the plays in question. While I would stand by the analyses of the other plays discussed in that book, as attempts to address the texts as a whole, the same could not be said of the accounts of *Titus* and *Hamlet*.

However, as I came to think about that material, if not anew, then at least away from the overridingly political concerns of that book, it seemed to me that what we had in *Titus* and *Hamlet* was an on-going discussion of the nature of true religion and of its relation not only to politics, but also to soteriology. What was at stake in these plays, but particularly in *Hamlet*, was the salvation not merely of states, but of persons.

Not only that, but it seemed that the generic question – the claim that these plays were first and foremost revenge tragedies – retained at least some traction. This was not because these plays did not also operate as plays about history and therefore as commentaries upon (and even interventions in) contemporary politics. In this, they were just like the other history plays analysed in *How Shakespeare Put Politics on the Stage*. Rather it was because there were similarities and continuities between *Titus* and *Hamlet*, so that one could regard them as discussions of a common set of issues; indeed, one might even read the second play as an attempt to revisit (and rewrite) the first.

Beyond the fact that they are both conventionally regarded as 'revenge tragedies', the two plays have a good deal in common. Both are set in elective monarchies. Both chart the course of events after a seemingly successful exercise in regime change. In both, central protagonists who could – or, in a strictly hereditary monarchy, would – have been kings are confronted by dreadful deeds, the precise nature and perpetrators of which are not immediately apparent. In both, those protagonists go 'mad', and in both cases, the precise nature and meaning of their 'madness' are unclear. Seemingly genuinely distracted, their distraction also serves as a mask behind which they can find out what really happened, can identify and threaten the guilty parties, while they decide precisely what form their revenge should take. Both plays feature a play within a play (admittedly designed in different ways) to entrap one of the protagonists. Hamlet's production of *The Mousetrap* echoes Tamora's little production of the prelude to a revenge tragedy, featuring a personified version of Revenge. Both of these performances enabled Shakespeare to evoke other examples of the genre, other ways of going about it. One thinks here most obviously of *The Spanish Tragedy*, but also of various Senecan revenge plays, many of which had been readily available in translation and print since the early Elizabethan period.[1] Having conjured those various predecessors – in *Titus* through direct reference; in *Hamlet* in passages of virtual parody – Shakespeare then proceeded, particularly in *Hamlet*, to distinguish between his current efforts and those other, lesser versions.[2] Both of the plays within a play go off at half cock, and in so doing are designed to send (admittedly diametrically opposite) messages about the role of providence in determining the outcome of Shakespeare's play. In both plays, the denouement sees plots devised to undo the revenger double back on the plotters themselves. In both, the fates visited upon all the guilty parties represent morally apposite inversions of the fates they had intended for their notional victims, and thus, as we might say, providentially appropriate comments and judgements upon their own particular style of villainy. In both, the successful realization of revenge serves a political, as well as a moral, purpose, with a purging regime change effected by invading forces from the north, justified in each case by essentially the same mixture of hereditary right, the workings of elective monarchy, and the new ruler's role in punishing and/or publishing the dark deeds which had undone their tyrannical and usurping predecessors.

But perhaps most significantly, both plays incorporate into their plots narrative strands that are central to the genre of the murder pamphlet, and thus elicit from their audiences a set of narrative and moral expectations derived therefrom.[3] As we shall see below, in so doing, the two plays both addressed and problematized basic assumptions about how, through the workings of both human and divine justice, and the ministrations of both the secular magistrate and the godly minister, order might be restored, and a world turned upside down by the most heinous of crimes, the most serious of rents in the moral and social fabric, could be turned the right way up again. At stake here were issues of (secular) order and social relations; but also – because of the seriousness of the crimes committed – the right relations between fallen humanity and an absolutely just, and absolutely merciful, God. Only through each and every element in the social and political, the secular and ecclesiastical hierarchies playing its part aright could equilibrium be restored not merely to society, but to the cosmic relations between creature and creator. In both these plays, those norms, assumptions and narrative expectations were evoked and animated, only then to be subjected to a sort of stress test: pushed to breaking point by being set in the midst of scenarios riven with tensions created by religious change and confessional conflict and dynastic crisis and regime change – tensions and anxieties of precisely the sort with which any politically sentient inhabitant of late-Elizabethan England had to live on an almost daily basis.

Thus, *Hamlet* can usefully be read as an attempt to rewrite *Titus*, with both plays staging precisely the same situations and dilemmas: the first time around, in a sedulously pagan setting; the second time around, in an equally carefully delineated Christian one. In some ways, *Hamlet* represented the second time that Shakespeare had done this. The first such pairing involved *Titus* and *Richard III*, with *Titus* being set in a completely pagan, explicitly elective monarchy, and *Richard III* in a Christian, free hereditary one. The second such pairing involved *Julius Caesar*, a play set in a carefully delineated Roman republican and pagan context, and *Hamlet*, which, of course, takes place in an explicitly Christian, indeed ostensibly Catholic, elective monarchy. And so, when the argument of this book requires, reference will be made to both *Richard III* and *Caesar* as points of departure and comparison.[4]

However, the focus will be on the two revenge tragedies themselves and on the ways in which they process and reprocess the relations between revenge, resistance and religion. In thus reading these two plays, the one against the other, we can watch Shakespeare conducting a sort of thought experiment. Placing different protagonists in similar situations – situations that seem to demand 'revenge' – he provided one with the sort of presuppositions and assumptions available to a Roman pagan, and the other with the residually Christian impulses displayed by Hamlet at the opening of the play. In the transactions between these two plays, we get to watch Shakespeare as he self-consciously deliberates on, and experiments with, not merely the nature of the revenge tragedy, but the role of the drama itself. We can watch him adverting directly to the development of his own dramaturgy in relation to evolving literary taste, both popular and elite, and we can watch him doing that while he stages some of the most urgently controversial theological questions of the day.

It is now widely acknowledged that Shakespeare wrote *Titus* in collaboration with George Peele, who, it is thought, wrote the first act (as well, perhaps, as act II scene I). But as Michael Neill and Colin Burrow have both argued, it is 'abundantly clear . . . both from the play's dramaturgical coherence and from the consistency of its linguistic and theatrical detail . . . that the two dramatists must have collaborated very closely, repeatedly exchanging ideas and perhaps even editing or revising one another's material'.[5] As Burrow points out, the play throughout makes 'much of relations between pietas, Roman duty, and pity' and creates 'oblique and indirect connections between the political debates presented in the early scenes' – notionally written by Peele – 'and the Ovidian rape and tragedy at its core'.[6] In short, while the differences between the bits written by Peele and Shakespeare might reveal themselves to the discerning eye and quantitative methods of the modern researcher,[7] the constituent parts of the play do not represent bleeding chunks of text, forced into an uncomfortable or incongruous union. Certainly, in performance, the audience does not experience any jarring transitions or shifts in tone or theme of the sort that would suggest that the play they are watching is the product of more than one pen. Rather, the bits of text written by Peele and Shakespeare form parts of a (jointly authored) whole. Accordingly, I have no qualms about including *Titus* in a discussion of Shakespeare's revenge tragedies, or in reading *Hamlet* as, in some ways, a later stab at themes and matter attempted earlier in *Titus*.

In both plays, among other things, Shakespeare is presenting a version of natural theology. He is setting up situations in which pressing questions – in *Titus* about persecution and religious violence, about the nature of true religion, the rights and wrongs of revenge and resistance; in *Hamlet* about providence and predestination, the force of conscience and the interaction between human agency, conscience (again) and divine providence and grace – are being posed. In both plays, central ethical and theological questions are, as it were, personified in the dilemmas, the actual or likely fates, of the central characters.

If, in watching the plots of the two plays unfold, the audience is also witnessing the working through of certain theological issues of pressing contemporary (i.e. post-Reformation) significance, in neither play are the theological questions being raised simply resolved. Rather, Shakespeare delineates them with an almost forensic precision, and then lets both the actions and the words of the individual characters (and the overarching structures of the plot) do their work. As ever, those structures are evident to the spectators in ways that are simply unavailable to the characters on stage. It is thus left up to the members of the audience to draw their own conclusions – in effect positioning themselves on one side or the other of the debates being staged. Moreover, in *Hamlet*, the complex relation of the play and the playwright to the audience(s) is directly staged and commented upon in the play-within-a-play-within-a-play scene involving *The Murder of Gonzago*, *The Mousetrap* and the play, *Hamlet*.

Both plays can be related to the political and polemical dynamics of the moments in which they were written and first consumed. And indeed, some of the differences – as well as the similarities – between them can be analysed in terms of the differences between those very different political conjunctures and Shakespeare's notional relation to them. I attempted to explain how that worked in my previous book. However, such issues of immediate political context and comment are entirely peripheral, if not irrelevant, to the argument of this book. 'Politics' features in the analysis only insofar as the choices and dilemmas faced by the central characters are embedded in events inherently political in nature. In both plays, the major characters are princes (and their kin and courtiers), and the foundational events with which both plays open involve managing contested or questionable successions, and thus the establishment of political legitimacy, under decidedly fraught circumstances. Necessarily, therefore, the impulses towards revenge experienced by the main protagonists immediately raise other questions about the rights and wrongs of resistance, and the (ethical and prudential) implications and consequences of the resort to political violence. These are, of course, inherently political issues of immediately contemporary relevance. But political as they are, viewed as these plays stage them, these topics also raise profound ethical and religious questions – questions that both plays leave for their audiences to resolve, by bringing to bear on the action of the play their existing opinions, prejudices and expectations, even as the plays themselves sought to unsettle and exploit those same predispositions and assumptions for their own dramatic and forensic purposes.

I want now to place the question of the relation between revenge, resistance and religion – the question that lies at the heart of both plays – in the wider social, cultural and political context constituted by the post-Reformation. Murder was conceived in the early modern period as the primal crime and sin. Not only did it cry to heaven for justice, but it created a rent in the social and moral fabric that demanded retributive and compensatory action, if social peace and moral consensus were to be restored. If the formal proceedings of public justice failed to deliver the goods, revenge could step into the gap. Indeed, revenge could be conceived as a means to do God's work, by bringing the culprit to a just end, while performing the compensatory – as well as punitive – work necessary to restore some sort of equilibrium to the human community.

But if revenge could be conceived of as a form of justice, then justice could also be conceived of as a form of revenge. The integral relationship between the two persists to this day in the modern obsession with the role of victims, not merely in the sentencing process, but – at least in the more barbarous parts of the United States, where Tamora's barb about 'a cruel and irreligious piety' could scarcely be more apposite – in the very execution of the condemned felon.

But while justice is public, revenge is private. In the early modern period (no less than today), though judicial punishment may have retained many of the lineaments of revenge (and may even have performed some of its social, symbolic and emotional work), the official ideologies of both Church and state sought to place (private) revenge itself way off limits.

From one view, although a way of seeing justice done and reparation made, revenge also almost always led to another crime being committed. Revenge could thus itself easily become the source not of social peace, but of continuing – indeed heightened –

conflict. Left unconstrained, the dynamic of action and reaction inherent in revenge – the mutually defining and confirming identities and enmities of revenger and revengee – could all too easily be perpetuated, almost institutionalized, in the feud.

In the most extreme situations, when the deeds involved took in the highest levels of social and political power, this process of escalation could culminate not merely in civil war, but in the complete breakdown of both moral and political order. That, of course, was the nightmare world that Shakespeare conjured up in the *Henry VI* plays, and which interested contemporaries could see working itself out in real time across the Channel in France. As Lisa Parmelee and others have pointed out, accounts – both long and short – of the dreadful course of the French wars of religion were a prominent presence in London bookshops, and indeed (in various forms) on the London stage.[8] One thinks here, most obviously, of Marlowe's *Massacre at Paris*, but, as Alan Stewart (among others) has pointed out, Marlowe's *Edward II* might be thought to have drawn on English history to stage French current affairs and depict a nightmare version of what could happen to England if events took a wrong turn.[9]

Historians of medieval and early modern Europe have been much concerned with the ways in which contemporaries – for the most part, agents of the Church and state – sought to constrain, contain and redirect the impulses released by revenge and instantiated in, and sustained by, the feud. While of long standing, such efforts were both accelerated and transformed by the two defining events of the 'early modern' period. For when clerics and lawyers, formed by the definitions of obedience, order and true Christianity produced by the Renaissance and Reformation(s), looked at the sort of peace produced by the feud, they did not like what they saw. Rather than the animosities and tensions of the feud being contained and diffused through the various ritual and social instantiations of Christian charity and community (which John Bossy put at the centre of his vision of the late-medieval Church), they tended to see nothing but sin and irreligion, disorder and conflict.[10] The result was both intermittently systematic, and cumulatively incremental, attempts to extend the jurisdiction of both the secular and the ecclesiastical courts, and, with that, the reach of various forms of (both coerced and internalized) spiritual discipline over areas of life hitherto controlled by more local, unofficial and collectively consensual (if not always consensus-producing) systems of arbitration, dispute resolution and the doing of justice.

When dealing with such questions over the *longue durée*, historians have tended to tell a series of success stories about these processes – stories centred on the inexorable spread of state power and the equally inexorable dissemination of various ideals of civility and piety.[11] Judged by these criteria, post-Reformation England was a remarkably centralized and intensively governed place, where these processes of moral and spiritual reformation, though still controversial and thus still capable of producing considerable conflict, were nevertheless relatively well advanced.

The dominant ideal was expressed in a somewhat idealized vision of the ways in which divine and human justice, the workings of the courts and of divine providence, the efforts of the ministers of God's word and of the secular magistrate all collaborated in the doing of justice, the maintenance of social peace and reaffirmation of the moral norms of the Christian community. The central belief was that, as the most dreadful of crimes, even when committed in secret by the most powerful or well connected of people, murder would out. If all else failed, and the flimsy, hand-to-mouth investigative powers of the authorities failed to reveal the truth of the matter, it was widely assumed that the demands of divine justice and the workings of divine providence would ensure that even the most secret (or successfully hidden) of crimes would eventually be revealed, along with the identities of the perpetrators – if necessary by miraculous means.

Once the crime and its perpetrators had been discovered, it was the task of public justice to bring the culprits to judgment, condemnation and execution, leaving their souls initially to the tender ministrations of the clergy, and ultimately to the perfectly just and perfectly merciful judgment of God. On this account, the secular authorities showed mercy – and discharged their spiritual obligations towards God and man – only if they ensured that condemned felons were put to death, in the process denying them any prospect of reprieve or pardon. Thus, facing the imminent judgment of God, they could be induced or enabled not only to admit their guilt (and hence acknowledge the justice of the verdict), but also to confront the dreadful reality of their current spiritual condition. Then, and only then, through the ministrations of the godly clergy, might they be brought to a potentially saving repentance.[12]

It has been widely argued that, over the *longue durée*, the Reformation and Counter-Reformation played crucial roles in the successful consummation of the processes of institutional, cultural and social change outlined above. But in the last third of the sixteenth century, the interaction between confessional, aristocratic and dynastic politics consequent upon the Reformation seemed to many observers to be not merely sending these processes into precipitate reverse, but actually plunging parts of Western Europe into moral chaos and social and political dissolution. Here the paradigmatic case was provided by the French wars of religion, in the course of which a variety of different forms of religious violence and confessional conflict was added to the always already violent and unstable course of aristocratic feud and dynastic civil war.[13]

One of the great claims made in defence of the Elizabethan regime was that the moderation and good government of our own dear queen had protected England from such a fate. And it was, of course, true that – with the possible exceptions of the revolt of the northern earls and the sad farce of the Essex rebellion – Elizabeth's reign saw no major aristocratic risings and no (successful) dynastic coups. However, throughout her reign, a succession of conspiracies and revolts was unmasked and frustrated. These almost always involved the assassination of the queen and, through various combinations of native risings and foreign incursion or invasion, the transfer of the crown from Elizabeth to some suitably Catholic claimant, more often than not Mary Stuart. Moreover, Mary's execution only settled the succession to the extent that it definitively removed Mary herself as a possible successor. As recent research has revealed, even after Mary's death in 1587, the issue of the succession continued to be a source of both actual and potential instability, anxiety and speculation.[14]

In addition, while England did not experience the outbreaks of religious violence that occurred in France, Elizabeth's reign was punctuated by outbreaks of annihilating state violence visited upon the bodies of certain English Catholics, normally priests. Admittedly, the authorities went out of their way to deny that what was involved here was any species of religious violence. Rather, the state claimed that its Catholic victims were being punished for the secular offences of disobedience and treason, not for their religious beliefs. But the Catholics on the receiving end of these policies vigorously denied that version of events, maintaining that those doing the dying were martyrs for their faith, and that those doing the killing were therefore, by definition, persecutors.[15]

Moreover, 'revenge' – conceived as some sort of religiously sanctioned, either providentially or papally sponsored, doing-of-justice – had a central role to play in how these issues were discussed. After all, for at least some English Catholics, as the offspring of the adulterous and allegedly incestuous union between Henry VIII and Ann Boleyn, Elizabeth I had always been a usurper and a tyrant twice over: first, through her illegal seizure of the throne from the true claimant; and secondly, through her subsequent conduct. Crucial here was her persecution of her Catholic subjects and, latterly, her judicial murder either of the 'real queen', or – if you accepted Elizabeth's initial right to the throne – of her one true heir, Mary Stuart. On such views of the matter, Elizabeth was guilty of crimes so rank that they positively demanded punishment not only by God, in the next life, but also (perhaps) by her subjects in this.[16]

On the other side of the confessional divide, by the early 1570s many of the English political elite believed that Mary Stuart was already guilty of crimes against the queen and realm of a seriousness that deserved, indeed demanded, death. From 1584 onwards, having taken the Bond of Association, a good part of the political nation was committed, in the event of Elizabeth's assassination, to taking summary 'revenge' – the word features prominently in the Bond of Association – not merely on the queen's killers, but also on anyone likely to benefit from the queen's death (i.e. Mary Stuart and quite possibly her son, James VI).[17]

Very often the dynastic and confessional politics of the period turned (or seemed about to turn) on assassination, both successful and attempted. One thinks here of Admiral Coligny, William of Orange, Henry III, the duke of Guise, and later Henry IV, not to mention the many unsuccessful plots against Elizabeth I. Given the political dynamics of the age, this meant that, at various times, in various places, and on both sides of the confessional divide, contemporaries felt a pressing need to cast or recast allegedly private acts of revenge – undertaken, it was said, by deranged, malcontent or fanatical individuals or factions – as inherently legitimate acts of resistance, that is to say as public acts of justice, committed in the name of some combination of 'the people', 'the commonwealth' or true religion, against peccant – variously heretical, tyrannical or persecuting – rulers.[18] Hence Cardinal Allen's claim that both Protestants and Catholics agreed that resistance was (or, rather, could be) legitimate. It was just that the Protestants then left it up to the people – all too often a rout of malcontent and heretical fanatics – to decide the case for themselves. For Allen, only the Catholics possessed an effective system of public justice, which referred all such questions to the divinely ordained authority, and determinative judgment, of the pope.[19]

But revenge as resistance and resistance as revenge always remained intensely controversial, and souls were always at stake. Thus, some Catholics hailed the killer of Henry III as a hero, regarding his action not as some petty act of revenge for the assassination of Guise, but rather as a glorious deed done in the service of true religion and the commonweal. But if Catholics consigned the soul of Henry's assassin to heaven, many Protestants, with equal certainty, sent him to hell. For them, the whole affair provided proof positive of the Antichristian nature of popery and its utterly corrosive effects on the ties that bound subjects to princes and princes to subjects.[20]

Indeed, on some views of the matter, even if the object of the revenger or regicide's attentions were a genuine tyrant, and therefore his death a providential working-out in this world of God's justice, the act of killing a king might still represent a sin so dreadful as virtually to ensure that the killer would be accompanying his victim to hell. In this scenario, God would be using the sin of one individual to punish that of another, before throwing them both onto the fires of eternal judgment.[21]

As Jessica Winston has suggested, these circumstances and the worries they prompted may well have had something to do with the vogue for English translations of Senecan revenge tragedy during the 1560s and thereafter. Indeed, 1568 saw the production at court (and then in print) of a play, *Horestes*, that may well have sought to comment – through a play based on ancient precedents – on the recent conduct and present status of Mary Queen of Scots. Even more pointed, of course, was *Gorboduc*, performed first at the Inns of Court and then before the queen at court in 1562, and then published twice later in the decade. This play took what Winston describes as a Senecan form to address the very pressing current question of the succession and how to settle it – and the likely dire consequences of failing to do so.[22] In the midst of a somewhat scatter-gun association between revenge plays and 'resistance', Linda Woodbridge asks, pertinently enough, 'was it a coincidence that the mid sixteenth century spawned resistance texts and tyrant plays?' 'Senecan tyrants,' she remarks, 'are outsized, unforgettable', and she asserts that 'anti-tyrannical tracts of the 1550s had a counterpart in mid-century plays'. Accordingly, Woodbridge reads the translations of Seneca of the 1560s to the 1580s as 'dissident plays'. 'Seething with tyranny, power abuse, and resistance, they were contemporary with much resistance writing' and, she maintains, 'did similar cultural work'.[23]

In this book, I want to argue that in his two revenge tragedies – *Titus Andronicus* and *Hamlet* – Shakespeare addressed the nexus of the theoretical and practical, political and religious, concerns outlined above. Both plays, I will argue, evoked the lost world of the old religion – of 'popery', as that notorious atheist and reprobate Aaron calls it in *Titus Andronicus*. In *Titus*, it is treated under the rubric of the 'cruel and irreligious piety' of the Andronici. In *Hamlet*, the old religion is evoked through a penumbra of beliefs about the nature of a good death and purgatory. These are evoked by the ghost and Ophelia, and, more generally, through the sanity- and soul-threatening demands made by lost fathers – Old Hamlet and Polonius – on their children. *Titus* staged the violence of religious persecution, and seeks to distinguish it from simple revenge, while denying it any claim to anything remotely resembling 'justice'. *Hamlet* staged the existential terrors of religious change and of the transition from one religious identity to another – a transition often organized under the rubrics either of conversion or apostasy; but in both cases very often associated with forms of melancholy, possession or despair. In *Titus*, Shakespeare examined the relationships between religion and revenge, and between revenge, resistance and an (emergently Christian) sense of justice. In *Hamlet*, he plumbed the depths of the soteriological politics of revenge and resistance. In both cases, he used the temporal and geographical distance afforded him by setting *Titus* in a remote, wholly pagan, and entirely made-up Rome, and *Hamlet* in an entirely foreign and temporally remote, albeit also remarkably contemporary, Denmark, in order to address questions that, in the context of a play about recent English history, might have proven a little too close to home.[24] In both plays, he was addressing central religious, affective and theological issues raised not merely by religious change, but also by confessional (and dynastic) change and conflict; and he was doing so at two moments when such concerns and anxieties might have been expected to be at the centre of his contemporaries' attention.

I should end by pointing out that I quote from the latest Arden editions of these plays: that of *Titus Andronicus* by Jonathan Bate and of *Hamlet* by Ann Thompson and Neil Taylor. In citing Hamlet, I quote from Q2, except on a couple of occasions where I prefer F.

PART ONE

TITUS ANDRONICUS

1

⊰⊹⊱

Succession and confessional politics combined

Titus Andronicus is not merely a revenge tragedy. Despite the fact that the play is overt about its origins in entirely fictional classical sources – it is suffused with evocations of, and references to, the *Aeneid*, and central elements in the plot are taken from Ovid[1] – when *Titus* was entered in the stationer's register, it was described as a 'noble Roman history'. Some of its central concerns – succession, tyranny, resistance and the nature and origins of monarchical legitimacy – echoed those of Shakespeare's history plays. As we shall see below, the play contains echoes of, and parallels with, the *Henry VI* plays and *Richard III*. It was, moreover, set within a meticulously evoked, although entirely fictional, version of *Romanitas*, a pagan Rome, composed of elements drawn from the imperial and republican periods. The result is a political system which the play goes out of its way to identify as a form of elective monarchy.

The action takes place in a period when Rome is engaged in a life and death struggle with northern barbarians, its polity an amalgam of republican and imperial forms. Since the barbarians in question are identified as Goths, we are, we might assume, dealing with the later imperial death throes of the Roman state – were it not for the fact that the setting is determinedly pagan, indeed, by all appearances, pre-Christian. The result is a chronologically unspecific evocation of pagan *Romanitas* in which Rome's endings and beginnings meet in the tale told by the play.

As T.J.B. Spencer famously observed,

the play does not assume a political situation known to Roman history; it is, rather, a summary of Roman politics. It is not so much that any particular set of political institutions is assumed in *Titus*, but rather that it includes *all* the political institutions that Rome ever had. The author seems anxious, not to get it all right, but to get it all in.

The result, as Spencer argues, was that the play 'would easily be recognized as a typical Roman history by a sixteenth century audience'. Despite the fact that, as Spencer put it, 'the claim that the play was "a noble Roman history" was a just one', on its printed title page of 1594 *Titus* announced itself as a 'tragedy'.[2]

Thus was the action of the play located safely in a sort of temporal and historical limbo, a never-never land, a very long way away from Roman (let alone English) history and, consequently, it might be thought, an equally long way away from Elizabethan England. And yet the action was set not merely within a carefully established and sustained version of *Romanitas*, but also in a polity and opening situation that spoke directly to pressingly contemporary Elizabethan concerns. As a 'history play' that was not about history at all, and a 'revenge tragedy' that was not only about revenge, *Titus* occupied rather mixed, even anomalous, thematic and generic territory.

Constitutional politics and the issue of succession

The play opens with an empty throne and a contested succession. The previous incumbent having died, the action starts with the succession disputed between the dead emperor's two sons. The elder, Saturninus, makes his pitch in terms of hereditary right. He appeals first to the patricians as the 'patrons of my right' [I, i, I] and then to the people, calling upon his 'countrymen, my loving followers, / Plead my successive title with your swords. / I am his first-born son that was the last / That wore the imperial diadem of Rome: / Then let my father's honours live in me, / Nor wrong mine age with this indignity' [I, i, 3–8]. The nature of Saturninus' pitch seems to leave the people and patricians no choice in the matter: on his view, they must accept his 'right', his 'successive title' to his father's throne. While accepting that this is an elective monarchy, then, Saturninus appears to think that it is also one in which the argument from hereditary succession and 'right' trumps all others.

But that view is immediately challenged by his own brother, Bassianus, whose claim is also based partly on heredity – after all he, no less than Saturninus, is his father's son. However, Bassianus also goes on to argue that his brother's moral failings in effect exclude him from the succession:

. . . suffer not dishonour to approach
The imperial seat, to virtue consecrate,
To justice, continence, and nobility:
But let desert in pure election shine.

In short, Bassianus' pitch is predicated on the right of the 'Romans' to make a free election or choice of their next emperor, and he exhorts the people to 'fight for freedom in your choice' [I, i, 17]. At this point, the tribune of the people, perhaps exploiting this outbreak of faction within the ruling house to interpose the people's (or his own) control over affairs, enters carrying the crown, as though it were in his, or rather in the people's, gift. Peremptorily he tells both 'Princes, that strive by factions and by friends / Ambitiously for rule and empery' to cease their contentions: '. . . the people of Rome, for whom we stand / A special party, have by common voice / In election for the Roman empery' chosen another. The tribune then enjoins both competitors to 'dismiss your followers and, as suitors should, / Plead your deserts in peace and humbleness' [I, i, 18–48]. Both Bassianus and Saturninus comply: Bassianus commits what he calls his 'cause' to 'my fortune's and the people's favour'; while Saturninus, still refusing to give up his hold on the hereditary principle, commits 'my right, my person and the cause' to 'the love and favour of my country' [I, i, 56–62].

The person the people have elected is the tribune Marcus' brother, Titus Andronicus, called Pius, who has just returned from ten years of war with the Goths. He comes bearing the bodies of two more of his sons, sacrificed in the defence of Rome, for honourable burial in the family mausoleum. But Titus, informed by his brother Marcus that the people have named 'thee in election for the empire' [I, i, 186], refuses the office. If this is a *coup de main*, worked by Marcus to install his brother on the throne as a compromise candidate, for the greater glory of the Andronici, it is a complete bust – a stratagem broken on the lack of imperial ambition, indeed on the Roman virtue, of Titus, who claims to have grown old in the service of the state and to now want nothing but an honourable retirement. Instead, Titus asks 'the people of Rome, and the people's tribunes here' for 'your voices and your suffrages. / Will you bestow them friendly on Andronicus?' When the tribunes accede to the request, Titus nominates Saturninus, 'our emperor's eldest son'. 'Then if you will elect by advice, / Crown him and say, "Long live the emperor!"' [I, i, 228–233]. To this, the assembled multitude, both 'patricians and plebeians', accede, and Saturninus is proclaimed emperor.

What we have here is a contested succession, about to break out into civil strife, if not civil war, with each of the rival candidates appealing to 'his loving friends' – to what Marcus and Bassianus both refer to at different points as 'factions' and 'friends' [I, i, 18, 218] – to enforce their claims with violence. The political system in which this is happening is portrayed as an elective monarchy, with power in the election lying formally, at least, in the people, whose representative, the tribune Marcus, is depicted as running the show. As should be clear by now, the word and concept of 'election' is used repeatedly in these exchanges. Titus at one point asks for the 'voices and suffrages' of 'the people of Rome' [I, i, 221–222]. As we have seen, Marcus announces at one point that 'the people of Rome . . . have by common voice / In election . . . Chosen Andronicus' [I, i, 20–22]. Titus urges the people to 'elect by my advice' [I, i, 232]. As we have seen, earlier in the same exchange Bassianus exhorted the Romans 'to fight for freedom in your choice' against his brother's claim to rule by hereditary right.

In short, throughout, the people's right to elect their emperor is made crystal clear, and – as Bassianus' claim for himself and the people's preference for Titus both show – that right trumps all considerations of, or claims to, hereditary right. Only Saturninus demurs, continually asserting that, as the emperor's eldest son, he must – and will – have the crown, and appealing to the patricians to vindicate his 'right'. Even after Marcus has announced the people's preference for Titus, and even as the election proceeds, while Bassianus pledges his loyalty to Titus, Saturninus makes to press his claim by force. When the tribune tells Titus that 'thou shalt obtain and ask the empery', Saturninus breaks in – 'proud and ambitious tribune, canst thou tell?' – and then appeals again to the patricians, exhorting them 'to draw your swords and sheathe them not / Till Saturninus be Rome's emperor' [I, i, 205–209].

Admittedly, in the process of choosing the successor, issues of hereditary right are clearly regarded as important. But crucially, they do not, at first, decide the issue. When Marcus the tribune announces the people's preference for Titus, both parties submit, to canvas their case by peaceful means. Everyone accepts that the people have the right to elect their emperor – except, to some extent, Saturninus, although even he is prepared to go through the external forms of an election (albeit one in which, on his account, there is no real choice left to the electors).

Of course, Saturninus does become emperor; but not because of the triumph of the hereditary principle, or the exercise of patrician force, but rather through the choice of the people, guided by Titus, whose political virtue, lack of ambition, respect for the hereditary principle and desire to save the state from civil dissension lead him to nominate Saturninus. In acting thus, Titus is being entirely consistent with his own value system.

For the play reveals him to be very attached to the hereditary principle: but while Titus cares deeply about heredity and nobility, the sort of nobility he cares about is defined not only (or even mainly) by blood, but also by honour, fame and virtue – qualities and attributes that are displayed and won in the service of the state. As he tells his sons (speaking of the family vault), 'here none but soldiers and Rome's servitors / Repose in fame' [I, i, 357–358]. It is a 'sacred receptacle of my joys, / Sweet cell of virtue and nobility' [I, i, 95–96]. Thus, for Titus, glorious death in the service of the state is no fit subject for grief. And so, of his 22 sons who have died in the defence of Rome, Titus claims, for them 'I never wept, / Because they died in honour's lofty bed' [III, i, 10–11].

He makes that remark as he is trying to prevent his brother and surviving sons from burying in the family tomb another of his progeny, Mutius, whom Titus himself has just slain for defying both paternal and imperial authority. Mutius and the rest of his kin have refused to allow the marriage between Titus' daughter Lavinia and Saturninus to take place, on the grounds that Lavinia is already betrothed to Bassianus. While Titus construes that refusal as an act of unforgivable disobedience to imperial authority, and consequently as the quintessence of dishonour, his sons and brother see it as both justified by the law – 'suum cuique is our Roman justice' [I, i, 284] – and necessary to protect the honour of Lavinia and of the Andronici.

Titus, of course, takes an entirely opposite view of the matter. For him, their action is treason pure and simple. When his eldest son Lucius reproves his father for having slain Mutius 'in a wrongful quarrel', Titus responds by disowning him: 'nor thou, nor he, are any sons of mine: / My sons would never so dishonour me. / Traitor, restore Lavinia to the emperor' [I, i, 298–301; also see I, i, 348–351]. To Titus, precisely because his brother and sons are traitors to the emperor, they are consequently also traitors to him and thus to the honour of the Andronici. What is being staged here is the conflict between a lineage-based version of honour and virtue, and one centred solely on obedience to the state and royal command – a conflict that Mervyn K. James has placed at the centre of the transition from a late-medieval to an early-modern state.[3] While Mutius and the rest take Bassianus' betrothal to Lavinia as having provided the Andronici with a 'right', a stake in lineal honour, so strong as to legitimate disobedience to royal command or state authority, Titus does not. While his kin seek to root their position in a version of 'our Roman justice', Titus bases his view of the situation on the straightforward demands of obedience to imperial authority, and shows the depth of that commitment by denouncing his sons as 'traitors' and by killing Mutius.

The play is very precisely staging here a situation taken from the centre of the Elizabethan political imaginary. We are being shown the dynamics of a potential interregnum and succession crisis, when, after the death of a monarch (the virtue and legitimacy of whose rule none doubted), the state faced an uncertain future. If we take Shakespeare to have written Titus in 1593, it is worth observing that at precisely this time Robert Parsons was constructing an account of the polity of England as just such a mixture of elective and monarchical forms. Peter Wentworth had planned to have the succession settled in parliament in 1593, and was consigned to the Tower for his pains.[4] These, then, were clearly issues that were very much in the air at precisely the moment when Peele and Shakespeare wrote their play.

They were also issues with a considerable Elizabethan backstory. Thanks to the researches of Patrick Collinson, we know that Burghley himself had considered construing Elizabethan England as something like an elective monarchy in the event of the queen's death, so that the commonweal could distinguish between the various claimants to the throne before selecting the best candidate. Such a prospect had been intermittently canvassed by elements at the very centre of the regime from at least the 1560s – indeed, almost as often as the imponderable issue of the succession had raised its increasingly unavoidable head.[5] On this basis, rather than an incompetent, incomplete or careless reconstruction of *Romanitas*, we should take the play as a deliberate attempt to address central questions about the nature of the English monarchical state in the early and mid-1590s, through, as it were, fictive Roman means.[6]

Religious violence, tyranny and revenge

Far from constituting any sort of end point, the election of Saturninus in fact provides the start of the series of dreadful events that constitute the play as a revenge tragedy of the most bloody and appalling sort. However, the roots of that descent into bloody mayhem, despair and revenge lie not in politics, but in religion. Titus is returning from ten years of war with the Goths, to bury his sons – killed in the war – in the family tomb. To appease the spirits of the dead, he also intends, as Bassianus describes it, to make a 'sacrifice of expiation', by killing the 'noblest prisoner of the Goths' [I, i, 37–38], who is also the eldest son of the captive queen of the Goths, Tamora. In an exchange with Tamora, Titus and his son Lucius explain the rationale behind this dreadful act:

> Give us the proudest prisoner of the Goths,
> That we may hew his limbs, and on a pile
> *Ad manes fratrum* sacrifice his flesh
> Before this earthly prison of his bones
> That so the shadows be not unappeased,
> Nor we disturbed by prodigies of earth. [I, i, 99–104]

Titus calls on Jupiter, 'the great defender of the capitol', to 'stand gracious to the rites that we intend' [I, i, 80–81], and selects just one Goth to be sacrificed. His reply to Tamora's plea for mercy is measured and stern, betraying no trace of the revenger's

22

passionate excess. Of his dead sons, he explains to Tamora that 'Religiously they ask a sacrifice. / To this your son is marked, and die he must,/ T'appease the groaning shadows that are gone' [I, i, 124–129]. Alarbus is then taken off to die, and Lucius returns, telling his father that 'Alarbus' limbs are lopped / And entrails feed the sacrificing fire, / Whose smoke like incense doth perfume the sky' [I, i, 145–148].

At this point, it is worth pointing out that the Romans regarded human sacrifice with horror, and so in establishing it as a central part of Roman *pietas* expressed towards the spirits of the dead, Shakespeare was making a very conscious decision to render the play's image of that *pietas* far more shockingly cruel and barbarous than it actually was. All of which might be taken to mitigate Christopher Crosbie's remark that, under the circumstances, and judged simply in terms of what Crosbie calls 'Aristotelian rectificatory justice', having lost 22 sons to the war against the Goths, and with multiple potential victims available to him, Titus might be thought to be displaying considerable self-restraint (even moderation).[7] To which one might reply, yes, but only in a belief system in which human sacrifice was normative, which was not the case among the Romans. Some critics have argued, plausibly enough, that in making this move the play is referencing what Megan Elizabeth Allen calls 'the extreme grotesque reading of *pietas* at the heart of books 10 and 11 of the *Aeneid*', thus, in effect, normalizing what she describes as Virgil's portrayal of 'Aeneas' perversion of ideal *pietas*'. For while Aeneas' 'momentary exaggeration of *pietas* into murder and vengeance is portrayed [by Virgil] as an aberration brought on by grief, even madness', Titus' sacrifice is no such thing.[8] It is as though the Romans of the play, in a misbegotten attempt to emulate Aeneas, have elevated his breakdown into furor, cruelty and revenge into some sort of normalized religious principle or duty. By making this move, the play does a number of things. It renders Roman *pietas* and *virtus* even more cruel and barbarous than they in fact were, while simultaneously removing Titus' sacrifice of Alarbus from under the rubric of revenge, and placing it in the realm of religion and the discharge of duty towards one's ancestors and the gods: an obligation which Titus discharges soberly, and without any of the excess of emotion, personalized cruelty or relish typical of the (Senecan) revenger.

The point is underscored by the fact that having sacrificed Alarbus, Titus freely gives the rest of his captives to the emperor. When Saturninus immediately frees them to celebrate his accession, Titus does not protest. When Saturninus' plan to marry Lavinia has collapsed in the face of the defiance of the Andronici, Saturninus marries Tamora, and still Titus does not repine.[9]

Titus, then, is no Clifford or Margaret of York. What we are seeing here is not the bloodlust, the orgy of revenge to be achieved through the almost indiscriminate violence that pervades the latter stages of the *Henry VI* plays. For Titus, what is at stake here is not revenge – some bloodlust to be taken out on all Goths, or even on all the progeny of Tamora – but rather the discharge of a religious obligation, owed both to the shades of his kin and to Rome. As Barbara L. Parker has observed, a London audience, steeped in the tropes of anti-popery, may well have seen more than a passing resemblance between the Andronici's expiatory sacrifice (of Alarbus) and the Catholic mass, which, as Parker observes, was also accompanied 'with a prayer for the dead, "take, O holy Trinity, this oblation, which I unworthy sinner offer . . . for the salvation of the living and for the rest or quietness of all the faithful that are dead"'. Moreover, the situation of Titus' 'unburied sons', stranded 'on the dreadful shore of Styx' [I, i, 88], parallels (Parker argues) rather closely that of Christian souls suffering in the 'Catholic underworld of Purgatory'. When Titus' statement that the sacrifice is 'religiously necessary' [I, i, 124] is added to Lucius' assurance that 'we have performed our Roman rites' [I, i, 145–146], we are left, Parker concludes, with something like 'a parody of the Roman Catholic Mass'.

If, as Tamora claims, 'mercy' were indeed the defining quality of the gods – a claim which, while it may well have been self-evident to the play's first (Christian) audiences, was anything but obvious to its pagan Roman protagonists – then the resulting form of piety might well appear (as she claims) both 'cruel' and 'irreligious' [I, I, 133].[10] But within the (pagan Roman) terms constructed by the play, rather than an act of revenge, Titus' sacrifice of Alarbus is a pious attempt to placate the spirits of the dead and to bring closure to the war with the Goths.

However, as both a Goth and Alarbus' mother, Tamora is in no position to appreciate the finer points of Titus' performance of either Roman *pietas* or Aristotelian 'moderation'. Rather, Titus' 'piety' provokes in her an unappeasable thirst for revenge against the Andronici. The two are thus placed at cross purposes to such an extent that Titus can, at one point, take comfort from Tamora's elevation to the imperial throne, because (so he reckons) she will regard herself as 'beholden' to him, since he is 'the man / That brought her for this high good turn so far' [I, i, 401–402]. Lavinia goes even further, later citing her father's generosity towards Tamora and her sons as she pleads with the Goth queen not to allow Chiron and Demetrius to have their evil way with her. But where Titus and Lavinia see the conferral of benefits and the exercise of mercy, Tamora can see only the most traumatic assault on her and hers, the occasion for the most terrifying and absolute revenge.[11]

Moreover, in terms of its immediate practical effects, all that Titus' performance of Roman piety and virtue – displayed both in his refusal of the throne and in his sacrifice of Alarbus – has done is to cede absolute power in Rome to the two people who are most dedicated to his destruction. From the outset, despite his effusive expressions of undying gratitude to Titus, Saturninus resents and fears him as a kingmaker: the person to whom he owes his crown and who may well later try to call in that debt. But Saturninus is also now married to Tamora, the queen of the Goths, who is motivated solely by desire for revenge – not only on Titus himself, but also on the Andronici and all their works.

Her revenge does not take the form of simple tyrannical oppression. Saturninus has impulses in that direction, but Tamora persuades him to 'dissemble all your griefs and discontents', and proceed by stealth:

> Yield at entreats – and then let me alone:
> I'll find a day to massacre them all,
> And raze their faction and their family,
> The cruel father and his traitorous sons
> To whom I sued for my dear son's life,
> And make them know what 'tis to let a queen
> Kneel in the streets and beg for grace in vain. [I, i, 447–460]

The form her revenge takes is a scheme, cooked up by her lover and evil counsellor, Aaron the Moor, out of the lustful pursuit of Lavinia by her two clueless sons. At Aaron's instigation, they murder Bassianus and rape and mutilate Lavinia – but the deed is brought off in such a way that two of Titus' sons are executed for the murder, while the fate of the now tongue- and hand-less Lavinia remains unknown. Titus' last remaining son, Lucius, is sent into exile for attempting to rescue his brothers from the executioner. Tricked into surrendering one of his own hands to save the lives of his sons, Titus is repaid by the return of the hand, along with the heads of his two now summarily executed sons. He is thus left childless, save for (the now mute and handless) Lavinia, whose 'lively body' [III, i, 106] in its newly disfigured form can serve only as a constant reminder of the fate and shame that have been visited upon both his daughter and his house.

The result, of course, is the maximum torment for Titus, who now descends into something like madness. As a result, Saturninus and Tamora have achieved their ends without the appearance of tyranny; the apparent guilt of Titus' sons ensures that, in punishing them, Saturninus does not seem to be guilty of tyranny or oppression, but merely of a (rather summary) doing of justice. As for Lavinia, the guilty parties remain unknown. Titus' descent into madness can thus be glossed as a regrettable, but also entirely predictable, effect of events of neither his nor the emperor's making.

We have here, then, a cycle of violence, of mutilation, murder and revenge, started by a religious act – the sacrifice of Alarbus to placate the shades of Titus' sons. But if the motivations for Titus' initial act of violence against Alarbus were religious, the subsequent campaign against the Andronici is prompted, on Tamora's part, solely by revenge; on Saturninus' part, by fear and resentment of any potential rival (typical of the tyrant); and on Aaron's part, by what emerges over the course of the play as a malign drive towards cruelty for cruelty's sake.

And yet the play talks about Lavinia's fate in the language of martyrdom. When her brother Lucius first sees her, he asks 'speak, gentle sister: who hath martyred thee?' [III, i, 82]. Later in the same scene, Titus laments that she has no tongue 'to tell me who hath martyred thee' [III, i, 108]. We have, then, the 'religious sacrifice' of Alarbus being met by the vengeful 'martyrdom' of Lavinia. While his limbs have been 'hewed' [I, i, 132] and 'lopped', and his entrails fed to the fire, her body has been 'lopped and hewed' and rendered bare 'of her two branches', her mouth turned into 'a crimson river of warm blood' [II, iii, 17–18, 22]. Later Titus refers to her mute and disfigured body as so many 'martyred signs'. She has become a 'speechless complainer', whose 'thought' he promises to 'learn':

In thy dumb action will I be as perfect
As begging hermits in their holy prayers.
Thou shalt not sigh, nor hold thy stumps to heaven,
Nor wink, nor nod, nor kneel, nor make a sign,
But I of these will wrest an alphabet
And by my practice learn to know thy meaning. [III, ii, 40–45]

And yet, for much of the play, Lavinia's disfigured body refuses to be deciphered; her tongueless mouth and handless arms remain a source of 'bootless prayer' [III, i, 76].

The right reading of the martyred signs or wounds of those consigned by the Elizabethan regime to a traitor's death was a matter of considerable interest and an object of bitter controversy for contemporaries. For the regime and its supporters – Protestants – the sufferings, the quartered limbs and the eviscerated bodies of the state's Catholic victims proclaimed that they were traitors indeed, since they had been forced, by a just and merciful Christian prince, to suffer the fate reserved for traitors alone. In their propagandistic or self-justificatory accounts of the death of these traitors, Protestants tended not to dwell on the nature of their punishment or sufferings. The distinctive nature of the disintegrative violence visited upon the bodies of these traitors, and of the body parts subsequently put on public display, spoke for itself: all the state needed to do to get its message across was to display the quartered remains, the severed heads and the boiled entrails to the public.

For Catholics, however, the message conveyed by the martyred signs and limbs of the state's victims was entirely the opposite: from a Catholic perspective, those same sufferings, those same wounds and signs, indicated that the person concerned had died not a traitor's, but rather a martyr's death at the hands of a persecuting – indeed, a tyrannical – state. And thus the Catholics could hardly stop talking about the bloody sufferings of their co-religionists; using, as they did so, the most emotionally charged and highly wrought language to evoke, and dwell upon, the physical torment, and the spiritual witness, of the state's victims.[12] A number of commentators have noted the seemingly otiose nature of her uncle Marcus' heightened – as some critics claim, Petrarchan – description of Lavinia's wounds, even as she stands mutilated and bleeding before us.[13] Many such critics see Marcus' florid rhetoric as jarringly inappropriate, part of an attempt to refocus his (and our) attention on his own (rather than Lavinia's) suffering. Eugene Waith observes that through Marcus' 'images of trees, fountains, and conduits . . . the suffering becomes an object of meditation'.[14] And that may be precisely the point. For in this, Marcus' over-wrought description of Lavinia's martyred limbs replicates rather closely the sensual, perhaps semi-pornographic, but also generalizing, aspects of Catholic martyr discourse: the reduction – or perhaps we should say the elevation – of the martyr's sufferings, body parts and lastly relics to the status of objects of contemplation, and even of (a form of) worship.

Indeed, John Klause has established a number of very close verbal echoes between Marcus' speech and Robert Southwell's tract of 1587 *An Epistle of Comfort to Those Restrained in Durance for the Catholic Faith*. Most notable are the parallels between Marcus' speech upon finding the mutilated Lavinia wandering in the woods [II, iii, 16–55] and Southwell's evocation of the eviscerated bodies of the martyrs. Hence, Klause finds Southwell lamenting that 'The lopping time has come' for martyrs who will soon be confronted by their own 'blood and slaughtered limbs'. Speaking of the martyrs' dismembered bodies, Southwell exclaims that 'the branches . . . of full growth are lopped', and figures the bodies of the martyrs as having been 'hewed' so that the tree of the Church may sprout more abundantly (93v–94r, 126r). He tells the martyrs that 'your veins are conduits, out of which [God] meaneth to drive the streams' (93v); streams which elsewhere become a scarlet river. 'Martyrdom is the river Jordan' (141r). Again, Southwell sees the 'wind' of persecution 'stirring', while the winnower comes with his fan to separate the wheat from the chaff (97v.). Elsewhere the martyrs are 'sweet roses' (114v), sweet with 'Sampson's honeycomb . . . taken out of the lion's mouth' (94v).[15]

The associations established through such phraseology between Lavinia's fate and that visited upon many Catholics under Elizabeth is, in fact, confirmed at several other points in the action, when the play goes out of its way to code the Andronici as 'Catholic'. In a crucial scene, Titus, his brother Marcus and his grandson Lucius fire arrows wrapped around with petitions for justice into the air. The conceit here, one redolent of Titus' madness, is that 'sith there's no justice in earth nor hell, / We will solicit heaven and move the gods / To send down Justice for to wreak our wrongs' [IV, iii, 50–52]. The Andronici will launch their suit for justice into the air towards the gods in heaven. Accordingly, Titus hands out arrows with messages 'ad Jovem', 'ad Apollinem' and 'ad Martem' – but 'not to Saturnine; / You were as good to shoot against the wind'. But, in fact, the Andronici do not shoot the arrows indiscriminately into the air, but 'into the court; / We will afflict the emperor in his pride' [IV, iii, 63–64]. This move is compounded when Titus sends the innocent clown with another message to the emperor. Significantly, with his invocations to 'God and St Stephen' to 'give you good e'en' and his references to the recently postponed executions of two separatists [IV, iv, 42; IV, iii, 80–82], the clown is a figure drawn directly from Elizabethan London, rather than from pagan Rome. The effect is to collapse the distance between the Roman past evoked by the play – itself, as we have seen, a remarkably temporally unspecific location – and the Elizabethan present. Titus enlists the clown to take a message to the emperor with a knife wrapped within it. The shift from petition to veiled threat here is clear. 'Mad' Titus may be, but he can still play mind games with the tyrant Saturninus.

What we have here is the Andronici acting towards the regime of Saturninus just as some Elizabethan Catholics reacted to the depredations of the Elizabethan regime – with petitions for justice to the gods, to the authorities and, indeed, to the people, and with complaints about the absence thereof in their current treatment. Saturninus' response to the petitions thus lobbed into his court is instructive. He characterizes the authors as 'these disturbers of our peace' who 'buzz in the people's ears' seditious thoughts, although in fact 'nought hath passed / But even with law, against the wilful sons/Of old Andronicus', who, for all his madness, has now crossed a line dividing acceptable eccentricity from sedition and treason. 'What's this but libelling against the senate / And blazoning our injustice everywhere?' [IV, iv, 7–18]. Thus, the play shows just complaints against injustice and oppression addressed to the heavens being construed as 'libels', populist appeals to the people and denunciations of monarchical rule. So Catholic complaints and laments about their treatment at the hands of the Elizabethan state were construed as acts of sedition, libellous and traitorous attempts to stir up the people against their prince.

Saturninus responds to the message wrapped around the knife by sending the innocent messenger, the poor clown, off to instant death [IV, iv, 44]. Klause compares the scene with the clown to the fate of Richard Shelley a Catholic layman who, in 1585, put into the queen's hand, as she walked in her park at Greenwich, a petition on behalf of English Catholics. Shelley was immediately thrown into prison for his pains and left to die there without trial.[16] Having not merely blamed the (entirely innocent) messenger, but actually slaughtered him, Saturninus proceeds to threaten even worse to Titus. 'For this proud mock I'll be thy slaughterman, / Sly frantic wretch that holp'st to make me great / In hope thyself should govern Rome and me' [IV, iv, 50–59].

This response is typical of the arbitrary means and methods, and the violent impulses, that throughout characterize Saturninus, who although not personally involved in the murder of his brother, the rape and mutilation of Lavinia, or the stitching-up of Titus' sons, is quite implicated enough in the savage, arbitrary and illegal treatment of the Andronici to have revealed himself to an Elizabethan audience as a tyrant.[17] As John Klause points out, Titus sends the clown to deliver what he calls a 'supplication' to the emperor. The Jesuit Southwell's pamphlet, which protested the loyalty and innocence of the English Catholics and denounced the policies adopted towards them by the regime as persecution, was also called 'An humble supplication to her majesty'. Dated December 1591, Southwell's text was a reply to the royal proclamation of autumn 1591, which denounced English Catholics as agents of the king of Spain and thus as a major threat to the security of the realm. It was not to be printed until 1600, but circulated in manuscript in the early 1590s.[18]

The most overt statement of the parallels between the situation and character of the Andronici and of Elizabethan Catholics is to be found in an exchange late in the play between Aaron the Moor and Lucius. One of Lucius' soldiers finds Aaron lurking with his son in 'a ruinous monastery' [V, i, 21]. Just like the clown's Elizabethan street speech, so this off-hand, and otherwise completely otiose, reference to the ruined monastery serves to collapse almost to nothing the temporal and conceptual distance between the play's make-believe Rome and Elizabethan England.

Apprehended in the monastery, Aaron and his son are dragged before Lucius. As Lucius prepares to kill first the child and then the parent, Aaron offers him a deal. If Lucius will spare his son, Aaron will spill the beans. If not, nothing will induce Aaron to talk. Lucius agrees; but Aaron, worried that Lucius will renege on the bargain, demands that he swear an oath. To this Lucius asks 'Who should I swear by? Thou believest no god; / That granted, how canst thou believe an oath?' To which Aaron replies that, while he is indeed an atheist, the crucial point is that Lucius is not:

I know thou art religious
And hast a thing within called conscience,
With twenty popish tricks and ceremonies
Which I have seen thee careful to observe,
Therefore I urge thy oath; for that I know
An idiot holds his bauble for a god
And keeps the oath which by that god he swears,
To that I'll urge him, therefore thou shalt vow
By that same god, what god so'er it be
That thou adorest and hast in reverence. [V, i, 74–83].

In a world as depraved as the Rome of Aaron, Tamora and Saturninus, and particularly in the eyes of a self-described atheist and Machiavel like Aaron, even the rudiments of religious sentiment, the barest signs of piety or conscience, look like superstition and can be written off as 'popish'. On the face of it, therefore, as an atheist and Machiavel, Aaron's might be taken to be the most unreliable of testimonies on the subject of religion. But we might well take the basic purport of this exchange to be that what the likes of Aaron (the Machiavels and evil counsellors of this world) call 'popery' is, in fact, nothing other than the operation of conscience; that is to say, the effects of true religion in its simplest, starkest (and purest?) form. If that is the case, then the use of 'popery' as a term of abuse – a 'boo-word' to excoriate and defame the exercise of conscience and the gratification of basic religious impulses and pieties – might be taken to be in itself a sure sign of atheism and ill will. Applied to the religious and political discourse of Elizabethan England, such a litmus test could lead to the most startling and disturbing of conclusions. Either way, Aaron's identification of the genuine (if flawed) piety of the Andronici with 'popery' remains the most attention grabbing of the moments when the play's carefully evoked pagan *Romanitas* is collapsed into post-Reformation England.

Admittedly, from the first, the antique Roman piety and virtue of the Andronici are presented as deeply flawed. However, imperfect as they are, the virtue and piety of the Andronici remain the only virtue and piety on offer in the play, which throughout offers us a stark contrast, an utterly unyielding binary opposition, between the (deeply flawed) piety of the Andronici and the cruelty, tyranny and atheism of Saturninus, Tamora and Aaron. And in this scene between Lucius and Aaron, we have, on the one side, labelled 'popish', the operations of conscience and religious scruple; and on the other, the desperate atheistical ravings of Aaron.

Of course, none of the asides or allusions discussed here mark the Andronici as anything like definitively or unequivocally 'Catholic'. Taken individually, they might easily be dismissed; even taken together, they are no more than suggestive. But there are enough such allusions scattered throughout the play to place such an association or identification before the viewer or reader as an option – a heuristic clue or device – through which the rest of the action of the play might be viewed. And if that association were to strike home, the trains of thought, of further association and argument, down which it might lead would end pretty quickly in what, in the context of late-Elizabethan England, were decidedly daring – even dangerous – conclusions.

What form might such conclusions take? Let us, as a thought experiment, take this association between the Andronici and the character and situation of Elizabethan Catholics, and run it through the workings of the play. We have here a cycle of violence, of sacrifice and martyrdom and counter-martyrdom, started by the quite literally Pius,[19] Titus Andronicus, acting, with merciless calm, in accordance with what he takes to be the dictates of true religion and his obligations to his kin and to Rome.

Here, we might suggest, is a version of the Marian persecution and its effects on the succeeding Elizabethan regime. The impulse at work is not to justify the Marian persecution, since, while the piety involved might be genuine, the play also reveals it to be both 'cruel and irreligious' in its nature and disastrous in both its moral and its political consequences. The point rather is to distinguish the Marian persecution from what follows in the next reign. Titus had at least been trying to do the right thing by Rome, his ancestors and their gods.[20] If Titus' sacrifice of Alarbus represents an attempt to emulate Aeneas' example at the end of the *Aeneid*, it shows him to be at least trying to find a precedent or model for his present conduct in a core text of *Romanitas*. Tamora, on the other hand, has demonstrated no interest in piety or the gods, still less in the fate of Rome: she wants only revenge. Thus, we have a 'cruel and irreligious' but genuinely pious, expiatory violence (of the sort displayed by the Marian Catholics), followed by a bloody, cruel, revenge-driven and politically motivated persecution of the sort conducted by the Elizabethan regime (or so various Catholic commentators claimed).

The play goes out of its way to demonstrate the extent of Titus' loyalty – not merely to the Roman state, but also to Saturninus. For his pains, he is repaid with the suspicion and enmity of the emperor and the undying hatred of the new empress. But instead of moving directly against them, Titus proceeds slowly, at first believing Tamora when, in public, she pretends to mollify the hostility of Saturninus, proclaiming at one point that 'this day all quarrels die, Andronicus; / And let it be mine honour, good my lord, / That I have reconciled your friends and you' [I, i, 471–472].

There are certain parallels to be observed here – both as regards the conduct of English Catholics at the time of Elizabeth's accession and the subsequent treatment of those Catholics by Elizabeth's regime. In 1559, English Catholics – acting here in stark contrast to at least some Protestants at the end of Edward's reign – had chosen not to oppose the claims of the Protestant Elizabeth Tudor. Rather, they had preferred the next lineal successor, Elizabeth, over Mary Stuart's combination of royal blood and Catholic faith – a point often made by Catholic authors like Robert Parsons to demonstrate the political loyalty and reliability of English Catholics, in contrast to the feckless zeal and serial disobedience of hot Protestants and puritans. Subsequently, despite that initial demonstration of loyalty and good faith, the Catholics fell under, first, the suspicion and then the hostile attentions of the queen and her counsellors. However, for years, they had been given a variety of assurances by the regime that, if they remained politically loyal and quiescent, all would be well. No one, it was claimed, was being persecuted for religion, but rather was being punished for disobedience and sometimes even treason. More particularly, the queen herself had, Tamora-like, made a series of gestures, to let it be known that she was no persecutor, and that indeed it was only she who stood between Catholics and the persecutory bloodlust of some of her more zealously Protestant counsellors and subjects.

But behind these public assurances of friendship, Tamora, her sons Chiron and Demetrius, and most notably Aaron the Moor, hatch the plot that will slaughter Bassianus, rape and mutilate Lavinia, and send two of Titus' sons to dishonourable deaths for the murder. While the crime is real enough, the trail that leads Saturninus to assume the guilt of the Andronici is entirely spurious. But not only are the Andronici done in by carefully laid accusations about crimes they have not committed, as Lorna Hutson has recently shown, their fate is also sealed by the perversion of proper judicial procedure and the rule of law by the exercise of arbitrary power – a combination that is entirely typical of Saturninus' tyrannical style of rule.[21] 'Were there worse end than death / That end upon them should be executed' [II, ii, 283–303, quote at 302–303]. This summary justice is compounded by the cruel trick whereby Titus is parted from his hand. Here, then, is Titus reduced to his lowest ebb, his situation summed up by the messenger sent to deliver the body parts:

> . . . ill art thou repaid
> For that good hand thou sent'st the emperor.
> Here are the heads of thy two noble sons;
> And here's thy hand in scorn to thee sent back:
> Thy grief their sports, thy resolution mocked,
> That woe is me to think upon thy woes
> More than remembrance of my father's death. [III, i, 235–241]

But, as we have seen, where the emperor's messenger sees cruelty and oppression, the emperor himself can see only justice [IV, iv, 7–8, 20].

And all this, of course, closely paralleled the ways in which English Catholics claimed that the Elizabethan regime treated them. The Jesuit Robert Southwell's *Humble Supplication* was an extended plaint that essentially loyal Catholics were being persecuted, to the point of death, on trumped up charges of disloyalty and treason. Spurious plots and chains of incriminating evidence were simply being invented and planted to justify the most dreadful persecution. Here, of course, Southwell's star exhibit was the Babington plot. This, he asserted, had in effect been invented by Walsingham, the more easily to send Mary Stuart to her death. But behind that single enormity, there lay a wider pattern of systematic perversion of the criminal justice system; at every turn it was being undermined by the regime and its agents, in their determination to part English Catholics from their lives, their liberty and their property. Just as with Saturninus' defence of his treatment of the Andronici, the state and its apologists insisted that the outward forms of the law were being followed; but, writers like Southwell argued, so patent was the perversion of the course of justice that those claims, even when made by the most exalted members of the regime, could not but ring hollow – just as hollow, in fact, as the parallel claims made in the play by Saturninus himself.[22]

The immediately contemporary resonance of the play's lament at the absence of justice from the workings of the political and judicial systems reaches its peak in the scene in which Titus and his fellows launch, into the court, their petitions to the gods for justice. As he calls his kinsmen to their task, Titus reminds them that '*Terras Astraea reliquit*: / Be you remembered Marcus, / She's gone, she's fled' [IV, iii, 4–5]. Astraea, of course, was the goddess of justice, and her presence on earth was often associated with the golden age. As Francis Yates famously pointed out, this persona was very often conferred on Queen Elizabeth, in panegyrics to her reign as a new golden age of justice, peace and good government.[23] Now we have a picture of tyranny and oppression, of martyrdom and injustice, being visited upon the Andronici in a situation where Astraea has fled from the earth. In so far as the situation staged in the play did recall at least some Catholic accounts of the regime's treatment of its Catholic subjects, the claim that Astraea was indeed absent from the earth might have been taken, by at least some contemporaries, to have had direct (and indeed rather radical) implications for the official account of the nature of the Elizabethan regime. For on this view, rather than living in the golden age of Astraea, Elizabethans were, in fact, living in a version of Ovid's iron age: an age in which Titus' rather crude and cruel caricature of true Roman piety and virtue might indeed represent the height of human moral achievement.

As Jonathan Bate has suggested, the claim that Astraea was absent from the earth might be taken to imply that the action of the play refers to a period after the death of the queen, and thus conjures up the sort of civil strife, disputed succession and vengeful religious war which many contemporaries feared would follow Elizabeth's demise. On this view, as Bate observes:

> the descent into imperial tyranny could well have looked like a warning as to what might happen once Astraea, the virgin Queen, had left the earth. Lucius brings back the light; in the shooting scene, his son, another Lucius, scores a direct hit on Astraea's lap. One of the writers who said that 'the christian faith' was received into Britain 'in the time of Lucius their king' was none other than [the famous Protestant martyrologist] John Foxe.

On such a Foxeian reading of the play, Bate concludes, 'the Goths who accompany Lucius, we may then say, are there to secure the Protestant succession'.[24] That certainly is one possible reading. But there is nothing in the text to require it. After all, if Titus' claim that Astraea had left the world is applied to the present, and not to the future – in other words, if it were taken as a comment on the patent absence of justice from a world ruled by a persecuting tyrant like Saturninus or (on certain Catholic views) Elizabeth – then it could be read as an ironic comment on the lack of justice to be found under the rule of 'Astraea' herself. And if that were the case, the light and the succession to be restored by Lucius at the end of the play might not be all that Protestant after all.

As with Bate's interpretation of the scene, nothing in the play compels such a reading; but nor is there anything to rule it out. As with other Shakespeare plays, it is left up to the viewer or reader to decide how to locate the action of the play in relation to current events. The play could be left safely in what was a distinctly distant, mythic Roman never-never land, the moral territory of the revenge tragedy rather than of the history play. More riskily, the action of the play could be applied to the immediate English past and present. Rather more safely, as Bate suggests, it could be construed as a (somewhat dystopian) gesture towards what might await the English after the death of Elizabeth. However, as we have seen, if the play was used in this way, as an interpretative tool – a moral and political template through which to view the current religio-political conjuncture – the reader or viewer was likely to find him or herself rather quickly confronted with some distinctly alarming conclusions. Unless, of course, he or she merely viewed the play, with pleasure tinged with horror, as a rather bloody drama, based heavily on recent box-office successes about revenge by Kyd and Marlowe.

2

⊰⊶⊱

Tyranny delineated

Tyranny as a conspiracy (of evil counsel)

If we follow through with the thought experiment that allows that the treatment of the Andronici *might* have recalled to at least *some* contemporaries the situation of Elizabethan Catholics, what can we say about the play's analysis of the regime at whose hands the Andronici are suffering? Its tyranny operates at a number of levels, through a series of linked networks of evil counsel and of sexual or sexualized corruption and influence. At its head, of course, stands the figure of Saturninus, who, from the outset, reveals himself as the stuff of which tyrants are made. But the malignity of the regime is not solely – or even mainly – a function of Saturninus' propensity to tyranny. It is also a product of the evil influence over events of Tamora and, through her, of Aaron the Moor. The connections here are pictured as sexual, a function of passion, indeed of lust. Impulses which link Tamora and Aaron both to one another and to Saturninus. The result is a love triangle of corruption and malignity. From the outset, as an archetypical tyrant, Saturninus is shown to be a creature of his passions, as evidenced by his instant attraction and attachment to Tamora. Even as he is becoming betrothed to Lavinia, he takes a shine to his new captive. 'A goodly lady, trust me, of the hue / That I would choose were I to choose anew' [I, i, 265–266]. As the projected match to Lavinia breaks down in the face of the opposition of Bassianus and of Titus' sons, Saturninus immediately takes Tamora for his queen; here anger and pride compound lust to push him into instant marriage [I, i, 331–333].

In response, she promises that 'if Saturnine advance the queen of Goths, / She will a handmaid be to his desires, / A loving nurse, a mother to his youth' [I, i, 335–337]. And thus she proves. We have already seen her schooling him in the arts of Machiavellian manipulation, as she urges him to pretend reconciliation with the

Andronici in public, while, in private, nurturing his (and her) desire to destroy them. But her role as evil counsellor goes beyond acting as a malign mother or nursemaid to Saturninus' worst impulses; she also uses her hold over him to mislead him into evils, the full nature of which he is unaware. Here the crucial examples are the murder of Bassianus, the rape and mutilation of Lavinia, and the summary execution of Titus' two sons, Quintus and Martius. Implicated in, indeed central to, the tyranny of the act, through his arbitrary and tyrannical subversion of the proper legal forms and his cruel manipulation of Titus, Saturninus yet remains innocent of the truth. He reacts with shock and anger when the real identity of the killers is revealed in act V. In this, the central action of the play and the quintessence of his tyranny, he remains Tamora's dupe.

Titus describes the relationship perfectly in act IV, when he observes that 'she's with the lion deeply still in league, / And lulls him whilst she playeth on her back, / And when he sleeps will she do what she list' [IV, i, 98–100]. Here the seduction into tyranny of an unvirtuous prince by an evil counsellor – able, at every turn, to anticipate his whims and gratify his passions – is given graphically sexual form in the relationship between Saturninus and Tamora. But Saturninus is undone by sex in more than the obvious sense. For the ultimate manipulation and betrayal of Saturninus, the prince, by Tamora, the evil counsellor, occurs in her affair with Aaron the Moor. This not only betrays and cuckolds the emperor, but it also nearly leads to his being saddled with an entirely supposititious heir. Throughout, the play figures the link between Tamora and Aaron in sexual terms. As Aaron enters the action contemplating Tamora's sudden rise to power in the Roman state and its likely consequences, he describes his own hold over the queen in the language of sexual seduction and mastery:

> Then Aaron, arm thy heart and fit thy thoughts
> To mount aloft with thy imperial mistress,
> And mount her pitch whom thou in triumph long
> Hast prisoner held, fettered in amorous chains
> And faster bound to Aaron's charming eyes
> Than is Prometheus bound to Caucasus. [I, i, 511–516]

Aaron, then, is to Tamora as Tamora is to Saturninus. Enabling, giving form and shape to her passions and malign purposes, Aaron is the ultimate Machiavel and evil counsellor. Through sexual lust enter corruption and evil counsel; and through evil counsel enter tyranny and oppression, violence and revenge. Saturninus' lust for Tamora, and for revenge on the Andronici, leaves him open to manipulation, corruption and betrayal at her (and Aaron's) hands; Tamora's lust for sexual pleasure and revenge leaves her and, through her, the Roman state, open to the utterly malign and destructive influence of that ultimate atheist and Machiavel, Aaron the Moor.

From the moment that Titus refuses Tamora's request to spare her son Alarbus, she remains determined, in the words of her son Demetrius, 'to quit the bloody wrongs upon her foes'. In the same speech, he exhorts her to

> . . . stand resolved, but hope withal
> The self-same gods that armed the queen of Troy
> With opportunity of sharp revenge
> Upon the Thracian tyrant in his tent
> May favour Tamora, the queen of Goths. [I, i, 138–142]

The rest of the play shows her in single-minded pursuit of that end. 'Ne'er let my heart know merry cheer indeed / Till all the Andronici be made away' [II, ii, 188–189].

The play presented the impulses that lie behind these aims as quintessentially 'feminine'. The sensual nature of Tamora's love for 'my sweet moor' represents the susceptibility of womankind to the pleasures of the flesh and the promptings of lust. Her impulse towards revenge is based upon a mother's love for her son, given passionate expression in her speech to Titus begging him to 'rue the tears I shed, / A mother's tears in passion for her son!' [I, i, 108–109]. There she appears as the epitome of feminine pity and motherly emotion. But the moment her pleas for mercy are denied, her nature is transformed, indeed inverted, into the mirror opposite of feminine softness and motherly virtue. She explains the nature of the change to Lavinia, who has just asked Tamora to have mercy for 'my father's sake', who 'gave thee life when well he might have slain thee'. Tamora replies that

> . . . hadst thou in person ne'er offended me,
> Even for his sake I am pitiless.
> Remember, boys, I poured forth tears in vain
> To save your brother from the sacrifice,
> But fierce Andronicus would not relent. [II, ii, 158–165]

The transformation of Tamora's nature into the opposite of itself, the perfect inversion of what a woman should be, is played out in the scene between Lavinia and Tamora in the forest. Lavinia tries to appeal to her fellow-feeling as a woman: 'O Tamora thou bearest a woman's face . . .' At first, Tamora will have none of it – 'I will not hear her speak; away with her!' However, her sons persuade her to listen to Lavinia's pleas, the better to demonstrate her ruthlessness. The exchange closes with Lavinia clinging to Tamora and begging for 'present death' at her hands, rather than a fate worse than death at those of Tamora's sons. Refused even that respite, Lavinia rounds on the queen of the Goths: 'no grace? No womanhood? Ah, beastly creature, / The blot and enemy to our general name' [II, ii, 173, 182–183].

On this account, then, perverted by revenge and lust, Tamora has become the symmetrical opposite of what a woman should be: inhuman, unnatural, just like Queen Margaret in the *Henry VI* plays, she has now become 'a beastly creature'. This is a verdict that the later action of the play confirms. Having started out begging for the life of her son, she ends up (in intention at least) as an infanticide, bidding Aaron to 'christen' their new born son 'with thy dagger's point' [IV, ii, 68–72].

As for Aaron, his motives and nature are even more purely malign than Tamora's. As we have seen, he enters the action with the speech of the classic, Marlovian over-reacher and Machiavel. There he announces his determination

> To mount aloft with thy imperial mistress,
> . . .
> Away with slavish weeds and servile thoughts!
> I will be bright, and shine in pearl and gold
> To wait upon this new-made empress.
> To wait, said I? – To wanton with this queen,
> This goddess, this Semiramis, this nymph,
> This siren that will charm Rome's Saturnine
> And see his shipwreck and his commonweal's. [I, i, 500–523]

Previous plays like Marlowe's *The Jew of Malta, Edward II* and *The Massacre at Paris*, and Shakespeare's *Richard III*, had introduced the audience to the figure of the utterly malign Machiavel; and, true to the expectations aroused by such characters as Mortimer or Guise, and, of course, by this speech, thereafter Aaron proves himself a classic example of the type. It is, as he explains to the warring Demetrius and Chiron, his 'policy and stratagem must do / That you affect' [I, i, 604–605] 'a stratagem / That, cunningly effected, will beget / A very excellent piece of villainy' [II, ii, 5–7]. Aaron's 'policy' thus turns a potentially disastrous feud over the sexual rights to Lavinia into an occasion for the slaughter of Bassianus, the ruin of Lavinia and the decimation of the remaining ranks of the Andronici [I, i, 561, 577]. Similarly, it is Aaron's 'villainy' [III, i, 203] that devises the scheme by which Andronicus is parted from his hand. And lastly, it is his 'deed of policy' [IV, ii, 150] in killing the only two witnesses to the birth of his son that keeps the existence of the bastard child whom he has conceived with Tamora a secret from the emperor. As a number of critics have noted, the word 'policy' is a key term in *The Jew of Malta*, its repetition there by the eponymous Jew himself signalling his status as a Machiavel indeed. As a Moor, Aaron's racial (and, at least to the Christian audience, his religious) otherness parallels that of the anti-hero of Marlowe's play, and marks him out again as the quintessential atheistical Machiavel.

Thus far, the ends of Aaron's scheming have been rationally self-interested – that is to say, explicable in terms of the urge to achieve revenge, both for himself and his mistress, on the Andronici; and of the need to avert an outbreak of internal strife and public scandal that could threaten them all, and to suppress all knowledge of his son's existence, coupled with the preservation of the baby's life, against the infanticidal preferences of the mother. However, the play hints throughout that there is more going on here than the mere pursuit – albeit the entirely corrupt and amoral pursuit – of self-interest. Aaron's first speech concludes with that reference to working the ruin both of 'Saturnine' and of 'this commonweal'. As he presides over the manoeuvres that dupe Titus into severing his own hand in a vain attempt to save his sons, Aaron observes to no one in particular that

. . . this villainy
Doth fat me with the very thoughts of it.
Let fools do good and fair men call for grace,
Aaron will have his soul black like his face. [III, i, 203–206]

As Tamora enters labour, Demetrius suggests that they 'go pray to all the gods / For our beloved mother in her pains', only to be told by Aaron 'pray to the devils; the gods have given us over' [IV, ii, 46–48].

What is emerging here is a picture of an atheistical Machiavel so sunk in sin, so thoroughly malign, as to have transcended even the entirely evil and corrupt pursuit of self-interest. Aaron is a man whose only pleasure lies in doing wrong, in inflicting pain, and in watching his own cunning come to fruition in the ruin and agony of others. That picture, suggested with increasing clarity as the plot progresses, is finally filled out in act V. As we have seen, in the exchange in which Aaron forces Lucius to swear that if he, Aaron, spills the beans, Lucius will spare the Moor's son, Aaron admits his atheism. After he has outlined the story of his own villainy – the murder of Bassianus, the rape and mutilation of Lavinia, the rigged evidence and false charges against Quintus and Martius, his cuckolding of the emperor, the trick played on Titus that parted him from his hand – he is asked by Lucius 'are you not sorry for these heinous deeds', only to be told that the only thing that Aaron is sorry for is that he has been unable to commit more such crimes:

> . . . as kill a man or else devise his death,
>
> Ravish a maid or plot the way to do it,
>
> Accuse some innocent and forswear myself,
>
> Set deadly enmity between two friends,
>
> Make poor men's cattle break their necks,
>
> Set barns on fire and haystacks in the night
>
> And bid the owners quench them with their tears.
>
> Oft have I digged up dead men from their graves
>
> And set them upright at their dear friends' door,
>
> Even when their sorrows almost was forgot,
>
> And on their skins, as on the bark of trees,
>
> Have with my knife carved in Roman letters,
>
> 'Let not your sorrow die though I am dead.'
>
> Tut, I have done a thousand dreadful things
>
> As willingly as one would kill a fly,
>
> And nothing grieves me heartily indeed
>
> But that I cannot do ten thousand more.

When Lucius responds to this tirade with the command 'bring down the devil, for he must not die / So sweet a death as hanging presently', Aaron replies with a riff on the notion of the devil: 'If there be devils, would I were a devil, / To live and burn in everlasting fire, / So I might have your company in hell / But to torment you with my bitter tongue' [V, i, 123–150].

By this point, Aaron has become the embodiment of evil, a principle of pure malignity. It is perhaps no accident that many of the crimes to which we see him pleading guilty with such enthusiasm were also precisely the sorts of crimes often imputed to that other agent of Satan – the witch. Indeed, the only thing that prevents Aaron from presenting himself as such an agent is that, as an atheist, he cannot quite bring himself to believe in the devil either. In Aaron we see the ultimate moral consequences of atheism: a delight in pure evil that would qualify him – 'if', as he says, 'there be devils' – for a leading role in hell. His status as the personification of evil – that is to say, as the perfect inversion of good – is confirmed in this final scene. When called to repentance, he repents only for evil deeds undone.

All this is figured in and through the colour of his skin, to which the play makes repeated reference. While he claims that others think black a dreadful, threatening hue, and his infant son 'a joyless, dismal, black and sorrowful issue', 'as loathsome as a toad / Amongst the fair-faced breeders of our clime' [IV, ii, 68–70], Aaron glories in his own and his son's blackness. As we have seen, at one point he expresses the wish that his soul might become as black as his face. Confronted with the demand that he kill his own son, the better to protect Tamora and her sons' hold on power, he rounds on Demetrius and Chiron in a tirade that simply inverts the traditional dichotomy, the binary opposition, between black (bad) and white (good):

What, what, ye sanguine, shallow hearted boys,
Ye white-limed walls, ye alehouse painted signs!
Coal-black is better than another hue;
In that it scorns to bear another hue;
For all the water in the ocean
Can never turn the swan's black legs to white,
Although she lave them hourly in the flood. [IV, ii, 99–105]

More constant than white, black is also more capable of dissimulation. 'There's the privilege your beauty bears. / Fie, treacherous hue, that will betray with blushing / The close enacts and counsels of thy heart' [IV, ii, 118–120].

If Aaron's blackness and moorishness stand, therefore, as an outward sign of his utter malignity and evil, of the complete moral inversion consequent upon atheism, his identity as a Moor also renders him even more radically other. His is an otherness that places him beyond the pale not only of *Romanitas*, but also, in terms of the experience and expectations of an Elizabethan audience, of a Christianity that, while utterly alien to the pagan world evoked by the play, yet hovers over (and at crucial points infuses) the action.

The tyranny of the regime that is persecuting the Andronici is thus composed of a number of strands. We have the pride, intemperance and suspicion of Saturninus. His potential for arbitrary and tyrannical action is turned into actual tyranny by the evil counsel, the corrupting influence and deceit of Tamora, whose own impulses towards violence and revenge are realized, in turn, by the 'policy', the stratagems and 'villainy' of her evil counsellor and lover, Aaron the Moor. The three of them are linked in a triangle of evil counsel, pride and revenge. The emperor's attachment to Tamora is paralleled by hers to Aaron, and the regime as a whole is pictured as a corrupt and corrupting love triangle, a lustful and tyrannical *ménage a trois*. The co-dependency, the appeals to whim and passion, that unite tyrant and evil counsellor, are here staged in explicitly sexual terms. Appealing to and exacerbating the others' worst impulses, their most degraded characteristics and instincts, each corrupts the others, enabling all of them to realize their full potential for evil.

Beyond evil counsel

It is worth comparing, for a moment, the play's account of tyranny, and of the forces and mechanisms that produce it in the play, first with a series of Catholic analyses of the tyranny of the Elizabethan regime, and then with the account of monarchical dysfunction given in *2* and *3 Henry VI*.[1] The Catholic accounts turned on the influence over an innocent queen of a variety of atheistical and Machiavellian evil counsellors – men who played on her susceptibilities and fears, the better to monopolize access to the queen, marginalize the ancient nobility, persecute their opponents, demonize the Catholics and kill Mary Stuart. The Catholic tracts portrayed the diversion of the succession either to the plotters themselves or to their creatures as the final culminations of these conspiracies. The men doing the plotting were presented as functional atheists, and, in the case of the earl of Leicester at least, notable sensualists, unable to check either their own (equally inordinate) lusts or ambitions. They were motivated entirely by the lust for power and position. Some Catholic polemicists, notably Cardinal Allen, reproduced and elaborated on the popular rumours that linked Elizabeth to Leicester as lovers, and indeed claimed that the queen had given birth to more than one bastard child by the earl.[2] As Carol Levine has shown, such rumours persisted at a popular level well into the 1590s.[3] When we add to the equation the fact that Elizabeth often referred to Walsingham as her 'Moor',[4] the argument that the drama was here playing off and exploiting a range of common knowledge and current rumour becomes rather compelling – particularly when we recall that Southwell's tract fingered Walsingham as the author of the trumped-up conspiracy that had sent not merely Babington and his mates, but also the queen of Scots herself, to an entirely undeserved traitor's death.

The *Treatise of Treasons* was the first statement of this Catholic view of the Elizabethan regime as a functional tyranny, based on a conspiracy of evil counsel. That tract identified the central conspirators as Cecil and Bacon, two men to whom it thereafter refers as Ulysses and Sinon. At the end of the play, as the villainy of the now dead Saturninus and Tamora is discovered, 'a Roman lord' demands that Marcus, the tribune, 'tell us what Sinon hath bewitched our ears, / Or who hath brought the fatal engine in / That gives our Troy, our Rome, the civil wound' [V, iii, 84–86]. Of course, the equation between Rome and Troy was very commonly spliced into foundation myths about London, England – and indeed Britain. Stories about the end of Troy and the origins of Rome were regularly applied both to English history and to contemporary events. These were associations that the *Treatise of Treasons* had exploited and which this play was arguably exploiting again.

These evil-counsel narratives had been produced, for the most part, by Catholic authors, who at least pictured themselves as 'loyalists'. They deployed the trope of evil counsel and conspiracy in order to save the queen from blame for the dreadful deeds and calamitous policies being committed and prosecuted in her name. If the regime was acting as a tyranny, that was not because it was headed by a tyrant, but rather because the queen was being systematically misled by a conspiracy of atheistical evil counsellors who had isolated her from her loyal (and often Catholic) subjects, told her lies about popery, Mary Stuart and the king of Spain, and presented themselves as her only hope of safety in an increasingly dangerous world. In the play, however, no such loop-holes remain.[5]

Again, in direct contrast to the analysis proffered by the Catholic tracts, but entirely in line with the *Henry VI* plays, the play reveals a central reason for the depravity of the regime to be the combination of monarchical weakness and an excess of female influence. Here Tamora plays the same role as Queen Margaret in the *Henry VI* plays – which also, of course, feature a love triangle linking a woman and a queen (Margaret), denatured by pride, lust and revenge, to her paramour, a corrupt courtier and evil counsellor (Suffolk), and finally to her terminally weak (but, in Henry VI's case, saintly and totally oblivious) husband and prince. In *Titus*, the balance between these three elements is shifted, for the worse. Suffolk has become the utterly malign and overtly (rather than merely implicitly) atheistical Aaron; Margaret has morphed into Tamora; and the central monarch-figure changed from the weak, but innocent, Henry into the weak, but vicious, Saturninus. We are now dealing with a fully fledged tyranny, centred on the figure of the prince, rather than merely on his evil counsellors and consort. Saturninus may indeed be oblivious to the deepest-dyed villainies being perpetrated in his name, and thus the victim of evil counsel, but he is more than violent, arbitrary, cruel and lustful enough to count as a tyrant in his own right. Moreover, since his evil counsellors are also his wife and her lover, it is neither practically feasible nor morally useful to draw nice distinctions between the roles played by these three partners in crime in the tyranny over which they all jointly preside.

Bad Queen Bess?

In the *Henry VI* plays, insofar as they existed at all, the connections between the resulting image of tyranny and the person of Queen Elizabeth had been left entirely implicit. *Titus,* however, gestures at such connections with considerably more daring. There is, of course, a striking resonance between the scene in which the vengeful Tamora taunts Lavinia before consigning her to a fate worse than death at the hands of her sons, and that in which Queen Margaret taunts York with the blood of his slaughtered son, before he, too, is slaughtered. Margaret is tormenting a man, but Tamora is shown doing the same to another woman. Lavinia is, of course, presented throughout as the epitome of feminine virtue. Beautiful enough to arouse the lustful desires of Tamora's dreadful sons, her virtue is such that Aaron can tell them in advance that anything other than a violent assault on it will prove fruitless. The epitome of daughterly and wifely duty, for Titus she is 'the cordial of mine age to glad my heart' [I, i, 169]. In this scene we see this personification of womanly virtue, and now of incipient victimhood, confronting the certainty of 'martyrdom' and begging a queen for that most feminine (and, of course, most royal and Christian) of virtues – mercy; pleas which are, of course, denied. The result is a starkly polarized diptych, in which archetypal feminine virtue, victimhood and martyrdom confront an equally archetypal image of feminine depravity and cruelty. In a play written at the height of the Elizabethan state's persecution of its Catholic subjects, and only a few years after the execution of Mary Stuart, this may not have been a scene devoid of immediate contemporary religious, moral and political resonance.

As Heather James has noted, the impact of this scene on an Elizabethan audience is likely to have been considerably compounded by the deployment within it of a number of classical figures and images central to the 'cult' of Queen Elizabeth as the poetry and festivals of the court constructed it. Coming upon Tamora and Aaron alone in the woods, Bassianus and Lavinia compare her to Diana, who 'habited' like 'Rome's royal empress' 'hath abandoned her holy groves / To see the general hunting in this forest' [II, ii, 55–59]. The chaste figure of Diana was, of course, often used to personate and praise the Virgin Queen. Earlier in the same scene, in the course of turning aside Tamora's amatory advances, her lover, Aaron the Moor, has just compared Tamora to that decidedly unchaste figure, Venus. For the audience, then, there is a considerable irony in hearing Tamora now compared to the archetypically chaste Diana. Thus is a figure conventionally used to praise the virtue and chastity of one queen, Elizabeth, converted into a means to exhibit the corruption and lasciviousness of another, Tamora. Trying to provoke the pair, Tamora takes up the Diana reference, replying that, if she really had Diana's powers, she would turn both of them into deer (as Diana had Actaeon), so that they could be punished for their presumption – 'saucy controller of my private steps' [II, ii, 60] – by being torn apart by the hunter's hounds. At this, Lavinia takes up the image of 'planting presently with horns' and the association of Actaeon with cuckoldry, directly to impugn the queen's own chastity:

> 'Tis thought you have a goodly gift in horning,
> And to be doubted that your Moor and you
> Are singled forth to try experiments.
> Jove shield your husband from his hounds today:
> 'Tis pity they should take him for a stag. [II, ii, 67–71]

This exchange James identifies as

> an obscene parody of Vergil's *Venus Armata* from *Aeneid I* where Venus disguises herself as a follower of Diana. In this paradoxically erotic and chaste form she appears to Aeneas and directs him to Carthage and Dido. The *Venus Armata*, who synthesized eroticism and chastity, was also incorporated into the iconography of the Virgin Queen.

Here, then, are two images used to praise Elizabeth, being used in the play to expose and denounce Tamora. Diana, of course, was also the huntress, and, as the following scenes show, Tamora's threatening classical allusions turn literal, as Aaron's plot comes to fruition and both Bassianus and Lavinia become her (and her son's) prey. The reference to Diana's chastity serves only to emphasize Tamora's lust, and Diana's role as a huntress only to emphasize her cruelty in hunting, not the 'panther and the hind', but that most innocent and defenceless of prey, the 'dainty doe' Lavinia [II, i, 26]. Thus, as James points out, the figures of Venus Armata and Diana join Astraea – all three 'guises' commonly 'appropriated from Vergil' to praise the queen – but used here for far from panegyric purposes.[6]

To this material can be added Tamora's fate at the very end of the play. Of the three principal malefactors, only Saturninus receives anything like an honourable burial. Lucius instructs 'some loving friends convey the emperor hence / And give him burial in his father's grave' [V, iii, 190–191]. Aaron the Moor has already been consigned to a dreadful fate: buried alive, he is to be left to starve to death. Anyone who relieves his agony is threatened with instant death. 'As for that ravenous tiger, Tamora', who was, after all, a queen and the emperor's wife, her corpse is to be left to rot in the street [V, iii, 194–199]. Thus, for all that she was a queen in her own right and the emperor's wife, her corpse receives treatment remarkably similar to that visited on the Catholic victims of the Elizabethan state, whose quartered remains were similarly left to rot on public display.

From tyranny to resistance

As Coppelia Kahn has observed, at the centre of the play's action is Titus' transition from Roman hero to revenging hero.[7] According to Kahn (writing about *Julius Caesar*),

> revenge . . . has a feminine character. Its matrix is pity and tears, the release of tender and passionate feelings, which are then easily transmuted into 'domestic fury and fierce civil strife' reminiscent of the Furies or the crazed female worshippers of Dionysius who in Euripides' Bacchae are capable of rending their children limb from limb.[8]

The same, of course, applied to Progne and Philomel, who were equally capable, in their revenging fury, of horrific violence and infanticide, and whose story features prominently in *Titus*. Thus, in Kahn's account, Titus' transition from Roman to revenging hero involves – or perhaps more precisely is effected through – a move from an inherently masculine, almost inhumanly controlled, Roman virtue, to a decidedly feminine emotional incontinence, an excess of feeling that eventually plunges Titus into something like madness.

In the opening acts of the play, secure in his role as Roman hero, Titus is able to contemplate the deaths of myriad sons with an extraordinary degree of emotional control. Hitherto everything that Titus has done and suffered has been both justified and rewarded by his service to Rome and her gods. His sons have either died in Rome's service, or, in Mutius' case, received the just deserts of disloyalty and disobedience. Now confronted first with the summary arrest and condemnation of two of his three remaining sons and the exile of the third, and then with the rape and mutilation of his only daughter, the exchange of mutual benefits, of service and sacrifice for gratitude and honour, which had hitherto structured both Titus' relations with Rome and his own sense of self, is shattered, and the result is something like a complete breakdown. A masculine, quintessentially Roman, control is now replaced by an emotional incontinence, an (over?) identification with the sufferings of Lavinia, in which he envisages himself, and his masculine kin, joining his daughter in turning 'some fountain' into 'a brine pit with our bitter tears' [III, i, 124–130]. Later he figures himself as the sea moved, and as the earth 'overflowed and drowned' 'with her continual tears' [III, i,

226–230], and insists, against all evidence to the contrary, that he alone 'can interpret all her martyred signs' [III, ii, 36]. When Marcus appeals to him to 'let reason govern thy lament', Titus replies that 'if there were reason for these miseries, / Then into limits could I bind my woes. / When heaven doth weep, doth not the earth o'erflow?' [III, i, 219–222].

But despite the intensity of his suffering, Titus' loyalism persists, even in the face of Saturninus' inherently tyrannical suggestion that he exchange the hand of one of the Andronici for the lives of his two sons. Here the play grotesquely parodies Titus' serial sacrifice of his family to the demands of the Roman state by recasting that sacrifice in absurdly over-literal terms, as he prepares, in return for the lives of his two sons, to part with 'that noble hand of thine / That hath thrown down so many enemies' and 'defended Rome' [III, i, 163–164, 168]. For all his malignity, Saturninus is here speaking a language that Titus can all too readily understand, and Titus embraces the offer with enthusiasm, even joy [III, i, 158–162].

And so, the return of his hand along with the heads of his two sons represents some sort of tipping point. Up until now, Titus has always been able to construe his own sufferings and those of his family as sacrifices to the good of Rome, direct consequences of his loyalty to the Roman state, and thus as enhancements to the honour of his lineage. But now that Rome (in the person of the emperor and his clique) has turned on him and his with such ferocity, that nexus of meaning, that source of ultimate value, has been utterly removed, and the service and sacrifice of the Andronici to the Roman state rendered meaningless – 'hands to do Rome service is but vain' [III, i, 81]. In the face of that meaninglessness, Titus finally turns to revenge, asking 'which way shall I find Revenge's cave?' [III, i, 271].

Earlier, even as he realized that Rome was 'but a wilderness of tigers' and 'tigers must prey, and Rome affords no prey / But me and mine' [III, i, 54–56], he had eschewed thoughts of active resistance or revenge, merely telling his banished son Lucius 'how happy art thou then / From these devourers to be banished'. Even after he discovered Lavinia's fate, Titus had held back. Now, however, with Saturninus' malice and deceit clearly established, Titus' thoughts turn, at last, to active resistance. He gathers his remaining kin about him 'that I may turn me to each one of you / And swear unto my soul to right your wrongs'. He now sends Lucius off – not to safety in exile, but rather 'to the Goths', to 'raise an army there' [III, i, 278–279, 286].

Titus now acknowledges for the first time that, as Kahn puts it, he must cease to be a Roman hero and become instead a revenging one. But that transition has dreadful emotional (as well as political) consequences. Not only are the service of Rome and the service of his family honour no longer coterminous, for Titus they have become mutually exclusive; for now, the pursuit of virtue, honour and justice seems to demand that he take action against the emperor himself. The result is the descent into madness, a complete lack of control, exhibited in the famous scene in which he reprimands his brother Marcus for the murder of a fly.

When Marcus observes, at the close of that scene, that 'grief has so wrought on him / He takes false shadows for true substances' [III, ii, 80–81], I think we must construe that grief as caused not only by his daughter's suffering and his sons' death, but also by the dissolution of the entire moral and political system that has hitherto enabled Titus to maintain the inhuman levels of self-control, Roman virtue and piety on display in the opening acts of the play. What we are seeing here is the breakdown of Titus, the honourable, pious and loyal Roman, into something else entirely.

But the result is anything but a continuing attack of emotional incontinence, a torrent of complaint addressed to the gods or his kin. That which the sufferings of his children and his own fate at the hands of the emperor and Tamora have deprived him of – his masculine *Romanitas* – his role as a revenger now enables him to reclaim. As a revenger, Titus does not give in to the extremities of passion, the spasms of emotion that characterize his grief and plaint in act III. Thus, even as he pledges himself to revenge, Titus rushes neither to judgement nor to action. He rather waits until he has discovered the precise nature of Lavinia's fate and the identity of her tormentors.

There is, of course, a contrast being drawn here between Titus' caution, his refusal to resort to violence until he has explored all other avenues and ferreted out the truth of the matter, and the addiction to precipitate, arbitrary and cruel action displayed throughout by the tyrannical Saturninus. Only once the extent of Saturninus' tyranny has become apparent, and the identity of the guilty parties established beyond doubt, does Titus move actively to seek his 'revenge'. For all his anguish and madness, there is something measured, judicious, even judicial, about Titus' approach to revenge and resistance.[9]

The political points being made here are clear enough. The play is set in an elective monarchy. And while it goes out of its way to establish the personal and political loyalty of Titus to the Roman state, the hereditary principle and indeed the person of Saturninus, the play also establishes that once the injustice of Saturninus' regime has been proven beyond doubt, once it is clear that Astraea really has left the building and that power is in the hands of Tamora and the Moor, resistance becomes entirely justified. Viewed in political terms, Titus' conduct thus shows that, even in an elective monarchy, mere injustice is not enough to justify violent resistance. If resistance is to be legitimate, the tyranny (and personal guilt) of those to be resisted must be patent, instantly recognizable as such to any and every observer, once the real truth is known.

The discovery of the identity of Lavinia's assailants enables Titus to turn the search for revenge into an exercise in rectificatory justice, creating, as Crosbie puts it, 'proportionate exchange, an equivalent return, even in his method of revenge'.[10] Moreover, because of the identity and status of its objects, Titus' powerful private impulse to avenge himself on those who have devastated his family becomes coterminous with his public duty to save the state from tyranny and destruction at the hands of Saturninus, Tamora and Aaron. As Coppelia Kahn observes, 'a political over-plot – the assault on Rome to unseat Saturninus . . . is paralleled and interwoven with the revenge plot against Tamora'.[11] It is now clear that the truest and last service that Titus can render Rome is to free her from the tyranny and injustice of Saturninus and Tamora. At this point, 'revenge' and the service of the Roman state, his personae as (in Kahn's terms) both a revenging and a Roman hero, as the agent of both private revenge and public justice, the vindicator of the honour of the Andronici and the servant of the Roman state, all come back into alignment, to form both a coherent plan of action and a unitary sense of both moral and political identity and purpose. The shift back from the 'feminine' emotional incontinence, the excess of human sympathy, to an inhuman and quintessentially masculine and Roman self-control is figured by Titus' cold-blooded and elaborately choreographed slaughter of Lavinia, the very person whose 'martyred signs' had provoked in him such an unwonted excess of emotion, but who now becomes the last of his progeny to be sacrificed to the honour of the lineage.

The transactions taking place here between public and private, the service of the state and the pursuit of personal revenge, between the 'feminine' role of revenging hero and the 'masculine' one of Roman hero, can be traced through the different 'patterns, precedents and warrants' culled from the canonical texts of *Romanitas* which Titus adopts – first, to make sense of his situation and order his emotions, and then to frame and legitimate his revenge. At first, as they learn just what has been done to Lavinia and who has done it, Titus and Marcus refer themselves to the fate of Lucrece at the hands of Tarquin [IV, i, 61–64]. Of course, if Lavinia is Lucrece, then, in taking revenge for her rape, Titus becomes Marcus Junius Brutus – and he was anything but a private revenger, but rather the saviour and re-founder of Rome as a republic. Thus, after Lavinia has successfully imparted what has been done to her and by whom, Marcus enjoins the other Andronici to swear an oath of the sort 'Lord Junius Brutus swore for Lucrece rape, / That we will prosecute by good advice / Mortal revenge upon these traitorous Goths, / And see their blood, or die with this reproach' [IV, i, 89–94].

But these scenes employ another literary template, taken from the Roman canon, to explain Lavinia's fate and what should be done about it. And that is Ovid's story of

Philomel and Tereus. Marcus is the first to adopt this tale as a means of interpreting Lavinia's fate, when he meets her, mutilated and bleeding, wandering in the woods. Titus has recourse to the same story in questioning Lavinia: 'wert thou thus surprised, sweet girl, / Ravished and wronged as Philomel was, / Forced in the ruthless, vast and gloomy woods?' [IV, i, 51–53]. And, of course, it is to these passages in Ovid's *Metamorphoses* that Lavinia points in her desperate attempt finally to communicate what has happened to her. But if Lavinia is Philomel, then, in taking revenge on her ravishers, the Andronici become not that epitome of masculine *Romanitas* – the state-saving and founding Marcus Junius Brutus – but rather Philomel and Progne, two female epitomes of a passionate revenge, worked through the private means of inhuman, almost bestial, cruelty and conspiracy. Even as he takes his revenge on Demetrius and Chiron, Titus homes in on precisely this textual precedent and warrant: 'worse than Philomel you used my daughter, / And worse than Progne I will be revenged' [V, ii, 194–195].

Here, then, are two very different models for action. While the one – masculine, public and entirely honourable – enables the roles of Roman and revenging hero to be squared, the other – private, feminine and inhumanly violent – does not. But the Andronici's political circumstances, labouring under tyranny, ensure that some combination of these modes of revenge will be necessary if the culprits are to be brought to book and justice done.

Thus, when in act IV the boy enjoins his elders and betters to adopt the course of open confrontation – 'if I were a man / Their mother's bedchamber should not be safe / For these base bondmen to the yoke of Rome' – Titus first praises his mettle and then demurs: 'I'll teach thee another course' [IV, i, 107–109, 119]. What that course amounts to is a subtle combination of political tactics designed to wage a war of nerves against the tyrant and his moll. As we have seen, under cover of Titus' madness the Andronici set out, slowly but surely, to undermine the stability of Saturninus' regime and thus prepare for the arrival of Lucius at the head of an army of Goths. Saturninus himself tells us that these appeals to the people have gained considerable traction. 'When I have walked like a private man,' Saturninus admits that he has heard the people say Lucius' banishment was unjust and that they 'wished that Lucius were their emperor' [IV, iv, 72–76]. Thus, while both Saturninus' summary execution of the clown and his denunciation of the Andronici's petitions for justice as seditious libels are indeed acts of tyranny, there can be no doubt that, by this stage, he is right about the Andronici: the intentions behind their increasingly threatening protests and petitions are anything but those of simple loyalists. The transformation of the pious, loyal and honourable Titus of the first half of the play into not only the revenger, but also the political insurrectionary, conspirator and rebel of the second, is well under way.

When the subtle subversion worked from within by Titus and his kindred is joined by the arrival of Lucius and his army from without, the result is overt resistance, assassination and regime change, and the purposive re-adoption by Titus of the persona of a genuinely Roman hero, a veritable saviour of the Roman state. Where, in the opening act, that persona had been underpinned by (notably imperfect) parallels with Virgil's *Aeneid*, it is now based on (equally imperfect) correspondences to Livy. Appearing before the emperor with a veiled Lavinia, Titus asks Saturninus whether it was 'well done of rash Virginius / To slay his daughter with his own right hand, / Because she was enforced, stained and deflowered?' Saturninus replies that 'it was . . . because the girl should not survive her shame, / And by her presence still renew his sorrows'. This, claims Titus, is 'a reason mighty, strong and effectual; / A pattern, precedent and lively warrant / For me, most wretched, to perform the like' [V, iii, 36–44]. With that he kills Lavinia and then reveals the identity of her ravishers. Having informed Tamora that she has just eaten the guilty parties baked in a pie, he then kills her.

As for Titus, he is now in the process of trying to shed the (feminized) persona of a revenger and conspirator to become, at last and again, a truly Roman hero. No longer citing the example of Progne – that feminine epitome of conspiracy, private revenge and passionate, indeed bestial, cruelty – Titus, now in public and before the emperor, adopts the aggressively Roman and patriarchal persona of Virginius and, through him, of Marcus Junius Brutus, both of them revengers of ravished daughters, vindicators of their family's honour and saviours of the Roman state from tyranny. But while he is happy enough to cut down the innocent Lavinia, loyal to the last, he will not do the same to the entirely evil Saturninus. Up to this moment, Titus' revenge has been directed solely at those guilty of framing his sons and ravishing and mutilating his daughter; at the evil counsellors surrounding the emperor, rather than at the emperor himself. His actions, bloody as they are, serve to inform the emperor of the true nature of the dark deeds that have been done in his name. Titus thus gives Saturninus a chance to acknowledge the nature of his tyranny and forswear his past crimes; a chance, in Christian terms (entirely familiar to the audience, but entirely foreign to the characters in the play) to repent. This is an offer that Saturninus proves himself only too able to refuse and, as a tyrant and a pagan, he responds by promptly killing Titus. This act identifies him as a tyrant twice over – the first time duped by Tamora and Aaron, the second entirely in his own right. In an act of virtual suicide, Titus provokes Saturninus into killing him. In so doing, he leaves the tyrant to his son, Lucius, who, in an act both of revenge and of justice, an assertion of the honour of the Andronici and the ultimate service to Rome, duly dispatches him.

By now, of course, the watching Roman populace is at something of a loss. The tribune Marcus addresses them, appealing for unity: 'O let me teach you how to knit again / This scattered corn into one mutual sheaf, / These broken limbs again into one body' [V, iii, 66–71]. This is all very well, but Lucius has just arrived at the head of an army of Goths, Rome's ancient enemies, and has slain the emperor, apparently in cold blood. Accordingly, a Roman lord demands a fuller explanation, which Marcus and Lucius provide, detailing the villainies of Tamora, Aaron and Saturninus in all their gory detail. To prove the point, they are able to provide both the physical evidence of Aaron and Tamora's bastard child and the promise of Aaron himself as a witness.

3

Beyond paganism and politics

Providential endings, political means

As in *Richard III*, the dreadful evil of the persons being removed from power might be thought to occlude or elide the very radical nature of the means being used to remove them: conspiracy, foreign invasion, assassination and regicide. In *Richard III*, that effect had been compounded by the presence throughout the play of a battery of providential signs, dreams, prophecies and omens.[1] However, in marked contrast to the English history play, in *Titus* providence – defined as the intervention of the supernatural and the prophetic directly into events – has had nothing whatsoever to do with it.

As Lorna Hutson has shown, *Titus* contains within it the structures of a typical criminal prosecution for murder, and Saturninus' failure to observe the conventional legal structures is a central aspect of his emergence as a tyrant.[2] But we can add to Hutson's basic narrative structure, culled from legal procedure, that of the typical providentialized murder pamphlet or play. In *Titus*, many of the central features of such narratives are counterfeited or staged by Aaron and Tamora. The 'discovery' of the 'crime' of Andronicus' two sons features a number of events that, in the average murder narrative, would have been presented as quintessentially providential. First, we have the discovery, by Andronicus himself, of the 'fatal plotted scroll' [II, ii, 47] that reveals the innerness of the plot to do away with Bassianus. Second, we have the discovery of the buried pot of gold, allegedly hidden to pay off the murderers under the very bush detailed in the letter. But all these seemingly evidentiary and 'providential' signs are shown being plotted and planted by Aaron and his allies. The comment on these events – 'what, are they in the pit? O wondrous thing! / How easily is murder discovered' [II, ii, 286–287] – passed by Tamora, of course apes the conventional 'murder will out' moral at the heart of many a murder pamphlet or trial

53

(and central to the structure of *Richard III*) – except that here the play reveals that comment to be not merely entirely false, but counterfeited, in order to create the appearance of a verisimilitude, of a moral and factual transparency, that in fact is entirely illusory.

Here, then, is the plot structure – if not that plotted by providence itself, then certainly as laid out in many a providential pamphlet or play – which *Titus* shows us being deployed by Machiavellian elements within the state to do down their enemies and lure an always already suspicious and violent emperor (Saturninus) into outright injustice and tyranny. The play shows us a knot of malign, evil counsellors exploiting the conventional plot structures and assumptions that shaped Elizabethan perceptions of the nature of murder and treason, and of the workings of both divine and human justice, to bring about effects and outcomes that are precisely the opposite of those that usually conclude such heavily providential narratives. Aaron and his accomplices are shown using such assumptions not only to cover their own sins, but to put the blame on others. Instead of the revelation of the crime and the criminal, and the due exercise of justice and punishment, we have murder not revealed, but hidden. This is followed not by the discovery of truth and the doing of justice, through proper observance of the relevant legal norms and forms, under the supervening influence of providence, but rather by the summary execution of innocent men by an arbitrary and tyrannical prince.

In Saturninus' malign hands, the procedures of judicial investigation or trial do anything but uncover the truth. Of course, the truth is eventually revealed, but not by conventionally pseudo-miraculous or providential means. On the contrary, incidents that in other accounts of these (or similar) events would undoubtedly have been recounted as miraculous or providential are, in this play, presented as having (we might say) entirely natural causes. Perhaps the best example is that of the tongueless mute speaking. Part of the point of the mutilation of Lavinia was to prevent her telling anyone what had happened to her. And, for much of the play, the ploy works. A whole variety of characters lament their inability to communicate with her, and to divine what her mute signs and displays of emotion mean. And, for all the talk about mute signs and wounds speaking more eloquently than mere words, for the most part, Lavinia remains a 'map of woe, that thus dost talk in signs' [III, ii, 12]. When Marcus asks 'what means my niece Lavinia by these signs', Titus can only answer 'fear her not, Lucius – somewhat doth she mean' [IV, i, 8–9].

At last, the code is cracked, but by anything but miraculous means. Rather, Lavinia manages to impart what has happened to her by seizing a copy of Ovid's *Metamorphoses* and homing in on 'the tragic tale of Philomel / And treats of Tereus' treason and his rape' [IV, i, 47–48]. Then she writes the word for rape – *stuprum* – and the names of her assailants in the dust, by manipulating a stick held in her mouth and moved by her two stump-like arms. Thus does the play enable Lavinia's tongueless mouth and handless stumps to speak. Quite remarkably, there exist two murder pamphlets from 1606, in which the perpetrators of the peculiarly vicious murder of a pregnant woman and her son are brought to justice through the testimony of a young girl whose tongue they had cut out to prevent her spilling the beans.[3] In the pamphlets, of course, this is presented as an unmitigated miracle; but in *Titus*, for all Marcus' invocation of the gods [IV, I, 66–67], precisely the same outcome is achieved by entirely natural means. To put the question in terms laid out by St Hilaire, the revelation of the truth has been effected through the Andronici's capacity as true Romans to interpret and apply aright the canonical texts through which the play repeatedly constructs *Romanitas*. And, as ever, those texts provide not merely the key to the interpretation of past events, but prescriptive guides about what to do next.[4]

Interpreting the purport of the martyred wounds of the state's victim was, as we have seen, a highly controversial and contested act in Elizabethan England. But in this instance, there is no room left for such controversy. Lavinia's martyred wounds have quite literally spoken, and what they have said needs no interpretation and brooks no denial. She names what has been done to her and who has done it. The result is an indictment not only of rape, but also of judicial murder and inhuman cruelty visited upon the most innocent of victims through the thoroughgoing subversion of the outward forms of justice. In short, precisely what English Catholics described as the persecution and tyranny visited upon them by the Elizabethan state. After the revelation of such crime, all that remains is justice and revenge.

But murder, rape and the perversion of justice are not the only secret crimes revealed. Another is the adultery of Tamora and Aaron. That, too, is brought to light by an event to which contemporaries habitually attributed miraculous force or providential significance – a monstrous birth. But here the monstrous birth in question is again shown to have been the outcome of perfectly natural causes. For Tamora's child is taken to be monstrous only because it is black; and it is black only because its father is a Moor. Again, providential ends are achieved, but by transparently natural means or causes.

While Lavinia is one source for the crucial information about what happened to her and Bassianus, the other is Aaron the Moor. But unlike in a properly providentialized murder pamphlet or play, his testimony is not secured through the operation of his conscience, forcing him – in the presence of his victims, or at the scene of the crime, or following the testimony of some accomplice or other – to tell all. On the contrary, his conscience has nothing to do with it. Rather, he is forced to spill the beans by Lucius' threat to slaughter his own child before his very eyes. Earlier in the play, Aaron has betrayed his willingness to risk everything to save his son: as the offending infant is consigned by Tamora to his tender mercies – as she thinks, to die upon his 'dagger's point' – Aaron baulks. Told by Demetrius that if he does not do as he is bidden, he will 'betray thy noble mistress', he replies

> my mistress is my mistress, this myself,
> The vigour and the picture of my youth.
> This before all the world do I prefer,
> This maugre all the world will I keep safe,
> Or some of you shall smoke for it in Rome. [IV, ii, 109–113]

Audiences inured to the structuring assumptions of a variety of providentialized narratives might assume that they were being shown that there was one crime – infanticide – too dreadful for even Aaron to commit. Such an audience might well presume that the workings of conscience were starting to take hold. But if the scene does indeed elicit such expectations, it utterly fails to fulfil them. For, as Aaron's subsequent exchanges with Lucius show, the impulses operating here are not those of conscience. The visceral emotional connection linking Aaron to his son is not the beginning of a chain of moral or emotional reasoning that will lead him to a sense of the evil of his other crimes. Far from it. His excess of finer feeling for his progeny prompts not repentance, but another 'deed of policy', the callous slaughter of the midwife [IV, ii, 148–152]. And later, even as he barters information about his past misdeeds in return for his child's life, Aaron betrays not the slightest sign of remorse or repentance, but rather the opposite.

Aaron is shown here acting according to what we might term 'natural' instincts: emotional, visceral – we might say, biological – affinities between father and son that even a man as sunk in sin and as lacking in moral sense as Aaron cannot resist. The play is thus devoid – indeed, it strips itself – of the conventional, providential, moralizing frameworks that, in the narratives about the inevitable disclosure and punishment of murder to be found in the pamphlet press and popular drama of the day, would have attended (or indeed would have caused) such events and outcomes.[5] We are not watching the semi-miraculous interventions of providence, the wildly improbable coincidences, the confluences of unintended consequence that, in many a murder pamphlet or play, routinely interrupted the 'natural' or intended course of events. Nor are we eavesdropping as the testimony of a conscience that can no longer be denied disrupts the best laid plans of even the most hardened of sinners. On the contrary, we are being shown the operation of a series of entirely natural causes.

That the play does all this in scenes in which the characters of Murder, Revenge and Rapine actually appear on stage merely heightens the effect, by emphasizing that the agent of Revenge is neither Revenge nor providence, but rather Titus himself, who sees through Tamora's ridiculous ruse and, in so doing, takes complete control of the play's denouement.

There is, of course, a wonderful irony (in Crosbie's terms, an inherent proportionality and justice) in the fact that it is Tamora's trap, set to lure Titus to his doom, that enables Titus to bring her, her sons and Saturninus to fitting ends. Such a perfectly symmetrical turning of the tables is quintessentially providential; but it has been brought about not through the workings of providence, but rather by the pertinacity and cunning of Titus, who now takes upon himself the role of Revenge – a revenge that mirrors precisely the original crimes of his enemies. His summary execution of Demetrius and Chiron, who are allowed no last dying speeches in the face of certain death – 'villains, for shame you could not beg for grace' [V, ii, 179] – reflects, indeed repeats, Saturninus' summary execution of Titus' sons. The grisly nature of their fate reflects the mutilation that they have inflicted on Lavinia, and indeed is referred to by the same loaded term – Titus is going, he says, 'to martyr' them. And the agony that he intends to inflict on Tamora by inducing her to feast on the flesh of her own sons reproduces, in intensely encapsulated form, the mental torment that he has had to undergo as his own sons have been executed and exiled; his own daughter raped and mutilated; and his own hand cut off before his very eyes.

At one level, then, the symmetrical fit between crime and punishment, together with the means whereby the true nature of those crimes has been revealed – the dumb speaking, the deepest-dyed villain being constrained to tell the truth, a monstrous birth – are all typical of both the revenge drama and the murder pamphlet. This impression is compounded by the fact that those outcomes are brought about by the active intervention of the figure of Revenge, here playing (as so often in this period) the role of a sort of paganized providence. At this point, Shakespeare is self-consciously locating his play in relation to the nascent genre of the revenge tragedy, mocking the tendency of such plays to reify the notion of revenge and the moral principles and lessons set in action on stage. One extant domestic tragedy from the period, *Two Lamentable Tragedies*, actually contains – at its beginning and its end – a personified dialogue between Truth, Homicide and Avarice, and the first version of *Hamlet* famously featured a ghost screaming 'Revenge! Revenge!' Here such absurdities occur not in the play itself, but rather at one remove from it, in an absurd play within the play, scripted and directed by Tamora, and designed to entice the seemingly mad Titus into destroying himself.

The ensuing scene does at least two things. First, it works to comment on the absurdity of such performances, and thus to distance Shakespeare's own exercise in the genre from other, lesser attempts. Secondly, and more importantly, it works to drive home the point that in this play it is not providence, personified in some abstract character or force called Revenge, but rather Titus himself who is bringing the play to its denouement.[6] Just as Titus is intended to take Tamora's little play literally, but sees through its childish obviousness immediately, so Shakespeare's audience is surely expected to see through the conventions of the revenge tragedy thus evoked, and perceive what is really going on in this play. Therefore, having seen through Tamora's pitiful attempt to deceive him, it is Titus who, quite literally, takes on the role of Revenge himself; and it is his planning, not the intervention of 'providence', that produces the 'providential' ending of the play – something which this scene seems designed to force the audience to acknowledge.

Not that the play defies anything like all the conventions of the emergent genre. As revenger – indeed, as the man whose sins started the whole cycle of bloody revenge that is ending here – Titus must, of course, die the death. But even that death is a product not of providential intervention, frustrating his plans, but of a last exercise on Titus' part of Roman virtue: a final demonstration of his residual loyalism in the face of imperial (but also tyrannical) sovereignty. Thereafter, even the final conclusion – the elevation of the king-killing Lucius to the imperial throne – is worked not by 'providence', but rather by the election of the Roman people. Even as the play delivers the goods of an audience- and justice-satisfying denouement in which the revenger and his victims all meet properly bloody ends – thus affirming its status as what it has, throughout, announced itself to be, a revenge tragedy – it undercuts some of the fundamental assumptions normally staged in and confirmed by such plays.[7]

What the audience is being shown is the triumph not of providence over human sin and deceit, but rather of the virtue, pertinacity and cunning of the Andronici over tyranny, persecution and atheism. 'Providential' outcomes have been reached, but through entirely this-worldly (indeed frankly political) means; through the self-help of deeply flawed, but – judged by the standards of the iron age conjured in the play – still 'pious' and 'virtuous' human agents. Thus, the play is anything but just another statement of the contemporary truism that under the beneficent influence – indeed often under the direct intervention – of providence, bad people will come to bad ends, murder will out and tyrants will meet a dreadful fate. Rather it is not merely an account of, but a positive justification for, political resistance. It ends as a vindication of purposive political action and of just political violence undertaken against tyranny by its victims, to punish sin and to free the commonweal from tyranny.

Atheism and its opposites

Not that the play's political denouement is devoid of religious significance. On the contrary, the play's political plot is underpinned by an argument about religion, albeit not one couched in terms of the confessional divisions of the post-Reformation. As a number of commentators have pointed out, the name of this new emperor is significant. For Lucius was the name of the mythical king, descended from Aeneas, who was credited with first introducing Christianity into Britain.[8] The return, then, of Lucius from an exile into which he has been thrown by the tyrant Saturninus might well be thought to have had a certain contemporary resonance, when the 'popish' Lucius – the phrase, of course, is Aaron's – returns in triumph, bringing true religion with him to a realm that has groaned under the persecutory violence of his tyrannical predecessor.

But the play is anything but explicit about the nature of the religion that is being restored. One thing does, however, emerge pretty clearly, and that is the dreadful consequences of religious violence. The whole cycle of revenge and regicide, of tyranny and resistance, described by the play has been unleashed by one original, not political, but religious act – the sacrifice by Titus of Alarbus. But while the subsequent violence, oppression and tyranny which that initial act provokes are responses to an (admittedly misguided) act of piety, they themselves lack any sort of religious motivation. Titus had been trying to appease the gods and the shades of his departed sons; but Tamora wants to appease neither her ancestors nor the gods. Nor does she have any interest in justice. She merely wants revenge.[9] The malign atheism latent in that impulse is taken to its logical conclusion and given its most coherent expression in the rantings of Aaron after his capture, and in the would-be infanticide of Tamora.

The play thus offers a stark contrast between the literal-minded legalism and idolatry of Titus' 'cruel and irreligious piety' and a reaction to it that is so extreme and atavistic as to amount (in Aaron's case literally) to atheism. That difference is revealed by the very different relationship enjoyed by the Andronici and their enemies to the core texts through which the play constructs both its vision of *Romanitas* and central elements in its own plot. As a number of scholars have pointed out,[10] the crucial texts range from the *Aeneid* to Ovid's *Metamorphoses*, from Seneca's *Hippolytus* and a fragment from Horace to crucial elements from Livy's *Ab Urbe Condita*. Rather than operating merely as source materials for the play, these texts 'are recognized explicitly and invoked by the play's characters themselves as the framework for the world in which they operate'.[11] Indeed, these continual references to central texts in the Roman canon serve not merely as a context through which events can be rendered intelligible after the fact, but also as a source of prescriptive guidance, offering 'a course of action for the characters to follow' and providing them with 'a pattern, precedent and lively warrant' for their actions in the present and future.[12] In contrast to the Andronici, who are always concerned to interpret their situation in terms of, and to align their actions with, appropriate precedents and exempla from the canonical texts of *Romanitas*, the Goths – being Goths and not Romans – show no interest in such matters. While they know the canonical texts, they persistently get them wrong; knowing well enough what the Roman sources say, they just do not understand what they mean.[13]

The contrast, then, is between a group – the Andronici – who are shown consistently trying to interpret, apply and, indeed, emulate a body of canonical texts, and another group who, while they might accept the canonical status of the same texts, and know what they say, are entirely incapable either of reading them accurately or of applying them aright. The one exception here is Aaron, who immediately detects the sinister undertone in Titus' citation of Horace. But as an unreconstructed atheist, Aaron has an entirely instrumental relationship to the relevant texts. He uses them not to extract and appropriate moral lessons and guidance, in an attempt, however imperfectly, to construct and continue a tradition of moral, political and religious thought and practice, but rather as a means to further his own entirely malign efforts to undermine and subvert that tradition. Thus, he applies the story of Tereus and Philomela entirely appropriately to his immediate circumstances, but only as a blueprint for the rape of Lavinia.

Such a contrast might well prompt us to see the Andronici as embodying the old religion, and their enemies as representing an ignorant and malign perversion and appropriation thereof. However, it remains the case that for all their dedication to the canonical texts, and for all their attempted fidelity to the key exempla of *Romanitas*, the Andronici's readings of those texts are consistently over-literal. Consequently, all too often they misapply, sometimes calamitously, the key exempla. That is to say, the Andronici are presented as disastrously flawed readers even of the decidedly barbarous – in Tamora's phrase, 'the cruel and irreligious' – version of *Romanitas* conjured by the play.

Thus, despite his protestations to the contrary, Titus' conduct corresponds neither to that of Brutus nor to that of Virginius. Far from killing Lucrece, her father had reassured her that, though her body was violated, she herself was innocent. In marked contrast to Lavinia, Lucrece's decision to take her own life was entirely her own. She did so both to save herself and her family from dishonour, and to provoke her male kin into taking revenge on Tarquin, and thus save the Roman state from tyranny. Virginius killed his daughter to save her from a fate worse than death, himself from dishonour, and Rome from the depredations of the tyrannous regime of the decemvirs. He did not murder her in cold blood to demonstrate his own Roman virtue. Titus is here reverting to type, sacrificing Lavinia, reduced once more to the role of her father's (necessarily) silently dutiful daughter, on the altar of his family's honour, just as he had earlier sacrificed Alarbus and Mutius. In short, even when he thinks he is simply emulating some of the great embodiments of Roman *virtus* and *pietas*, the virtual patron saints of *Romanitas*, Titus only succeeds in producing a skewed, cruel and over-literal reading of their example. His is a cruel and irreligious parody even of the barbarous version of *Romanitas* conjured in the play.

As such, it provokes the gruesome cycle of revenge, mutilation, ravishment and horror that constitutes the action of the play. Thereafter, while Titus' pursuit of revenge does indeed result in a form of justice, not to mention at least the prospect of a return of order to the Roman state, that outcome has only been brought about through the most appallingly cruel and duplicitous of means. As Crosbie points out, within the moral universe conjured by the play, the only available versions of piety and virtue, of justice, and even, bizarrely enough (and it is more bizarre than Crosbie's account allows), of 'moderation' are those personified by the Andronici. But by the same token, the play leaves us in no doubt that, while they remain the only game in town, the versions of virtue and piety evidenced by the Andronici are also appalling in their savagery and idolatry, their crude legalism and lack of human feeling. Certainly, when viewed from the perspective provided by the Christian standards and aspirations of the play's audience, there remains something deeply defective, indeed horrifyingly inhuman, about the virtue and piety of the Andronici.

Here the child-killing propensities of Titus represent the key element. As Culhane argues, 'the close connection between filicide and exemplarity in this play suggests that Shakespeare is responding to Livy's *Ab Urbe Condita*, a text in which Livy presents the willingness of virtuous Romans, like Titus Manlius Torquatus, to sacrifice even their own sons on the altar of *Romanitas* as the quintessence of Roman virtue. Culhane describes Livy's account of Manlius' filicide as carefully calculated to render 'something that might be considered unnatural . . . heroic and consistent with admirable standards of piety and discipline'.[14] Shakespeare uses Titus' similar propensities to exactly opposite effect. After all, the play opens with Titus killing someone else's child and concludes with him killing one of his own, having killed another, Mutius, in between. If the play is conceived as a contest to see who can kill more of Titus' progeny, the result is a two-all draw between Titus and Tamora. Moreover, while Tamora ends the action as a failed infanticide, Titus has succeeded in committing that most unnatural of crimes twice over. All three of Titus' victims – Alarbus, Mutius and Lavinia – have been sacrificed on the altar of the honour of the Andronici. Moreover, it is not only his piety that leads to murderous deeds and awful outcomes; his dominant moral and political virtue, his loyalist dedication to the Roman state, also prompt both appalling crimes (here the murder of Mutius stands out) and calamitous mistakes and misjudgements – mistakes and misjudgements that have the most dreadful consequences not only for him and his family, but also for Rome. Thus, if Titus' religious piety and political virtue remain genuine forms of piety and virtue, the play presents them as deeply flawed.

The point is driven home, as we have seen, by Titus' slaughter of Lavinia – an act which Shakespeare's (Christian) audience was far more likely to view (with Saturninus) as 'unnatural and unkind' [V, iii, 47] than as an example of any kind of virtue. And yet, of course, while identified in the play with pagan Rome, a whole series of parallels and resonances serves to bring the inhuman cruelty taking place on stage very close to home indeed. Just as (as a number of commentators have observed) the action of the play breaks down the assumed dichotomy between a civilized Rome and a barbarous Gothic other, it also undercuts any assumption of a vast gulf separating the inhuman cruelty taking place on stage in a remote pagan Roman and barbarian past from the realities and practices of post-Reformation England.[15]

There are, then, two master oppositions in play here. The first is that between religion (defined as the force of conscience and a basic respect for the demands of the divine) and atheism; and the second is that between the over-literal – the 'cruel and irreligious' – pagan piety of the Andronici and Christianity. Christianity, of course, has no direct presence within the play. The outline and prospect of distinctively Christian values figure only fleetingly, most notably when Tamora, of all people, posits mercy as the master attribute and value of the gods. In another sense, however, distinctively Christian values and expectations are omnipresent, imported into the action by the reactions elicited from an audience made up of Elizabethan Christians by the dreadful events being played out on stage. But if the reactions provoked in such an audience do indeed serve to position the action of the play in relation to Christianity, that same audience also knows – and again the name of Lucius is there to remind them, should they be tempted to forget – that Christianity is coming; that pagan *Romanitas* will be succeeded by Roman Christianity.[16]

The play appears to present its audience with a binary opposition – between the atheism of Saturninus, Tamora and Aaron, on the one hand, and the defective, cruel and irreligious piety of the Andronici, on the other. Despite the presence of Goth and Moor on the really dark side, as a number of commentators have pointed out, the play does not present us with a straight choice between Rome and a Gothic barbarous other – between, as it were, inside and outside; rather, the choice is between actual presences and potentialities situated at the heart of Rome and, of course, by extension, of Elizabethan England. That stark either/or choice ensures that any vision of a more properly Christian piety or virtue that might emerge from the play will not represent some mean between extremes – some precisely calibrated *via media*, poised elegantly between differently corrupted versions of essentially the same thing. In terms of a search for a religious mean where, in that formulation, Protestantism ought to be, we find instead the atheism and tyranny of Aaron, Tamora and Saturninus; and in the place of Catholicism, the deeply flawed pagan Roman piety and virtue of the Andronici. The way out of the nightmare of violence and conflict conjured in the play cannot, therefore, lie in a process of compromise and accommodation, but rather in an inevitably violent, inherently dialectical conflict between the two extremes, out of which might emerge, at least and at last, the dim prospect of something better, as the dreadful battle between thesis and antithesis finally manages to produce at least the outlines of a synthesis. If the play does indeed offer us such a possibility, it will surely be based on 'the thing called conscience' which Aaron discerns operating within Lucius, now perhaps purged of the 'twenty popish tricks and ceremonies' [V, i, 75–76] which Aaron – that most unreliable, but also that most perspicacious, of witnesses – sees attending it. But, the play suggests, 'conscience' alone will not be enough.

Here the scene between Aaron and Lucius is crucial. Aaron knows that Lucius possesses a conscience which will be bound by a solemn oath. For Aaron, the atheist, such faith is mere weakness – superstition and 'popery' in fact. But that faith is also, he acknowledges, a force strong enough to prevent Lucius from taking his revenge on Aaron's bastard son. Here is religion, dismissed as superstition and popery by Aaron, triumphing over the impulse to take revenge – an impulse which the play has otherwise shown wreaking the most terrible havoc on Rome. It may have taken the perverse atheistical logic of Aaron to do it, but – almost alone among the central characters in the play – Lucius has been saved by the force of religion and the demands of conscience from his own atavistic impulse towards revenge – an impulse that, up to this point, has been leading him inexorably towards that most monstrous of crimes, the slaughter of an innocent child.

We might pause for a moment here to consider just how Lucius' 'conscience' has been activated. He is certainly not saved from baby killing by any feelings of compunction or natural sympathy of his own; that is to say, by any either residual or emergent belief that killing babies is wrong. On the contrary, what holds his hand is the force of the oath that Aaron has induced him to take. Lucius' 'religious' instincts continue to take the cold, legalistic forms that have thus far characterized his father's – and indeed his own – conduct. When bound by certain obligations towards the gods, the Andronici discharge those obligations, whatever the human cost, with a chilling absence of affect. In the opening act, religious duty has led them to slaughter in cold blood another of Tamora's children, Alarbus. Here, once bound by his oath, that same sense of religious obligation leads Lucius to spare the life of another. The difference between the two outcomes has no sympathetic or affective content or cause: it is purely a function of differently structured obligations towards the gods.

If there is an element of human sympathy, of moral compunction, in operation here, it comes not from Lucius, but from Aaron, in whom (as we have seen) a natural – we might say, instinctive – impulse to save his son has not prompted any wider awakening of conscience, moral sense or human sympathy. As his murder of the midwife shows, whatever finer feelings his ties to his new-born son might be provoking in Aaron, they include neither a heightened respect for human life nor a propensity to repent and abandon the ruthless promptings of 'policy'. But in the iron age in which the play's actions take place,[17] it is precisely because of Aaron's lack of a 'conscience', as he defines it – and therefore because of his consequent freedom from the legalistic structures of religious obligation that frame and constrain the ethical and emotional lives of the Andronici – that Aaron is able to experience and obey the promptings of the basic human solidarity that binds a parent to his or her child – a basic impulse which Titus and Lucius' austere *Romanitas*, their idolatrous religious rigorism and literalism, has all but entirely suppressed.

For if Aaron lacks even a spark of the sort of conscience that animates both Titus and Lucius, they are similarly devoid of the sort of instinctual human bonds that have prevented even Aaron from killing his own son. These, of course, are precisely the sort of basic human emotions and impulses that, for all his (considerable) piety and virtue, Titus – that piously inveterate murderer, that sacrificer of his own (and other people's) children – never displays. Or rather, insofar as he does experience such emotions, he does so only as a result of a complete breakdown in the control mechanisms imposed upon him by his identity as a pious and loyal servant of the Roman state. The result, as we have seen, is an emotional incontinence, an excess of feeling, so extreme as to constitute a form of madness. That Titus can only reinsert himself within the canons of Roman virtue and piety from which this outbreak of emotion has excluded him by killing both himself and, in Lavinia, the primary (and entirely innocent) object of those emotions, merely serves to drive the point home. In

Lucius, too, the natural human responses, the sympathies and solidarities that might otherwise have prevented coldly cruel acts – such as the sacrifice of Alarbus or his projected slaughter of Aaron's new-born son – have, to this point, been altogether suppressed by the demands of (pagan Roman) piety, virtue and, latterly, revenge.

On the one hand, we might see in these exchanges between Lucius and Aaron a basic human sympathy – that between parent and child – saving an overly rigid, legalistic and idolatrous religious system from its own worst excesses. On the other hand, we might see a defective, but effectual, notion of conscience – a determination to obey the dictates of a 'cruel and irreligious' but still genuine form of piety – attaching itself to the most basic of human sympathies, like those that bind parents to their children and children to their parents. In and of themselves, such sympathies are too particularizing, too intensely personal, to form the basis for any more general notion of human solidarity or moral community. Indeed, unattached to notions of conscience, as they clearly are in Aaron's case, the very intensity and particularity of such emotional attachments were likely to produce actions and reactions quite as desperate, as immoral and violent, as those taken by Aaron to preserve the life of his son. But when such sentiments became attached to a sense of conscience, an acknowledgement of a wider obligation to obey the demands of divine authority – of the sort that Aaron discerns in Lucius, but entirely lacks himself – the basis of a more general set of constraints and solidarities might emerge. For only forces as strong as Lucius' Roman conscience and Aaron's nakedly human attachment to his son would be both powerful and capacious enough to limit, indeed perhaps even to avert, the sort of atavistic and vengeful violence that otherwise constitutes so much of the action of the play.

Lucius' decision not to kill Aaron's son is the first (and only) time in the play that 'conscience', the active force of religion, inhibits the impulse to kill – either (as with Titus and the death of Alarbus) in the pursuit of piety, or more often (as with Tamora's vendetta against the Andronici) in pursuit of revenge. As St Hilaire observes, Lucius is 'the first character in the play to purposefully refrain from killing a child' thus 'putting a break in the chain of vengeful murders of progeny' and perhaps 'suggesting the possibility of a more merciful society'.[18] Nor is the religious conclusion devoid of significance for the political aspects of the play; for, saved by a combination of his own 'conscience' and Aaron's natural instinct to preserve his child from an atavistic pursuit of revenge for revenge's sake, Lucius is freed to do genuine justice. Accordingly, even though Lucius gets to kill the king, at play's end it is Titus who must die, while Lucius survives to rule the Roman state.

What we are seeing here (again, for the first time in the play) is the operation of a version of 'conscience' – indeed, perhaps even a version of religion – that might have been recognizable as such to an Elizabethan Christian audience. But 'conscience' and its demands are not presented as being introduced into the pagan locale evoked by the play from (a Christian) outside. Rather they are shown being reconstituted through the dialectical – indeed the violent – clash of opposites: on the one side, the atheism of Aaron; on the other, the cruel, legalistic and idolatrous piety of the Andronici. Ostensibly, of course, the iron age being conjured in the play is situated in a distant pagan Rome – indeed, in a Rome that never existed; but, as we have seen, at several points the play's invented Roman past is collapsed into a version of contemporary post-Reformation England that is quite as much in need of a combination of this sort of raw human sympathy and broader religious obligation, if its own violent confessional passions and extreme religious violence – evoked so brutally in the play – are to be controlled.

A more precise sense of the dialectical progressions being sketched here can be gleaned from the scene in which Titus slaughters Tamora's sons, bakes them in a pie and serves them up to Tamora. As he cuts the throats of Chiron and Demetrius, Titus tells his daughter – in what many commentators have seen as a 'dark parody' of the language of the eucharist – 'Lavinia come, / Receive the blood' [V, ii, 196–197]. Similarly, the scene in which Tamora is induced to eat the bodies of her own sons recalls the crudest Protestant assaults on the Catholic doctrine of transubstantiation, which, some polemicists claimed, rendered taking the sacrament an act tantamount to cannibalism. Thus John Jewel maintained that while 'Christ spake spiritually of eating with faith', the Catholics spoke 'grossly of eating with the teeth: as though they would swallow down his flesh into their bodies, as with other meats'.[19] When Protestants made such claims about popery, they were accusing it of what Glyn Parry has termed 'gentilism' – that is to say, of adulterating Christianity with beliefs, assumptions and practices taken from the heart of paganism. For some Protestants, this accounted both for the penumbra of idolatrous outward forms and superstitions associated with popish worship and for the papists' thoroughly pagan, over-literal, indeed savagely cannibalistic notion of the sacrifice of the mass.[20]

The mass, the sacrament of Christ's body and blood, was the rite intended to affirm the integrity and unity of the Christian community, conceived as the mystical body of Christ. Titus uses a blasphemous parody of that rite symbolically to expel Tamora from the bounds of the human, immediately prior to her expulsion from the land of the living. As Barbara Parker points out, 'Tamora's consumption of the pie – "eating the flesh that she herself hath bred" (V, iii, 62) – becomes a literal parody of eating the Son.'[21] Here, then, is a travesty of the eucharist or mass, something indeed like a black or anti-mass, being used to inflict on the demonic figure of Tamora the precise opposite of the spiritual benefits conferred on ordinary Christians by the sacrament.

But this blasphemous parody also serves another function. It reveals, perhaps even more starkly than his sacrifice of Alarbus, the literal-minded crudity and legalism, the inhuman cruelty and rigour, that render Titus' (pagan Roman) piety so 'cruel and irreligious' (in Tamora's words). Titus' forcing Tamora to eat her own children represents the apogee of the crude literalism that characterizes the play throughout. Even if, as Crosbie suggests, there is a certain symmetry or reciprocity – even a sort of rectificatory justice – inscribed in the form of Titus' revenge, the crude literalism (and extreme cruelty) through which those rectificatory symmetries are realized cannot but call into radical question the justice and virtue (let alone the moderation) of Titus' actions.[22] Over-literalism of this sort, applied consistently to a canon of texts of even the greatest inherent wisdom, cannot but lead to the most catastrophic of mis-readings, as examples are pulled out of context, misapplied and subjected to the most crude and literal-minded 'emulation'. Indeed, pushed too far, such literal-mindedness cannot but lead to idolatry; and it is, of course, a form of idolatry that leads Titus literally to sacrifice – not so much to Rome, as to the honour and standing of his own lineage – not only Alarbus and a whole slew of his own sons, but even his beloved Lavinia. In so doing – as the contrast set up throughout the play between Titus' conduct and that of Tamora and Aaron is designed to show – he *is* displaying forms of honour and nobility, of patriotism and piety; but only of the most savage, bloody- and literal-minded – or, as Aaron puts it, 'popish' and 'superstitious' – sort.

Thus, if, as Nicholas Moschovakis has argued,[23] the play can be read as an indictment of religious violence (Titus' sacrifice of Alarbus) and persecution (the treatment by Saturninus et al. of the Andronici) as pagan attributes, utterly unworthy of Christians, then the religion to be restored at the end of the play by the returning King Lucius – however 'popish' it might seem to the Aarons of the world – would surely have been a 'popery' reformed or remade by the traumas of the recent past. If the gesture here is towards a genuinely Christian future, there is, of course, a wonderful irony in the fact that that gesture is almost literally embodied in a new-born infant – in this case, the black, bastard progeny, indeed the monstrous birth, produced by the adulterous couplings of Aaron the Moor and Tamora. Here the sins of the fathers are *not* being visited on the sons. Rather, a vision of a human (indeed, perhaps of a prospectively Christian) community, capaciously merciful enough to take in even the offspring of that match, is being conjured.

On this account, therefore, the religious logic of the play is anything but crudely confessional. Rather, by opposing religion to atheism, and paganism to the prospect of Christianity, and by associating the expiatory religious violence of Titus first with paganism and then with Catholicism, and then by associating the revenge-based persecution of Tamora and Aaron with atheism, the play is trying to transcend the theological and confessional differences that were dividing contemporary Christians into warring factions and thereby creating the conditions for the outbreak (among Christians) of acts of violence and revenge easily as dreadful as anything being staged in this play – actions so bloody, in fact, as to be shocking even when transposed from the Christian present to the pagan Roman past, as conjured by the play.

Thus, the play's moral argument is not being made in the name of one religious grouping rather than another, but in the cause of religion rather than of atheism; of Christianity rather than of paganism; of virtue and the service of the commonweal rather than tyranny. Put succinctly, we are being told that a pious paganism is better than atheism, and that Christianity is better than both. Stated in a vacuum, such claims were mere commonplaces, the equivalent of elaborate panegyrics to the moral excellence of motherhood and apple pie. But to make such claims in a play that might be taken to equate the treatment being meted out to English Catholics by the Elizabethan state with the conduct of Saturninus, Tamora and her Moor towards the Andronici – which, in short, might be taken to render Elizabethan England itself a repository of both atheism and tyranny – was to turn moral platitudes of the kind to which everyone could (and would) assent into the basis for the most radical and dangerous rethinking. Moreover, if the pitch being made seems moderate, even irenic – designed to unite, in moral revulsion and cathartic release, an audience made up of very different sorts of Christians, of various sorts of Protestants and various sorts of Catholics – its immediate results (on stage) are anything but moderate, irenic or peaceful. This, after all, is a revenge tragedy and, in the concluding sections of the play, such emergent principles and solidarities lead not to peace or unity, but to an outbreak of the most annihilating political violence.

We are not dealing here with a *via media* of the classic 'Anglican' or 'Erasmian' sort; a position of exquisite balance and equipoise, located at Canterbury and positioned between extremes represented by, say, Rome and Geneva; an inherently moderate and irenic form of 'mere Christianity', entirely removed from the confessional passions and partisanship of the post-Reformation world, of the sort often imputed to Shakespeare by modern critics of a similarly irenic, sceptical, moderate and/or 'Anglican' cast of mind.[24] As Crosbie and now Ethan Shagan[25] have both, in their different ways, pointed out, in extreme times and circumstances, an Aristotelian search for the mean will not produce anything remotely like 'moderation' in the common-sense meaning of the word. Indeed, as Shagan has pointed out, in such circumstances the quest for moderation often prompted campaigns of violent suppression directed against the extremes that were taken to threaten, and define, the 'moderate' middle ground. Shagan places that paradox at the centre of much post-Reformation thought and action. This reading of *Titus* might be taken to imply that he is right.[26]

But necessary though it was, the violence involved here could not be described as 'religious'; that is to say, it is not prompted by the drive of the devotees of one religion to satisfy the demands of a jealous god through violence directed against the devotees of another. The sacrifice of Alarbus had been designed for just such god-satisfying purposes. What was at stake then had not been human justice – the punishment of crime or sin and the re-establishment of peace thereby – for, as Tamora points out to Titus at the play's start, the only crime that Alarbus and her other sons have committed is to perform 'valiant doings in their country's cause'. 'O if to fight for king and commonweal / Were piety in thine, it is in these' [I, i, 116–118]. Titus, of course, proves implacable in the face of these (irrefutable) arguments; but he does so not to punish crime, or even to exact revenge, but, as he puts it, 't'appease their groaning shadows that are gone' [I, i, 129]: in other words, to discharge what he takes to be a religious obligation. The deaths that conclude the play are very different. All those who die – even Titus (indeed *especially* Titus) – are simply guilty of the most appalling crimes; and if their deaths satisfy a religious need or imperative, it is a duty to vindicate both human and divine justice by unmasking and punishing the most crying of crimes and sins.

Moreover, the only 'religious' opinion being punished here is atheism; and atheism, of course, represented a limiting case, the exception that proves the rule. For, while atheism is an opinion about religion, to contemporaries it represented – as Aaron's case shows perfectly – pure negation. Atheism was not a form of religion, but its very opposite: a position that removed all the moral bases of social and political life and led, almost immediately, to moral and political chaos – indeed, to the sort of pure evil articulated at the end by Aaron's ravings from the scaffold. As such, it was a position that all truly religious persons – whatever their particular confessional allegiance or identity – should (indeed would) agree must be extirpated. Once, that is, they had been taught (by the play) to recognize its true nature, presence and effects. Confronted with the spectre of pure unbelief, there was only one side to be on and only one thing to do. The patent justice of the punishments and degradations handed out to Titus, Saturninus, Tamora and Aaron renders not only the acts of revenge with which the play concludes, but also the political means – the sedition and conspiracy, the foreign invasion, resistance and regicide – that have brought that outcome about, not merely legitimate, but also morally satisfying; not merely political, but also religious, and thus genuinely expiatory.

With both Saturninus and his father dead, and his own fate in the hands of a decidedly confused populace, Lucius is able triumphantly to demand that the people 'judge what cause had Titus to revenge / These wrongs unspeakable, past patience'. Lucius backs up that request with a pledge that should the people find that 'the poor . . . Andronici' had done 'aught amiss', they will hurl themselves and 'on the ragged stones beat forth our souls and make a mutual closure of our house'. Not only do the people reject Lucius' offer, but by 'the common voice' they elect him 'Rome's royal emperor' and 'gracious governor' [V, iii, 124–133, 139, 140, 145]. Thus, the result of the political self-help, the sedition and violent resistance of the Andronici is neither death and disgrace nor a further descent of the Roman state into violence and civil war, but rather the virtual re-foundation of that state, under what promises to be the beneficent rule of Lucius. After all, just like Richmond at the end of *Richard III*, Lucius ends the play promising to 'heal Rome's harms and wipe away her woe' [V, iii, 147].

PART TWO

HAMLET

4

<--->

Hamlet with the confessional and succession politics left in

Hamlet is conventionally regarded as a revenge tragedy. Certainly, a great deal of the critical commentary on the play, most notably that centred on the *topos* of Hamlet's 'delay', is predicated upon that assumption. However, considering the question of genre, we might remind ourselves that on the title page of the quarto, *Hamlet* proclaimed itself a 'tragical-history'. 'This is not to say,' as de Grazia points out, 'that these quartos classified the play as history rather than as tragedy, for that would presuppose that the two classifications were already generically distinct.'[1] Rather, this hybrid term shows us that before the Folio distinguished so rigidly between tragedies and histories, the two genres or categories were closely associated the one with the other. 'With the introduction of the genre called the Histories, the Folio dissolved the kinship between tragedy and history. The tragedies, traditionally drawn from historical materials, appeared ahistorical when segregated from the new genre.' On de Grazia's account, the notion of the four great Shakespearean tragedies emerged relatively late. What rendered these plays – *Hamlet, Lear, Macbeth* and *Othello* – 'pure' was 'their dissociation from history. Disencumbered of matters of state, the "pure tragedies" are free to concentrate on the suffering of great individuals.'[2] But if we free *Hamlet* from these later presuppositions, and reintegrate it into the immediate moment that produced it as the 'tragical history' it initially proclaimed itself to be, it looks rather different.

To begin with, we need to remind ourselves just how directly the play speaks to immediately contemporary political concern and circumstance. It does so no less than any of the other history plays, and it does so through the staging, from Danish history, of a crucial moment of dynastic change. Denmark is portrayed as an elective monarchy. Old Hamlet has not been succeeded by his lineal heir and son, but rather by his brother Claudius, who has, in Hamlet's words, 'popped in between th'election and my hopes' [Q2, V, ii, 64; F, V, ii, 65].

We are confronted here with an issue which Parson's great succession tract *A Conference about the Next Succession* (and, among others, James VI's reply to that text, *The True Law of Free Monarchies*) had made an intensely current and controversial one for contemporaries: was the English monarchy – indeed, were all monarchical polities – essentially elective in their structure, or was there such a thing as a free hereditary monarchy? Of these different forms of monarchy, which was better? Did – as the likes of both Parsons and Buchanan insist – even elective monarchy confer a right on the people or commonwealth to resist the usurper or tyrant?[3] If England were taken to be such an elective monarchy, whether such a reading of the polity could be used to legitimate the diversion of the succession from the rightful heir to the throne – first Mary, and then James, Stuart – to another figure already established within the English political system (or even to the infanta) had been the subject of a great deal of contemporary speculation. Robert Parsons, for one, had spent whole tracts attempting to feed such fears, and many contemporaries, up to and including James VI and the earl of Essex, were mightily afraid of just such manoeuvres being contemplated or effected by the people they regarded as their enemies, chiefly the Cecils. At precisely the period when *Hamlet* was probably being written, such fears were rampant among Essex's inner circle, and were to provide the animating drive behind the Essex conspiracy. More generally, as a variety of scholars have shown, the years between 1598 and 1601 were rife with all sorts of rumours about the succession – about Spanish and Scottish plots to force the issue and about Essex's caballing.[4]

Moreover, at least as far back as the famous Catholic libel of 1584, *Leicester's Commonwealth*,[5] concerns had been expressed that just such a court putsch to divert the succession would be effected through the secret murder of the queen by an inner circle of evil counsellors, well able to time their run at the throne for the best, or most propitious, moment and prepared to go to any lengths to do so. Of course, among the central figures in – and the most rabid supporters of – the Elizabethan state, there was an equal and opposite propensity to worry about the seditious potential of the Catholics, and, at moments of crisis, to plan feverishly to withstand a Catholic attempt on the life of the queen. As Helen Gardner pointed out years ago, the most famous expedient adopted by the Protestant state and its supporters to perpetuate itself in the event of such a calamity was the Bond of Association, which introduced the notion of revenge into the very centre of the politics of the regime. Each signatory to the bond undertook to wreak instant and bloody revenge not only on anyone who might act against the queen, but also against anyone else who stood to gain from the queen's death. The bond invoked the imperatives and obligations of revenge to justify the instantaneous slaughter of the woman – Mary Stuart – who, on certain views of the matter, was, if not already the rightful queen of England, then certainly the present incumbent's rightful successor. From 1584 on, therefore, dynastic politics – the politics of the succession – was also the politics of revenge and of the private bond. Early in 1600, James VI urged his nobles to enter into a bond to help him pursue (by force, if necessary) his dynastic right in England and in Ireland. He also petitioned his parliament for supply to enable him to take military action, if such action were called for. As James told his parliament, he was not certain 'how soon he should have to loose arms; but whenever it should be, he knew his right, and would venture crown and all for it'.[6] *Hamlet*, of course, ends with the successful (and armed) exercise, by a claimant from a neighbouring kingdom to the north, of certain 'rights of memory' to the Danish crown. At the turn of the sixteenth century, this was not an outcome – or rather, not a prospect – likely to be unfamiliar to a London audience.[7] For not only was such a prospect the subject of perfervid political speculation, of both the hopes and fears of a range of contemporaries, but it was also entirely familiar from certain of Shakespeare's own recent plays: in particular, from *Richard III* and *Titus Andronicus*, two plays from which, as we shall see below, Shakespeare was reworking certain central materials and questions in *Hamlet*.

Hamlet portrayed a situation in which the secret murder of the sitting incumbent had prompted the diversion of the succession from the obvious hereditary candidate to someone else deemed (because older, wiser, or more experienced) better suited to the exercise of rule. This occurred within a monarchical state construed to be elective rather than simply hereditary. This was a scenario all but identical to that predicted by a range of contemporaries (some of them Catholics certainly, but others not). Those predictions had been attended with hope or dread, depending on whether the prognosticators in question liked the Elizabethan regime or not. Crudely Protestants did, while (most) Catholics did not. But whether they liked it or not, everyone knew that the reign of good Queen Bess was now clearly nearing its end, in a plethora of differently constituted hopes, fantasies and fears. *Hamlet*, then, was not only precisely directed at pressingly present political circumstances, but it was also staging the most threatening version of where the present dynastic and political conjuncture might well be leading, either then or in the very near future.[8]

Patently, more was at stake in the play than the timing, the nature and the immediate (both spiritual and temporal) consequences of revenge. The fate of the kingdom and the crown of Denmark was involved, as was the vexed issue of 'providence' and its role in shaping the fortunes not only of the individual protagonists of the drama, but also of the states whose fate those protagonists were, in their turn, shaping. The play, therefore, was a history not only in the sense that it was a story 'about real or imaginary men and women who lived in the remote or the recent past', but also in the sense that it was a story 'about a nation's past'.[9]

Ostensibly about Denmark's past, the play was also about England's present and future. To quote de Grazia again, 'there is no denying that the play produces a sense of contemporaneity'. Hamlet's alma mater, the university of Wittenberg, was founded in 1502; the play references various aspects of modern warfare – 'rapiers, petards, ordnances, Swiss mercenaries' – as well as contemporary theatrical practices. 'Topical events', too, are glancingly referred to – the war of the theatres and 'more conjecturally, Essex's political "innovation" or insurrection of 1601'.[10]

But the play's range of historical reference is not limited to these immediately contemporary concerns and events. Like *Titus Andronicus*, 'through scattered allusions, tropes and puns, the play also references events of world historical magnitude, all bearing on England's own remote and recent history'. The play invokes the siege of Troy and the death of Caesar. In short, to quote de Grazia again, 'history of empire, ancient history, history of the Four Rules, salvational history all impinge upon the play's contemporaneity, saturating it with the past in preparation for another imperial fall' – or, we might say, dynastic transition.[11]

Hamlet, then, can be read perhaps not as a play simply about politics, but certainly as a play with an essentially political problematic or dilemma at its core. In its basic outlines, that dilemma resonated intensely with – and in some respects replicated rather closely – both the political situation of the moment and the modes of discourse adopted in the other 'history plays' to discuss that situation. But, as we shall see below, unlike in many of those other 'history' plays (but quite like *Titus Andronicus*), that basic political problematic is refracted through a series of essentially religious concerns – in this case, about the relations between divine providence generally conceived (and more particularly the divine decrees of election and reprobation) and human 'free will' – that is to say, the capacity of fallen humanity to determine outcomes, both political and salvific, in this and the next life. In that sense, the play returns to the basic problematics underlying its immediate predecessors, *Henry V* and *Julius Caesar*. The question of how far even men of the greatest virtue can determine their own fate and save or re-found the state certainly remains central to *Hamlet*. But it is joined as an organizing concern with the question of the compatibility of decisive political action and effective rule with the basic values of Christianity. Can rulers who do the things necessary to achieve power and maintain order in a fallen world go to heaven? In Hamlet's case, this last question is ratcheted up to hitherto unexplored levels of intensity, until it becomes, for both Hamlet and the audience, the central dilemma of the play – the issue from which the play draws most, if not all, of its very considerable emotional and dramatic energies. In what follows, I want, in short, to read the play as a theological thriller about succession politics.

The topical matrix: dynastic politics gets personal

Of course, the play reveals Claudius to be a murderer (indeed, a fratricide and a regicide) and, as such, a sort of usurper – except that he has been chosen king, in an election whose legitimacy is accepted by all. Hamlet may grieve for the loss of his father, and may resent, indeed denounce, the incestuous marriage of his mother to his uncle; but even he entirely accepts Claudius as the legitimate ruler. So much so that his melancholy, and then his apparent madness, are interpreted by others as having personal and emotional, rather than political, origins.

Throughout, Hamlet is clearly regarded as having some sort of hereditary claim to the throne. Claudius tells him that 'you are the most immediate to our throne' [Q2, I, ii, 109; F, I, ii, 107], and Rosencrantz reminds him that 'you have the voice of the King himself for your succession in Denmark' [Q2, III, ii, 332–334; F, III, ii, 331–332]. And in a number of asides, the play does hint that there might be a political element to Hamlet's discontent. Asked by Claudius, 'how fares my cousin Hamlet', the prince replies that 'I eat the air, promise-crammed. You cannot feed capons so.' Claudius is defeated by the remark – 'I have nothing with this answer, Hamlet. These words are not mine' – [Q2, III, ii, 89–93; F, III, ii, 91–95], but some commentators have taken that line to represent a deeply coded, subliminally threatening, allusion to Hamlet's role as a frustrated candidate for the throne, forced to feed his hopes of power on 'the chameleon's dish' of empty promises of future favour. Later, Hamlet replies to Rosencrantz's assurance that he has Claudius' support as next successor to the throne with the first half of a proverb that, he says, has grown 'something musty' – 'while the grass grows', he mutters and then breaks off without uttering the second part – the horse starves [Q2, III, ii, 335–336; F, III, ii, 333–334].

These asides apart, there is nothing in the play to lead us either to suppose that there is a general sense or suspicion at the court that the malcontent Hamlet is harbouring a suppressed ambition for the throne, or to believe that Hamlet's discontents are, in any obvious sense of the word, political. The reasons for his supposed madness remain a mystery – a mystery which Rosencrantz and Guildenstern are planted to fathom, but which no one so much as suggests has been caused by anything other than what his mother describes as 'his father's death and our o'er-hasty marriage' [F, II, ii, 56; Q2, II, ii, 57] or what Polonius insists is the prince's frustrated love for his daughter. However, the existence of such barely voiced suspicions does help to explain the urgency of Claudius' quest for the real cause of his nephew's malady.

Meanwhile, the formal legitimacy of Claudius' claim and rule is accepted implicitly by all. To Hamlet, Claudius may be an entirely unworthy successor to his father's throne and wife, but even for Hamlet (until the intervention of the ghost calls everything into question) Claudius is a ruler whose claim to the throne remains entirely legitimate. However, the play does make it clear that, alone of the inner circle of the regime, since his father's death Hamlet has been stubbornly resisting integration into the new order. The implication of the famous exchange between Gertrude and Hamlet – when she exhorts him to 'cast thy nighted colour off, / And let thine eye look like a friend on Denmark' [Q2, I, ii, 68–86; F, I, ii, 66–84] – is clear. Through the accession of the new king and his marriage, and indeed into the opening days of the new regime, Hamlet has continued to wear black and project all the outward affective and sartorial signs of mourning. Given the circumstances, such behaviour is not – indeed cannot be – devoid of political significance. It represents a public display of disaffection and dissent which, if sustained, might well render Hamlet (who is, after all, the next heir to the throne) the centre of an equally disaffected reversionary interest. Viewed from a political perspective, such a performance of grief might well invite suspicions of hypocrisy. Indeed, Hamlet might be taken to be trying to head off such suspicions, when he replies to his mother's initial question by famously turning it into an accusation of hypocrisy – a suggestion that has not, in fact, been made. But even if (especially if) Hamlet's threateningly public performance of grief is, as he claims, but the imperfect external expression of an entirely genuine internal state, it remains the case that his public enactment of mourning has ensured that that internal emotional state has remained anything but a private matter, but has rather taken on the form of a public rebuke to both his mother and his uncle, or rather to the new king and his queen.

For all his nephew's disaffection, the play shows us Claudius rather impressively assuming the reins of power. He deals expeditiously, through diplomatic means, with the threat from Norway posed by young Fortinbras. He deals out avuncular, sensible, temperate and admonitory advice to Hamlet on the need to control his grief at his father's death. But his performance of monarchical sagacity and beneficence is not limited to the public pronouncement of the appropriate moral platitudes. In sharp contrast to his decision to allow Laertes to go back to France, Claudius refuses to allow the malcontent Hamlet to return to Wittenberg. Instead, he intends to keep him under the royal eye in Denmark as 'our chiefest courtier, cousin, and our son' [Q2, I, ii, 117; F, 1, ii, 115]. When Hamlet replies to this royal command/request by talking only to his mother, Claudius puts the best possible gloss on the exchange. Hamlet's, he claims, is a 'gentle and unforced accord', 'a loving and a fair reply' (which, on the whole, it is not) [Q2, I, ii, 121, 123; F, I, ii, 119, 121]. Here is a new king doing his best to sound regal; dealing both subtly and decisively with the immediate potential threats unleashed by his accession to the throne both abroad (by Fortinbras) and at home (by Hamlet); struggling to control and reintegrate the malcontent Hamlet into the structures of the new regime and of the rapidly reconstituted royal family.

The play, then, offers us a picture of a returning monarchical normality and marital harmony. A potentially dangerous shift in regime, a 'cease of majesty' of the sort that Rosencrantz later opines might well, if mismanaged, produce the 'boisterous ruin' of the state [Q2, III, iii, 15, 22; F, III, iii, 15, 22] is being managed firmly and is going well. And everyone, except Hamlet, seems pleased and relieved by the outcome. Of course, what throws all this into radical question is the intervention of the ghost. That exchange takes place as the king feasts in drunken celebration of his nephew's agreement not to return to Wittenberg, but rather to stay in Denmark under the royal eye. We are being presented here with the juxtaposition of a political establishment, a royal family and court society – indeed, of a monarchical body politic – celebrating its own renewed integrity and unity, and the transmission on the castle battlements of the secret knowledge that there is indeed something 'rotten in the state of Denmark'. Hamlet – who, if Denmark were a free hereditary monarchy, would be king, and is anyway heir presumptive to the throne – is now in sole possession of the knowledge that the new king is not only a usurper, but a fratricide and a regicide to boot.

At a stroke, this puts Hamlet at radical odds with his social environment. For the bearer of such knowledge, monarchical normality and political legitimacy have been transformed into their polar opposites. The normal appears corrupt and sinister. Quotidian procedures and assumptions, designed to maintain order and reproduce authority, take on a corrupting, threatening and even deadly aspect. For Hamlet, newly burdened with the ghost's message, even normal social relations, the ties and reciprocities of everyday social life, are loaded with threat and danger. Old friends and familiars – for Hamlet, Rosencrantz and Guildenstern – become potential spies and informers. Such doubts are pervasive. Less a function of the trustworthiness of the individuals concerned, the doubts are, in effect, structural – a necessary part of Hamlet's relations with his entire social world. No one in the king's service, however well meaning, can be trusted now.

The result, as Timothy Rosendale has observed, is that '*Hamlet* is a play particularly saturated with falsely acting selves . . . who are relentlessly investigating and probing one another to determine the truth or untruth of their postures'.[12] Since the stakes are so high – lives and quite possibly souls are, quite literally, at stake – these exercises in mutual interrogation can take on the overtly hostile and potentially bloody form of the hunt. And, as Rhodri Lewis has pointed out, in an exhaustive examination of hunting imagery and reference, the play is saturated in such material.[13]

Even those like Rosencrantz and Guildenstern, of old acquaintance, once they have been caught doing the king's bidding, can never be trusted again. The structural necessities of monarchical rule demand that this should be so. From the moment that Claudius tells them that 'the need we had to use you did provoke / Our hasty sending' [Q2, II, ii, 3–4; F, II, ii, 3–4], Rosencrantz and Guildenstern are bought and paid for. Rosencrantz's later speech about the dreadful consequences of the 'cease of majesty', which 'dies not alone; but like a gulf doth draw / What's near it with it' and his comparison of the king's safety with 'a massy wheel, / Fixed on the summit of the highest mount, / To whose spokes ten thousand lesser things / Are mortised and adjoined' [Q2, III, iii, 15–20; F, III, iii, 15–20] represent but high-flown accounts (and legitimations) of the basic political realities, the asymmetries of power, that ensure that the likes of him and Guildenstern will – indeed, must – allow themselves to be used by the king to defend the state. It is also, of course, an eerie prophecy of their own fate, pulled to their deaths by the undertow of Claudius' failed schemes to destroy his own nephew.

As such, Rosencrantz's speech both presages and confirms the ruthless realism of Hamlet's moral accounting, as he tells Horatio of their fate in England. In response to Horatio's horrified question/exclamation 'so Guildenstern and Rosencrantz go to't', Hamlet famously replies:

> why, man, they did make love to this employment.
> They are not near my conscience. Their defeat
> Doth by their own insinuation grow.
> 'Tis dangerous when the baser nature comes
> Between the pass and fell incensed points
> Of mighty opposites. [F, V, ii, 56–62]

Of course, it is by no means clear that his two former cronies had made 'love to this employment'; but, as subjects and aspiring courtiers, they had no choice but to serve the king's purposes – purposes which, of course, seemed to them to be entirely beneficent. But it is equally the case that, as the king's creatures, sent to worm what they could not know was potentially fatal knowledge out of the prince, and then to accompany Hamlet to a certain death in England, they have immediately and inevitably become Hamlet's mortal enemies. From Hamlet's perspective, they were not mere instruments of Claudius – innocent bystanders, as it were – but as former friends now bent on betraying him to his mortal enemy, they were guilty not merely of malice, but of treachery. The situation ensures that, just as Rosencrantz and Guildenstern had no choice but to 'side' with the king, so Hamlet has no real choice but to destroy them. That they are oblivious to all this, just as Hamlet is necessarily oblivious to their obliviousness, merely serves to render explicit the fog of unknowing into which the fallenness of human nature has plunged all of the characters in the play.

The same logic applies, of course, to Polonius. A sedulous purveyor of conventional wisdom and a practised server of the purposes of both prince and state, a past master of the court arts of surveillance and 'indirection', a doddering intelligencer and counsellor of vast experience, considerable self-regard, and a certain soiled worldliness, all of which prove entirely unequal to the extreme circumstances in which he unknowingly finds himself, he blunders into the search for the real causes of Hamlet's 'madness', and in so doing he, too, becomes a potentially mortal enemy.[14] Less insidious, and therefore less threatening, than either Rosencrantz or Guildenstern, he becomes the object of the prince's contempt, rather than of his loathing. The outcome, however, is the same. Polonius' activities on the king's behalf put him in the same structural or objective relationship with Hamlet as that enjoyed by the prince's two former intimates. By spying for Claudius, trying to entice from Hamlet the real cause of his madness, Polonius, Rosencrantz and Guildenstern all become, in ways that they cannot possibly even guess at, Hamlet's mortal foes. And, of course, they all come to share the same fate – death at the hands of the prince. We might see Polonius' accidental death as a darkly comic presage to the more calculated fate visited upon Hamlet's erstwhile friends in England. Either way, Hamlet's response to Polonius' death is not, on the face of it, much more contrite or charitable than his response to the fate of his former companions. He 'repents' the deed that sent the old counsellor to his grave – something he conspicuously fails to do about the fate of Rosencrantz and Guildenstern – but his comment on the departed is scarcely respectful of the dead: 'This councillor / Is now most still, most secret and most grave / Who was in life a most foolish prating knave' [Q2, III, iv, 211–213; F, III, iv, 188–190]. But both responses register the iron logic imposed on Hamlet's situation by the information imparted by the ghost. Such ruthlessness is essential to Hamlet's continued survival in a court now filled (by definition, and whatever the good intentions or finer feelings towards the prince of the individuals concerned) with spies, intelligencers and (potentially as well as actually) mortal enemies. No one can be trusted; nothing is as it seems.

The same applies even to 'the fair Ophelia', who precedes his mother as bait in the on-going trap set by Polonius and the king to extract from Hamlet the cause of his malady. Of course, not only does she have no choice in the matter – as a dutiful daughter, she must obey the instructions of patriarchal authority – but she also has every reason to think that she is acting in Hamlet's best interests. But objectively, viewed in terms of the likely effects of her actions, she has gone over to the dark side, and the savagery of her treatment at Hamlet's hands registers that fact.

Given the centrality in personal monarchies of the family romance of hereditary succession and lineal legitimacy, when the politics of succession raises its ugly head, even (indeed especially) the closest of kin become peculiarly intense objects of suspicion and loathing. And, of course, foremost among those whom Hamlet can no longer trust is his mother. After all, the play famously poses (and never quite answers) the central question of just what Hamlet's mother knew and when she first knew it. The seemingly all-knowing ghost – and he certainly knows a good deal more about these things than Hamlet – uses the most ambiguous of language to describe the extent of Gertrude's complicity with Claudius, 'that incestuous, that adulterate beast' [Q2, I, v, 42–46; F, I, v, 42–46]. While he exhorts Hamlet to avoid all violence towards his mother, this is only to 'leave her to heaven, / And to those thorns that in her bosom lodge / To prick and sting her' [Q2, I, v, 86–88; F, I, v, 86–88]. In short, the ghost does anything but exonerate Gertrude. Indeed, he leaves Hamlet in no doubt that, although unspecified, her sins are dreadful. It comes, then, as no surprise that throughout, Hamlet continues to suspect her of deep involvement in Claudius' plotting; his demand at the height of the closet scene that she 'confess yourself to heaven' and 'repent what's past' [Q2, III, iv, 147–148; F, III, iv, 140–141] implies as much, and as late as act V he can still be found referring (almost casually) to Claudius' having 'whored my mother' [Q2, V, ii, 63; F, V, ii, 64].

The topical matrix and providential politics

The ghost had not, of course, only imparted knowledge or information to Hamlet; he had also enjoined him to act – 'to revenge his foul and most unnatural murder' [Q2, I, v, 25; F, I, v, 25]. But this injunction involved something other than a merely private revenge to be wreaked by the heir of one man upon his killer. Claudius was not only the perpetrator of a murder 'most foul, strange and unnatural' [Q2, I, v, 28; F, I, v, 28]: he was also a regicide and arguably a usurper. But now a legitimately elected king, safely ensconced on the throne, he ruled as the epitome of legitimacy and the fount of all justice and honour. Precisely because Claudius' crime and its immediate moral and political effects had consequences far wider than the murder of a private individual, the role of avenger, imposed by the ghost on Hamlet, had a far wider significance than the revenge of a private wrong, or the revelation and punishment of a common or garden crime.

Ghosts, apparitions and dreams appearing to reveal otherwise hidden crimes were a standard part not merely of revenge tragedies, but also of murder pamphlets. There God's providence compensated for the inefficacies of human justice and knowledge. Often through supernatural or miraculous means – ghosts, apparitions, extraordinary coincidences, the impact of the bad conscience of the perpetrator, provoked, perhaps years later, by the pulpit, or theatrical performance or the death-bed testimony of an accomplice – God revealed not only crimes unknown or long forgotten, but also the identity of the perpetrator(s). Thereafter, however, the baton was passed to God's vice-gerent, the Christian prince and his representatives, the secular magistrate and the godly minister. Thus, through the interaction between divine providence and the efforts of both magistrates and ministers, a world turned upside down by the enormity of murder – a crime, as the ghost tells Hamlet, 'most foul, at the best' – was righted, and the legitimacy and efficacy of royal government and the justice and mercy of God vindicated.[15]

In *Hamlet*, however, the normal structures of secular and spiritual authority are in abeyance precisely because the otherwise unknown, indeed unsuspected, murder revealed by providence is regicide, and the structures of human authority to which the task of bringing the murderer to book would normally be delegated are now headed by the murderer himself. This leaves the person to whom the crime has been revealed as the only means whereby the workings of divine justice can be embodied in this-worldly acts of accusation, trial and punishment. But in order to do that, Hamlet has not merely to circumvent the normal structures of human authority, in the person of the murderer, Claudius – he has directly to assault them. Claudius' dual status as both king and felon entirely stymies the usual interactions between divine providence and human action – the happy coordination between human and divine justice and mercy routinely celebrated in the murder pamphlets. On this account, 'the time' is indeed 'out of joint', and Hamlet is the only person available 'to set it right'. Indeed, as he says, he has been 'born' to do so, because, as old Hamlet's son, he is the person best qualified and most intensely obliged to revenge his father's death, and also because, as the son of the murdered prince, he is the person best placed to restore legitimate rule, by punishing and displacing the usurper. Thus, in wreaking revenge on Claudius, Hamlet will not merely be fulfilling the private role of avenger, vindicating his father, his lineage and his own honour, but will also be 'protecting the state' – acting, in short, as an instrument not so much of his father, as of divine justice or providence.[16] That is a role played in the murder narratives by both the secular magistrate and ministers of the word. Here those roles are collapsed into one and thrust onto Hamlet. As we shall see below, a great deal not only of the action, but of the dramatic and intellectual energy and tension that animate the play, stems from Hamlet's desperate attempts to fulfil all these multiple roles and functions, while also saving his own soul.

Under the circumstances, Hamlet's is a destiny or fate likely to prove as fatal to the chosen agent of revenge or justice as it is to his victim. If he is to act on the knowledge imparted to him – whether through insurrection, court conspiracy or an isolated act of assassination – he is going to have to kill a regnant monarch, and then navigate the forces and conflicts that such acts always unleash. For all the relish that he displays on having his earlier suspicions confirmed by the ghost – 'oh my prophetic soul! My uncle!' – Hamlet's words at the end of act I register his acknowledgement of and dismay at these realities: 'The time is out of joint: O cursed spite, / that ever I was born to set it right!' [Q2, I, v, 186–187; F, 1, v, 188–189]. Hamlet may at certain moments, and in some moods, talk a good game about his future starring role as revenger – 'now could I drink hot blood, / And do such bitter business as the day / Would quake to look on' [Q2, III, ii, 380–382; F, III, ii, 380–382] or again 'from this time forth / My thoughts be bloody or be nothing worth' [Q2, IV, iv, 64–65]; but at other times he views his as a desperately dangerous (indeed, potentially fatal) destiny – almost literally a fate – put upon him by exterior forces beyond his control and from which he would gladly escape.

Nor are the dangers inherent in the revenger's role purely secular or political. For in order effectively to revenge his dead father, discharge his role as the 'minister and scourge of heaven', thus putting 'the time' back into 'joint', Hamlet will have to commit a series of acts that might well be thought to be in themselves sinful – sins, which, while in terms of their immediate effects may well serve as punishments on the guilty, might also rebound on Hamlet, to his considerable detriment not only in this world, but also in the next. It is, of course, no accident that Hamlet's most coherent and fully formed realization of this fact comes at the same moment that he first explicitly conceives of himself not merely as the avenger of his father's murder, but also as the 'scourge and minister' of 'heaven', a self-description prompted by his own murder of Polonius. For all the ironic bluster and levity with which, both at first and subsequently, he greets that deed, it is an act that he immediately registers as a sin, and one that will weigh heavily upon him [Q2, III, iv, 170–175; F, III, iv, 155–161].

As Robert Weimann has pointed out, the speech in which Hamlet makes these observations is directed as much at the audience as it is at his mother:

The passage begins as genuine dialogue that leads to Hamlet's first 'Good night', which being repeated a second and a third time indicates that the passages in between suspend the convention of dialogue in favour of a more generalized, chorus-like kind of monologue.

Since, as Weimann observes, the subject at hand is nothing less than 'the significance and the consequences of Hamlet's thoughts and actions', 'the manner of delivery and prophetic content'

> so broaden the nature of Hamlet's speech that it supersedes the immediate context of dialogue and functionally becomes a direct address to the audience, in this case, something like a chorus. The change from one convention of speech to another does not come unannounced, however; for the expressive statements that transcend the illusion of one-to-one conversation follow the dramatic representation of leave-taking. In moving beyond the limitations of the illusion of conversation, and so in moving away, physically and psychologically, from his partner in dialogue, Hamlet also distances himself from the illusionistic modes of causality and locality and assumes a theatrically more neutral position from which he, as it were, collaborates with the audience.

While for Weimann, the point here is to establish that 'an old popular stage convention is impressed into the service of a new kind of realism', for the current argument the point to emphasize is the way in which Hamlet's direct address to the audience serves to advert to – and to awaken in them – a set of providential principles and expectations derived not so much from the revenge tragedy as from the murder pamphlet and the jeremiad.[17]

The topical matrix and confessional politics

At this point, it is worth pausing for a moment to recast Hamlet's dilemma in slightly more abstract terms, in order to see which group, if any, in Elizabethan England might be thought to be similarly trapped between, on the one hand, the claims of the past, of conscience, of both divine and human justice, and on the other hand, their current relationship to the structures of power, and indeed to the political and moral assumptions of the majority of their contemporaries. English Catholics, too, knew (or rather, some of them thought they knew) things about their queen that their contemporaries did not. They thought (or some of them did) that, as the murderer of a regnant queen (Mary Stuart), Elizabeth was a regicide and perhaps a usurper; that the regime under which they lived was illegitimate; that there was something rotten in the state of England; and that the time was indeed radically out of joint. Such knowledge was as potentially dangerous to them as it was to Hamlet: it turned the environment of even the noblest and most honourable Catholic into something hostile, full of intelligencers and informers. They, too, could trust no one – except, of course, people who shared their knowledge, and yet trying to share that knowledge with others might itself prove fatal. Their knowledge, too, if true, might be thought to demand action – action which constituted, or could be taken to constitute, a form of revenge for a murdered monarch and butchered co-religionists, and the discharge of sacred obligations towards God, man and the commonweal, to boot. But any such action was also treasonous in the eyes of the regime and of many of their fellow Englishmen (both Protestant and Catholic), and accordingly fraught with physical, material and, of course, spiritual danger. Resistance or regicide might or might not be, under current conditions, a sin; but either way, these were deeply dangerous acts, with untold consequences not only for the immediate perpetrator (who might be acting with his or her eyes not so much on this life as on the next), but also for the entire commonweal. There were, moreover, very different schools of opinion on the topic of political resistance, and its appropriate means and modes, to be found even among English Catholics.[18]

In short, in confronting the ghost's claims about Claudius' right to rule and its injunctions to revenge, Hamlet was confronting a nexus of choices and dilemmas that precisely paralleled that which had confronted English Catholics, if not since the death of Mary Tudor, then at least since the moment in 1570 when the pope had excommunicated Queen Elizabeth. That dilemma had (arguably) taken on redoubled force when Mary Stuart's head had parted company with her shoulders at Fotheringhay and the Spanish had bent their considerable efforts towards the conquest and reconversion of England. Moreover, with the end of the reign now imminent, things were only likely to get worse. For years, certain Catholics had been claiming that there was a plot among various of her counsellors to do away with Elizabeth and divert the succession from her natural hereditary successor, first Mary and now James Stuart, to A.N. Other (Catholic) claimant.

As the century and the reign neared their end, such fears were rampant, and were spread and exploited by that old hand at black propaganda, Robert Parsons. If Parsons was right, soon many English people might find themselves confronted with a regime headed by someone who, according to strict hereditary principles, would be a usurper, but who would base his or her claim to legitimacy on election by the commonweal. In fact, he or she would have been put on the throne by, and in order to serve the interests of, a narrow faction of self-interested courtiers and Machiavels. Elizabeth would be dead; the natural heir, James VI, would have been excluded from the throne; and a usurper (a Claudius lookalike) installed. We know from remarks made at his trial that this was precisely the fatal prospect that Essex thought his enemies at court were about to visit upon the realm, and from other sources (and the researches of Helena Stafford) that James VI shared these anxieties. In short, the situation in post-Elizabethan England would be very like that in Hamlet's Denmark, and the question of what to do about such a state of affairs would be quite as pressing and dangerous for those who understood the realities of the situation, as it was for Hamlet, confronted by his uncle's murderous usurpation. On this basis, the scenario laid out in the play, and Hamlet's dilemma in relation to it, can be read as an encapsulation, an intensely distilled version of and commentary on, the past, present and quite probable future dilemmas of English Catholics (and as the examples of Essex and James VI show, by 1599 not only of Catholics) as they waited for the end of the reign of good Queen Bess and worried about who might succeed her.

Such a reading becomes more likely when we remember that the information – and the injunction to act – that set up Hamlet's dilemma are based on the testimony of what the play goes out of its way to describe as a witness of distinctively 'Catholic' provenance: the ghost of Hamlet's father. From the outset, the precise ontological status of the ghost – and thus the epistemological status of everything it says – is placed under the most radical question.[19] The play's first words – 'Who's there' – set the tone here. At the ghost's first appearance, Horatio addresses it as an 'illusion' [Q2, I, i, 125; F, I, i, 108]. On its second, Hamlet sets out the parameters within which he assumes that he (and we) must decide the ghost's ontological status. The ghost, he claims, is either 'a spirit of health or goblin damned', bringing with it either 'airs from heaven or blasts from hell' [Q2, I, iv, 40–41; F, I, iv, 19–20]. Horatio tends towards the demonic end of this spectrum of possibilities when he tries to dissuade Hamlet from following the ghost: 'What if it tempt you toward the flood, my lord, / Or to the dreadful summit of the cliff' [Q2, I, iv, 69–70; F, I, iv, 48–49], Hamlet, self-consciously (and provisionally) suspending disbelief, takes the ghost to be what it seems and claims to be: 'I'll call thee Hamlet, / King, father, royal Dane' [Q2, I, iv, 42–45; F, I, iv, 21–24].

But having been raised at the outset, the possibility of the ghost's demonic origins, its status as an 'illusion', refuses to go away. For all the impact of the ghost's initial revelations, for all the closeness of their fit with Hamlet's own suspicions and emotional instincts – indeed, in many ways because of the closeness of that fit – Hamlet continues to nurse the suspicion that 'the spirit that I have seen / May be a devil' [Q2, II, ii, 533–534; F, II, ii, 593–594].

In thus positioning the issue of the ghost's status, the play is faithfully representing the larger cultural and intellectual framework within which such phenomena were viewed in post-Reformation England. As Stuart Clark explains, both Catholics and Protestants, intellectuals and ordinary believers, held that

Satan could easily 'represent the lykenesse of some faithfull man deceased', counterfeiting in outward show 'his words, voice, gesture, and such other things'. Devils could feign themselves to be dead men back from hell and represented 'unto our sighte' by magic, and they could also 'bleare and beguile the outward eyes' just as easily as dazzling the inward sight of the mind.[20]

According to Clark, both Catholics and Protestants subscribed to 'a shared demonology' that 'permitted to demons the assumption of bodies that were, as one discussion put it, "solid to the senses"'.[21] This was a world in which 'apparitions could be real visual phenomena, which waking people might see under normal visual conditions'. It was just that, for Protestants at least, 'they were never what they seemed' and 'certainly not ghosts of the dead. Even if seen normally, they were demonic simulations of visible forms, while abnormal conditions could easily be created by the artificial manipulation of visual objects, by alterations of the visual medium and by the malfunctioning of the organs of perception' – in all of which Satan was, of course, exceptionally, indeed preternaturally, skilled.[22] Keith Thomas sums up the situation thus: 'although men went on seeing ghosts after the Reformation they were assiduously taught not to take them at their face value'.[23]

But, as Peter Marshall has persuasively argued, there is good reason to doubt whether that lesson was ever fully learned, at least at a popular level. As late as 1659, 'a full hundred years after the Elizabethan Settlement, it could be asserted that examples of people returning as ghosts after their death were "numerous and frequent in all men's mouths"'.[24] Nowhere was what Marshall terms the 'failure of the Reformation to eradicate' the popular belief in ghosts clearer than in the propensity of the victims of unsuspected or unsolved murders, recorded (as Malcolm Gaskill has shown) in many a murder pamphlet and play, to return in order to reveal the details of the crime or the identities of the murderers.[25] Thus, one of the few things we know about the earlier *Hamlet* play, upon which Shakespeare's was almost certainly based, is that it contained a ghost that clamoured for revenge. This was by now a relatively common feature of the genre, common enough to be satirized as such in the introductory passages of another play – *Two Lamentable Tragedies* – written at just about this time. However, such conventional figures of revenge tended not to produce the sort of self-justificatory ontological account of themselves, the elaborated theological pedigree, which the ghost in *Hamlet* provides for itself. As Peter Marshall says, 'most dramatists who placed ghosts on the stage did not unduly agonize over their precise ontological status, or they evaded sensitive theological issues by rationalizing them as spirits from Hades in the Senecan tradition'. Marshall concludes by citing the claim of R.H. West that 'ghost and spirit scenes in contemporary drama are there to serve dramatic not expository ends'.[26]

But this is most decidedly not the case in Shakespeare's version of *Hamlet*. There, confronted by the fear, suspicion and scepticism evinced by both Horatio and Hamlet, the ghost has to come up with an account of itself likely to induce belief in the otherwise incredible claims it is about to make about the death of old Hamlet and the crimes of the current king and his new queen. And in order to do that, it gives an impeccably 'Catholic' account of what it is, whence it has come and whither it must return [Q2, I, v, 9–20; F, I, v, 9–20]. On its own account, the ghost is a soul, as it were, on night release from purgatory; allowed out to tell those it has left behind in the world the facts of old Hamlet's dreadful death, and thus to alert young Hamlet to the need to bring his killer to book and thus set the world to rights.

In addition, the ghost's account of the dreadfulness of its death is drenched in imagery and vocabulary taken from the old religion. He was, the ghost explains,

cut off even in the blossoms of my sin,

Unhousel'd, disappointed, unanel'd,

No reckoning made, but sent to my account

With all my imperfections on my head.

O horrible! O horrible! Most horrible! [Q2, I, v, 76–80; F, I, v, 76–80]

Here is a panoply of distinctively Catholic beliefs about the nature and necessity of a good death, involving the last rites and formal confession to a priest, coming out of the mouth of a tormented soul from purgatory. Shakespeare, then, goes out of his way to have this ghost give an impeccably and distinctively Catholic account of itself. This marks the play out from the many others that also contain the souls of the dead denouncing their killers or seeking to intervene in the lives of the living.[27]

Shakespeare was doing all this in a play written for a London audience at the turn of the sixteenth century; in other words, at a time when the official ideology of the Church and state held that purgatory was an illusion or fiction; a fact of which the entire audience – even (especially) those who were themselves Catholic – would have been acutely aware. And he was doing so at a time when, as Stuart Clark has shown, the fundamental disagreement between Catholics and Protestants over the existence or otherwise of purgatory meant that 'the Catholic Church and its opponents now disagreed crucially over the distribution and activities of spirits'. Accordingly, what Clark terms 'the apparitions debate' intensified (at least among the learned) 'to the point where it became fundamental to confessional polemics'. As Peter Marshall cautions, Keith Thomas might be going slightly too far when he claims that in the sixteenth century, the question of 'whether or not one believes in ghosts' was 'a shibboleth that distinguished Protestants from Catholics almost as effectively as belief in the Mass or the Papal Supremacy'.[28]

But it remains the case that the ghost question resonated with confessional significance – significance which *Hamlet* both draws upon and plays up, by making the ghost's credibility turn upon its claims to be a soul in purgatory. This at least appears to confront its first audiences and readers with what amounts to a confessional, as well as an epistemological, choice. For the early scenes with the ghost set up a situation in which, if Hamlet is to believe the ghost, he must also believe that it is what it claims to be. But if it is indeed 'an honest ghost', then purgatory must exist. For if the ghost is lying about that, why would it be telling the truth about anything else? By the same token, if it is found to be telling the truth about Claudius, would there not then be at least a presumption that it is also telling the truth about the rest? In believing the ghost, Hamlet and (more importantly) the audience at least appear to be being asked to take a gamble on, indeed almost to make a commitment about, the existence of purgatory and hence the truth of Catholicism.

For Hamlet, portrayed as living in a Catholic country, there was no difficulty in that. If the ghost was telling the truth, it probably was what it said it was, rather than a devil or a demonically inspired figment of Hamlet's own melancholy. For most of the audience, subjects of a Protestant queen and members of a Protestant national Church (to which such beliefs about purgatory were anathema), the stakes were rather higher.

In this way, the play might be thought to be putting the confessional conflict between Protestantism and Catholicism somewhere near the centre of the action. Just like *Titus Andronicus*, but unlike any of the other history plays, this one locates its account of the dynastic, political situation at its core against, or on top of, a polarized version of the contemporary religio-political scene. It thus sets up a situation in which the resolution of the dynastic/political plot must have direct consequences for the confessional issues raised in and through the ghost – and, of course, vice versa. That is the first sense (as we shall below, there are others) in which the play can legitimately be seen as a theological thriller about succession politics; or, if you prefer, a political thriller – or, less anachronistically still, a history play – about theology.

The topical matrix and religious politics

However, the play's engagement with issues of theology and religion does not end with the ghost or with ghost-related questions of confessional identity or conflict. For the situation into which his conversation with the ghost plunges Hamlet, also plunges him into a spiritual crisis. The emotional effects and expressions of that crisis are discussed in the play, both by Hamlet and by others, under the rubric of madness. That is a subject upon which Hamlet himself is ambivalent. As he leaves his fellow ghost watchers, he makes his famous remark that later he may well 'think meet / To put an antic disposition on' [Q2, I, v, 169–170; F, I, v, 170–171], which might be taken to imply that his subsequent displays of mental disturbance, eccentric demeanour and outspoken word play are a mere device, a cover, put on for some secret (undisclosed) purpose. And yet he himself talks elsewhere of 'my weakness and my melancholy'. Melancholy, of course, was a condition regarded by contemporaries as quite serious enough on its own to subject the sufferer to illusions, apparitions and obsessions of precisely the sort being experienced by Hamlet. On this account, then, Hamlet himself, as well as feigning madness, is (entirely understandably) afraid that he may be, in effect, mad; not so mad as to be unable to tell a hawk from a handsaw, perhaps, but certainly quite mad enough to be subject to melancholic delusions that make his description to Laertes of his killing of Polonius as an action of his madness rather than of his real self something more than an exercise in courtly obfuscation and politesse.

Hamlet's melancholy also raised the spectre not only that his experience is delusional but rather that it is a product of Satan's drive to lure him into damning sin. For, as Stuart Clark explains, it was a commonplace that, even left to its own devices, 'an imagination damaged by melancholy was one that "will see what is not, and create an infinite number of false and monstrous ideas"'. That propensity left those suffering from melancholia peculiarly exposed to the delusions of Satan. Thus, the polemicist and future bishop Samuel Harsnet argued that 'the melancholic saw more demons and witches than the sane'; and Robert Burton, author of the *Anatomy of Melancholy*, identified the activity of the devil 'as one of the causes of general melancholy and as an obvious explanation for many of the symptoms of its religious subtype, notably (and unsurprisingly) the fear of Hell'.[29] Timothy Bright agreed, explaining that Satan was always ready to 'embrace' the 'opportunity' offered to him in those 'already under the disadvantage of the melancholic complexion'.[30]

Thus, insofar as Hamlet is dissembling, i.e. feigning madness (and of course he tells us that he is), that may well be a function of (and an attempt to hide) his incapacity effectively to dissemble. That is to say, the situation into which he has been plunged, instantaneously and uncontrollably, by the ghost's revelations sets off reactions and effects in him that he is quite unable entirely to suppress or hide. In other words, he continues to have 'that within which passes show' [Q2, I, ii, 85; F, I, ii, 83], but now in a situation in which he cannot allow anyone to even suspect for a moment what or why that is. 'Madness' becomes, therefore, a convenient way both to display and to conceal by displaying in a certain way, just what he has within him. It also represents an all too tempting explanation for what is happening to him. If he is mad, a genuine melancholic, then the ghost may well be a (satanic) delusion, both an expression of his own obsessions and a demonic attempt to exploit those obsessions for altogether malign purposes. If so, then he has good reason not to act: delay is a sign not of weakness, cowardice or even madness, but rather of prudence. In such circumstances, his current apprehension of his situation and destiny as a revenger becomes itself a delusion, and he can hope to return from the nightmare world of isolation, suspicion and loathing into which the ghost's revelations have plunged him to something like normal. Hamlet's madness is thus, at once, a reality, a fake and a temptation; it fulfils multiple functions for him, and for the audience, as they try to work out just what it is that they are experiencing and watching.[31]

I want now to turn to the forms which Hamlet's madness takes in order to argue that what he and the other characters take for madness, can be re-described – and, more importantly, would have been recognizable to a contemporary – as a form of religious melancholy, an affective state that could indeed end in desperation, suicide and damnation, but that could also provide the starting point for a process of spiritual growth or conversion, ending in spiritual assurance and salvation.[32]

We are offered only a retrospective view of Hamlet as he had been before his father's death, his mother's over-hasty remarriage and the ghost's revelations had soured his relations with the world. According to Ophelia, he had been 'the courtier's, soldier's, scholar's, eye, tongue, sword, / Th' expectation and rose of the fair state, / The glass of fashion and the mould of form, / Th' observed of all observers' [Q2, III, i, 150–153; F, III, i, 152–155]. In short, Hamlet had been the epitome of the renaissance gentleman or aristocrat; a master of all the arts and attributes – martial, social, intellectual – that made up the late-Tudor courtier and man of honour. The play lays out those attributes very clearly. Hamlet's interest in swordsmanship is matched by the intensity of his passion for the drama, and indeed by his own literary pretensions and abilities. This is a man as able to compose (admittedly execrable) love poetry to Ophelia as he is to write lines for insertion in the players' performance before the king. His literary tastes are *avant-garde*. On his own admission, he likes plays not loved by the million, and can deliver a disquisition on the correct way to play that is at direct variance with popular tastes and common practice. He is a scholar, trained at Wittenberg to extract from the best authors the essence of human wisdom and philosophy. Osric's commendation of Laertes as 'an absolute gentleman, full of most excellent differences, of very soft society and great showing . . . the very card and calendar of gentry' [Q2, V, ii, 92–95] might just as well apply to Hamlet as to his doppelganger Laertes. Certainly, Hamlet's appraisal to Horatio of Laertes as a 'very noble youth' [Q2, V, i, 213; F, V, i, 221] implies his continuing appreciation of such qualities and the easy move from the observation of such attributes and accomplishments to the conferral of true 'nobility' or 'honour' on those perceived to possess them. And yet the effect of the ghost's revelation on the prince was to empty all such worldly considerations of their value.

Told by the ghost to 'remember me', Hamlet replies that what the ghost has told him, and indeed enjoined him to do, will henceforth drive from his mind the memory of all humane learning [Q2, I, v, 97–112; F I, v, 97–112]. In the face of what the ghost has told him, all Hamlet's previous gleanings from the various sources of humane wisdom, the fruits of the humanist education which he opened the play wishing to continue at Wittenberg, count for nothing. The only commandment or moral imperative worthy of remembrance in the tables of his memory is now the ghost's injunction to revenge. In the face of the villainy of his uncle and his mother, he sees that the humane virtues and accomplishments surrounding him at the court are a mere sham. As he tells his accomplices, seemingly in jest, the purport of the honest ghost's message to him – and at this point, for Hamlet, it is 'an honest ghost' – is 'there's never a villain dwelling in Denmark / But he's an arrant knave'. On the face of it, this is mere tautological nonsense: at best, the sort of festive, biting taunt that henceforth characterizes the discourse of Hamlet's 'madness'. As Horatio comments, 'there needs no ghost, my lord, come from the grave / To tell us this' [Q2, I, v, 122–124; F, I, v, 122–124]. But in fact, just as the knowledge imparted by the ghost to Hamlet does objectively transform his relationship with his entire social world, with his own past, his present and his future, so the nature of the sin and corruption revealed to him by his father's shade transforms a world he has perceived hitherto through the frame of courtly humanist culture into a place utterly debased, a sink of corruption, full of 'villains' who are indeed all 'arrant knaves'. As Timothy Rosendale observes, his 'description of the world as "an unweeded garden . . . rank and gross" evokes a postlapsarian anti-Eden, entirely ("merely") corrupted by sin'.[33]

Hamlet's subsequent demeanour, and indeed explicit commentary on the world, reflect this new insight. His appearance, as Ophelia describes it to Polonius, is hardly that of the dapper young man about court, 'the glass of fashion and the mould of form' of the recent past:

with his doublet all unbraced
No hat upon his head, his stockings fouled,

Ungartered and down-gyved to his ankle,
Pale as his shirt, his knees knocking each other,
And with a look so piteous in purport
As if he had been loosed out of hell
To speak of horrors. [Q2, II, i, 75–81; F, II, i, 76–82]

His remark to Rosencrantz and Guildenstern that 'Denmark's a prison' reflects a similar alienation from 'the world', which itself is 'a prison' 'in which there are many confines, wards, and dungeons – Denmark being one o' th'worst' [F, II, ii, 243–245]. That remark is followed, of course, by a longer description of Hamlet's mood and a disquisition on the nature of 'the earth' and of 'man'. The former, for all its glories, now seems to him 'nothing to . . . but a foul and pestilent congregation of vapours' and the latter, for all his god-like capacities, a 'quintessence of dust' [Q2, II, ii, 261–276; F, II, ii, 295–309].

Throughout, these insights and feelings are attributed to a radical change within Hamlet's affective state – 'I have of late, but wherefore I know not, lost all my mirth' – and are discussed under the rubric of a radical subjectivism: 'There is nothing either good or bad, but thinking makes it so. To me it is a prison' [F, II, ii, 247–249]. They take place in a series of exchanges between Hamlet and the two spies, sent to inform on him by the king and queen, in the course of which Hamlet needs to continue to maintain that he is, in fact, 'mad', a melancholic in the grip of a textbook example of melancholia: 'O God, I could be bounded in a nutshell and count myself a king of infinite space – were it not that I have bad dreams' [F, II, ii, 252–254]. And yet what these speeches also register is the completeness of Hamlet's alienation from the temptations and pleasures of 'the world'. And, of course, alienation from 'the world', the capacity to see through its surface allurements and attractions to the 'quintessence of dust' underneath, was not only a sign of madness, but was also – within both Catholic and Protestant cultures – a necessary prerequisite for, and effect of, conversion to a true Christian faith.

So too, as his remark to Rosencrantz and Guildenstern about being no more 'delighted' by women than by men implies, was a visceral disgust at the blandishments and pleasures of the flesh. Hamlet, of course, could speak as admiringly as anyone of the pleasures of married love, but he did so only in describing the relations between his dead father and his mother. That vision was now defiled by the descent of 'the royal bed of Denmark' into 'a couch for luxury and damned incest'. This is the fruit of 'lust', which 'though to a radiant angel inked. / Will sate itself in a celestial bed / And prey on garbage' [Q2, I, v, 82–83, 55–57; F, I, v, 82–83, 55–57]. The words, of course, are those of the ghost; but they are immediately endorsed and developed by his son into a visceral sexual disgust. For Hamlet, just as for his father's shade, the prime object and provocation of that disgust is the mere thought of the sexual act performed between Gertrude and Claudius. In the closet scene, Hamlet famously tortures both himself and his mother with images of the royal couple going at it. They are pictured, as Hamlet puts it elsewhere, in 'imaginations' as 'foul / as Vulcan's stithy' [Q2, III, ii, 79–80; F, III, ii, 81–82].

In these speeches, love has become lust; sexual desire and pleasure a form of corruption and decay – an attribute not of man as demi-god or angel, but rather as beast, wallowing in the sty of his filthy lusts and impulses. Of course, the sexual relations being pictured between his mother and his uncle are, at least in Hamlet's and the ghost's view, by their very nature incestuous. But Hamlet uses the same sort of imagery to describe sexual relations between men and women more generally. As in his interactions with his mother, lust is figured as female; and Hamlet's disgust at and distrust of his own sexual impulses are evacuated onto the woman in the case – Ophelia – who is figured by Hamlet as necessarily without virtue precisely because she is beautiful, and therefore an object of his and other men's desires [Q2, III, i, 110–114; F, III, i, 111–115]. Women, as the objects of desire, are here depicted as the prime movers in the process of corruption:

> I have heard of your paintings well enough. God hath given you one face and you make yourselves another. You jig and amble and you lisp, you nick-name God's creatures and make your wantonness your ignorance. [Q2, III, i, 144–148; F, III, I, 143–147]

But Hamlet's analysis of the generality of the corruption and sin inherent in human sexuality transcends an assault on the brevity and untrustworthiness of 'women's love'. Even if Ophelia herself remains 'as chaste as ice, as pure as snow' [Q2, III, i, 135–136; F, III, i, 136–137], if she marries she will neither escape calumny nor avoid becoming 'a breeder of sinners' [Q2, III, i, 121; F, III, i, 122]. And at this point, Hamlet, for the first time, includes himself in the analysis:

> I am myself indifferent honest but yet I could accuse me of such things that it were better my mother had not borne me. I am very proud, revengeful, ambitious, with more offences at my beck than I have thoughts to put them in, imagination to give them shape, or time to act them. What should such fellows as I do crawling between earth and heaven? We are arrant knaves all – believe none of us. Go thy ways to a nunnery. [Q2, III, i, 121–128; F, III, i, 122–129]

The result of these exchanges is a social and sexual world in which virtue for either sex is all but impossible, and the only proper response to such enmeshing corruption is withdrawal into celibacy – for Ophelia into a nunnery; for his mother into a refusal to sleep any more with Claudius; and for Hamlet into a rejection of all thoughts of marriage: 'Go to, I'll no more on't. It hath made me mad. I say we will have no more marriage. Those that are married already – all but one – shall live. The rest shall keep as they are' [Q2, III, i, 145–148; F, III, i, 147–149]. While there can be no doubting the misogyny that runs through these exchanges between Hamlet and both his mother and Ophelia, the extent of the corruption involved here cannot be limited to women. There is, in fact, an inextricable connection between Hamlet's denunciation of the corrupting influence of female weakness and beauty and his overpowering sense of his own sinfulness and corruption.

In theological terms, what we have here is a characterization of the sexual instinct, of desire and all that it leads to, as concupiscence; and of concupiscence as simply sin – indeed, we might surmise, as the source of all sin, connecting an always already sinful humanity to its fallen progenitors, Adam and Eve, through generations of corrupting desire, procreation and death. On this view, Hamlet's 'madness' takes the form of an intense alienation – on the one hand, from both the attractions of 'the world', of all humane learning and accomplishment, of everything that, on one view of the matter, renders man more like an angel or a god than a mere creature; and on the other hand, from the pleasures of the flesh. Again, viewed in theological terms, all this might be seen to represent a peculiarly intense, almost paralyzing, apprehension of the nature and extent of (both original and personal) sin.

From his claim to Horatio and the others that 'there's never a villain dwelling in Denmark but he's an arrant knave', through his bitter denunciation to Ophelia and his repudiation of his own seemingly honest nature as a sink of corruption and vice, to his injunction to Polonius to treat the players far better than their desert, because 'use everyman after his desert and who shall scape whipping' [Q2, II, ii, 467–468; F, II, ii, 525–526], Hamlet's discourse is pervaded by a sense of the encompassing nature of human sin. For, as he tells Ophelia, 'virtue cannot so inoculate our old stock but we shall relish of it' [Q2, III, i, 116–118; F, III, i, 118–119]. All the characteristics being displayed by Hamlet here were, as we shall see, frequently discussed by contemporaries under the signs of madness or melancholy; but there was also an alternative reading of such affective states and senses of the self in a fallen world. For versions of precisely such attitudes and states of mind were regarded by certain styles of rigorist Christian as a desirable, indeed a necessary, condition or stage through which unregenerate sinners, in urgent search of true saving faith and assurance of salvation, had to pass.

On this account, Hamlet may not be mad or melancholic at all, but in the throes of the sort of spiritual crisis that could provide the starting point for a soul-shattering and life-altering conversion to true saving faith.

What the play has done, therefore, is to arrange on top of one another four distinct political, confessional and spiritual areas of intense and immediate contemporary concern. First, we have the political, dynastic nexus, centred on the fact of Claudius' regicide and usurpation, Hamlet's knowledge thereof and on the course of action proper to such knowledge. Second, we have the confessional issue, related to the truth or falsehood of Hamlet's knowledge of Claudius' crime and to the credibility of the entirely popish source of that knowledge. Third, we have the providential aspect of the case. All of these cruxes spoke directly to pressing contemporary, religious and political concerns, anxieties and dilemmas. Taken together, they provided the grounds for the spiritual crisis experienced by Hamlet – a crisis acted out and described in the play in terms of madness and melancholy, but couched in (and certainly available to contemporaries for interpretation in terms of) the language of original sin, spiritual despair and the search for assurance: the language, in short, of evangelical conversion, or of what William Perkins once termed 'A case of conscience, the greatest that ever was, how a man may know whether he be a son of God or no' (the title of his famous tract of 1592). We have here, then, a gesture to a fourth nexus of directly contemporary, evangelical concerns about the nature of true Christianity, of true Christian conversion, and about the spiritual despair consequent upon religious change, apostasy and the activity of the devil.

5

◄◄┄►►

The generic matrix
Revenge tragedy, history play, murder pamphlet and conversion narrative

Revenge tragedy and history play

Just as it brings together and processes a variety of different sorts of contemporary concern – political, confessional and religious – the play elicits from its audience, and then manipulates, a series of narrative expectations derived from a range of different contemporary genres. Put another way, as Lee observes, the irruptive intervention of the ghost has cut Hamlet off from the 'values and traditions out of which the narrative quest for life is sustained', and has thus rendered him unable to find a 'story to render satisfactorily intelligible his life' and current circumstances.[1] Put in more immediately contextual or historical terms, as Rhodri Lewis has pointed out, it has utterly undermined all the canons of Renaissance humanist assumption that had hitherto underpinned his existence and sense of himself as an actor or social, political and moral agent in the world.[2] The play exploits this void by offering Hamlet (and, of course, the audience) a variety of different sorts of story or narrative template with which to make sense of what is happening to him and them.

The first of these is provided by the revenge tragedy. This genre has dominated discussion of the play – and for good reason.[3] We know that Shakespeare's *Hamlet* had been preceded by an earlier version of the story, central to which had been a ghost screaming for revenge, revenge. Audiences coming to see Shakespeare's version would have done so with certain expectations in mind – expectations which the play does a good deal to encourage, even as, for its own dramatic advantage, it frustrates and exploits them. After all, the one thing that was certain in a revenge tragedy was that revenge was the main event; whatever else happened, revenge would be achieved in ways that would bring both revenger and revengee to deserved and bloody ends. The audience therefore knew that revenge was coming, but the question was when and how: in what form and with what consequences, in this life and the next, would revenge in fact be achieved?[4] As

William Empson has observed, that question was rendered the more pressing for Shakespeare by the fact that, in deciding to write *Hamlet* in the first place, he was reworking an old play, the basic contours of which would not only have been well known to his audience, but which, Empson surmises, had become something of a by-word for the risible predictability of the genre as a whole. In Empson's formulation:

> you had a hero howling out 'Revenge' all through the play, and everybody knew the revenge wouldn't come till the end. The structure is at the mercy of anybody in the audience who cares to shout 'Hurry Up', because the others feel they must laugh, however sympathetic they are; or rather, they felt that by the time Shakespeare wrote *Hamlet*, whereas ten years earlier they would have wanted to say 'Shush'. This fact about the audience, I submit, is the basic fact about the rewriting of *Hamlet*.[5]

I would like to suggest that it was to address precisely this predicament that Shakespeare had recourse to the other genres – or rather to the sets of audience expectation that attended the other genres – that shaped the plot of his version of *Hamlet*, the second of which was, as we have seen, the history play. By this point, especially in Shakespeare's hands, the history play had become indelibly associated with issues of dynastic right, succession and the re-establishment of order and right rule after interludes of usurpation, tyranny and revolt. In this generic context, the fate of the revenger and the revengee was indelibly linked to the fortunes of the state and future of the realm.

The murder pamphlet

The third set of narrative expectations and thematic associations evoked and exploited by the play was that derived from the providentialized murder pamphlet or play. There the issue was not so much revenge as justice. The dominant narrative task such texts set themselves was the demonstration of a complete compatibility, indeed synergy, between human and divine justice. This was to be achieved through the workings of the criminal justice system, aided, as and when necessary, by the irruptive interventions of divine providence. Together, these were supposed to unmask the crime and the criminal, and then to bring him or her to justice. Thereafter, the workings of human justice had to be rendered compatible with those of divine mercy, as the convicted criminal was confronted with his guilt and current spiritual condition, and, if possible, through the ministrations of the clergy and the intervention of divine grace, brought to a saving repentance – a repentance to be expressed fully and freely on the scaffold.[6] The means used to effect such interventions were often, in Horatio's phrase, 'wondrous strange' – that is to say, supernatural and indeed sometimes frankly miraculous: 'There are more things in heaven and earth, Horatio, / Than are dreamt of in your philosophy' [Q2, I, v, 163, 165–166; F, I, v, 164, 166–167]. And, of course, the play opens with just such a 'wondrous strange' visitation by an entity (whose precise ontological status is unknown) to reveal an otherwise entirely unsuspected crime.

In at least some of the murder pamphlets, not only the revelation and punishment of the crime are at stake, but so also are the spiritual state and fate of the condemned. But what is never in doubt is the spiritual state or fate of those doing the punishing and admonishing, whose status as public persons, magistrates, agents of the state, render their violent acts not merely entirely free from sin, but in fact embodiments of divine (as well as human) justice.

There were available at least two immediately contemporary accounts of the commonwealth and of monarchical right through which Hamlet could have claimed such a public status. The first was associated with the notions of elective monarchy and resistance theory. On this view, as an inferior magistrate or prince of the blood, Hamlet might well have been able to claim a public status sufficient to enable him legitimately to right the wrongs committed by Claudius. The second is an absolutist rationale, articulated, as András Kiséry points out, by none other than Belleforest, the author of one of Shakespeare's probable sources for the play. Belleforest was a virulently absolutist opponent of all such monarchomach theories, and yet at the end of his account he has Amleth declare the righteousness of his act in killing his usurping uncle. Since Amleth is the rightful prince, while his uncle is a usurper and a tyrant, in this instance killing the king is not tyrannicide, but merely the exercise of royal justice, as the true prince punishes the dreadful crimes of one of his subjects.[7]

It is surely significant that at no point does the play make any gesture in either of these directions. Hamlet is pictured throughout operating in a mental, moral and political world in which no such claims to a legitimate – as it were, 'public' – right to resist exist. While the situation confronting him is quintessentially political, his response to that situation remains entirely 'private', utterly cut off from any structure of argument or assumption through which he could claim a public status as either the representative or saviour of the commonwealth, or indeed as the true king – both positions that could legitimate an overtly political, public challenge to Claudius' standing as king. As we shall see below, precisely such a challenge *is* made, with entirely disastrous results; but it is made by Laertes, not Hamlet, who sedulously avoids all such claims and expedients.

Of course, to Hamlet, if he has done what the ghost claims he has done, Claudius is no sort of king at all. Various editors have construed Hamlet's jibe, when asked where he has stashed the body of Polonius, 'that the body is with the king, but the king is not with the body' [Q2, IV, ii, 25–26; F, III, v, 28–29], as a slighting reference to the doctrine of the king's two bodies, designed to distinguish between Claudius' private person or body and the crown itself, to which he has no right. Certainly, Hamlet's next remark to Guildenstern that 'the king is a thing . . . of nothing' [Q2, IV, ii, 26–28; F, III, v, 29–31] would seem to bear out such an interpretation, as would his earlier claim to Gertrude that Claudius is 'a cutpurse of the empire and the rule', 'a king of shreds and patches' [Q2, III, iv, 97, 99; F, III, iv, 90, 92]. But while that may well be Hamlet's view, as we have seen, it is no one else's. Elected king according to the norms of the Danish monarchy, Claudius' legitimacy is accepted by all. In fact, even in the face of open rebellion he remains the residual beneficiary, as he tells Laertes, with no trace of irony, and with immediate effect, of 'the divinity that doth hedge a king' [Q2, IV, v, 123; F, IV, i, 122]. All of which inevitably raises the question of whether, even if Claudius is as guilty as the ghost claims, in killing him Hamlet would be committing a crime that would put not merely his life but his very soul in jeopardy.

For, even if the ghost is telling the truth – indeed, even if the killing of Claudius does not merely serve the ends of private revenge, but also in some sense those of public, and even divine, justice – precisely because he *was* the king, the sin committed in killing Claudius might still be grave enough to send his killer to hell. Immediately after having killed Polonius, Hamlet observes that God often uses the sins of one person to punish those of another. Under those circumstances, even the scrupulous discharge of his ascribed role of scourge and minister of divine justice would be no guarantee of his own spiritual safety. Indeed, among those contemporaries most practised in discerning and justifying the workings of divine providence to their fellow Christians, it was a commonplace that, having used his nominated scourge to punish the sins of his people, or to restore order to a world thrown into chaos by sin, God could just as easily proceed to throw both the scourge and his victim onto the fire of divine judgment and eternal damnation. He could, in short, use the sins of one group or individual to punish those of another, and then wash his hands of both of them. For an audience coming to the action of the play with such models, maxims and expectations in mind, Hamlet's soul, as well as his temporal fate and that of the Danish state, would have been very obviously at stake.

At this point, concern with providence morphs into concern with that subset of providence, predestination. Murder pamphlets sometimes ended with accounts of the repentance and conversion of the felon; in those cases, murder – followed as it was not only by conviction and death on the gallows, but also by sincere confession and true repentance – is turned into a *felix culpa*. The crime, no matter how dreadful, becomes itself providential, providing the grounds both for the salvation of persons who previously may have led lives sunk in the direst sin, and for the spectacular demonstration of God's justice and mercy. The telling of such tales could sometimes turn into vindications of the doctrines of absolute election and reprobation, providing spectacular examples of the extent of divine mercy and of the power of free grace to save even the deepest-dyed villain from what appeared to all the world to be a richly deserved damnation.[8] In *Hamlet*, of course, the issue is not only the spiritual fate of the perpetrator(s) – although, as we shall see, that is an issue – but also that of the revenger, the instrument of God's justice.

The conversion narrative

In foregrounding these issues, the play turns to matter that is central not merely to the more evangelically engaged and theologically explicit of the murder pamphlets, but also to a fourth genre, the 'conversion narrative'. We need to be careful about what we mean by the phrase 'conversion narrative', because the literary form that has subsequently become known by that term had yet to be developed, and *Hamlet* could scarcely be said to be shaped by (still less to be feeding off) the audience's familiarity with a genre that did not yet exist.[9] However, at the end of Elizabeth's reign, certain modes of practical divinity, forms of introspection, ways of speaking about conversion and of describing and handling the experience of religious doubt or despair were being developed by a range of contemporaries. The results of all this experimental divinity were as yet only slowly finding their way into print. We can see that process starting in the early 1590s, with the publication of, for instance, Edward Dering's letters of spiritual advice to various godly women, or of Thomas Wilcox's *Discourse Touching the Doctrine of Doubting*.[10] Dering's letters were first printed on a puritan exile press in Middelburg, in the Netherlands, but then included in an expanded edition of his works, printed in London in 1597. Wilcox's *Discourse* was described on the title page as 'written long since and now published for the profit of the people of God' by the Cambridge University printer in 1598. However, even by the 1590s, what was getting into print was but the tip of an iceberg of pastoral activity, and the circulation, through word of mouth and manuscript – the manuscripts, for instance, of Richard Greenham's table talk were but anecdotes, polished, arranged in sequence and transcribed for a wider audience – of the techniques, axioms and achievements of the great puritan doctors of the soul, men like Greenham himself or William Perkins, many of whose works and sayings were only printed posthumously, through the efforts of their epigones and proteges.[11] However, the fact that those works did find their way into print so quickly, and in such numbers, proves both the fame which these men had achieved among the godly, and the demand for such works among the reading public. But the prevalence of such activities long pre-dated the careers even of Greenham and Perkins. Divines like Wilcox or Thomas Cartwright, more famous today for their agitation for the Presbyterian platform, were also active among the godly as doctors of the soul.[12] Similarly, the famous Protestant martyrologist, church historian and anti-papal polemicist, John Foxe, had a very widespread popular reputation not only as just such a doctor of the soul, but also as an exorcist.[13]

Conversion took two forms: evangelical conversion – from an unregenerate to a regenerate state, from unbelief or a merely formal Christian profession (from what many divines described as a merely historical faith) to a truly justifying and effectually saving one; and conversion from one ecclesiastical allegiance or confessional identity to another. The two types of conversion could be – indeed often were – conflated; but they were conceptually and practically separate. Both forms of conversion were, however, in their different ways associated with spiritual distress, doubt and even despair.

In the case of evangelical conversion, despair – or at least extreme spiritual distress – was often induced by the pastoral efforts of divines, anxious to shock those who heard them into a properly urgent sense of their own spiritual condition, of the extent of their own sins, and hence of their desperate need for a saving faith. The standard means to convert unregenerate sinners, or merely formal Christians, was to apply to them what became known as the hammer of the law. This was done to convince the sinner of the extent and gravity of his or her sins, and thus of his or her complete powerlessness to do anything to merit salvation in the face of the perfect justice of God. Only thus could worldlings be weaned away from their thraldom to the world, the flesh and the devil, and from the damning belief that salvation could somehow be won through their own efforts or merits. For it was only when they had been convinced of their own utter depravity, and of the certainty, in their current state, of eternal damnation, that Christian professors could be induced to throw themselves on the mercy of God in Christ in the utterly unconditional way that might lead to a true saving faith. It was therefore only after the preacher had beaten down his charges with the hammer of the law that he would then apply to their bruised souls and afflicted consciences the balm of the gospel, laying out, in calming detail, the extent of God's promises to save repentant sinners no matter how dreadful their sins might be. Moved, then, to understand that a lively faith entailed both repentance for sin and amendment of life, thereafter the Christian could be led up the ladder of repentance and amendment to a greater and greater sense of assurance of salvation and the experience of that growth in grace that was always supposed to attend, and was thus also taken to be the crucial sign of, a true, lively, saving faith.[14]

Problems arose when this progression, this narrative, stalled. This could happen at any stage: suffering under the lash of the law, Christians could become convinced that their sins were so great that they could never be saved. Later, failing to achieve a settled sense of assurance, or to experience the approved growth in grace, they could conclude that theirs was either a false faith or that a once true faith had been lost, perhaps irretrievably. The result could be doubt, even despair; the conviction that one was damned, a reprobate soul beyond help. Much of the practical divinity, the case law and spiritual counselling and casuistry being developed and disseminated at this time was concerned with how to induce this sort of conversion experience, and how then to contain and control the consequences, if it spun out of control.

Problems could also arise within conversion from one ecclesiastical affiliation to another. As Michael Questier has demonstrated, throughout the post-Reformation period there was much traffic across the boundaries that separated Protestantism from Catholicism.[15] High-profile conversions were topics of great interest, and both sides tried to extract the maximum polemical advantage from them. For evangelical Protestants, the goal in converting a Catholic was not mere outward conformity to the rites and formularies of the national Church, but rather the construal of such a change as also an evangelical conversion from a false to a true faith, a move from damnation to salvation. With the stakes this high, there was, of course, a considerable risk of pretence and hypocrisy, of self-deception and mistake. Here the great danger was apostasy, and perhaps even the sin against the Holy Ghost, the only sin that placed the sinner beyond the saving efficacy of Christ's sacrifice.

As Michael MacDonald has shown in a seminal article, for late-Elizabethan Protestants, the paradigmatic example of the integral connection between false conversion, apostasy and despair was provided by the dreadful fate of Francis Spiera.[16] Spiera was an Italian Protestant who, having been denounced to the Inquisition, renounced his faith. After his second recantation, he heard a voice 'admonishing him for denying God and sentencing him to eternal damnation'. Convinced that he was guilty of the sin against the Holy Ghost, and that God had forsaken him, Spiera fell into despair. Taking to his bed, he refused food and drink. Convinced that he was a 'reprobate like Cain and Judas, who casting away all hope of mercy, fell into despair', he resisted all attempts to persuade him that he was not damned. Latterly he became convinced that he was also possessed by the devil, and when a priest came to try and exorcise him he refused his ministrations, telling him that the spirits who possessed him could not be cast out with mere spells. He tried to kill himself, before finally, after nearly eight weeks in this state, expiring from hunger.

As a number of commentators have pointed out, the play itself contains a reference to another similar case, the highly publicized suicide of Sir James Hales. An Edwardian Protestant, Hales had converted to Catholicism under Mary, only to drown himself in despair in 1560. As Alison Chapman observes, the gravedigger's hair-splitting discussion of the rights and wrongs of death by drowning 'presents a parody of the legal arguments used at Hale's postmortem trial' and comes a mere 20 lines after Gertrude's account of Ophelia's 'muddy death'.[17]

Spiera's case was widely known in late-Elizabethan England. John Foxe included a brief account of his fate in the *Acts and Monuments*. Thomas Beard included another in his *Theatre of God's Judgements* of 1597. In 1587, a ballad based on his life had been published. A clergyman named Nathaniel Woodes wrote a late morality play based on the case, of which two editions appeared in 1581. Finally, a recension in English, based on the original Latin accounts of the case, was produced by the leading puritan layman Nathaniel Bacon. This was not printed until the 1630s, but circulated in manuscript in the late sixteenth century, another example of the widespread circulation in manuscript, as well as in print, of texts concerned with the interiority of despair, the internal dynamics of conversion, and demonic possession.[18]

The association in the Spiera case between religious despair and demonic possession was a common one. Timothy Bright, the author of a 1586 *Treatise of Melancholy*, saw Satan as the cause of religious despair, with the fiend all too often exploiting the symptoms of the melancholic to plunge him or her into a desperation so deep as to constitute something akin to the sin against the Holy Ghost. Such demonic temptation could take various forms, of which actual possession – what Bright termed 'the corporal inhabiting of Satan' – was 'the greatest'. In cases of 'corporal possession', Bright explained, 'it seemeth there needeth no means; when Satan possesseth all parts of the house', he could, as 'master', command 'at his pleasure'. But in other cases, Satan had perforce to resort to other methods. Drawing on what Bright termed his 'long experience and practice of our misery from age to age', Satan was 'able with ease to work our annoyance in all respects' by playing on our susceptibilities, our innermost weaknesses and compulsions, all of which the fiend could apprehend 'by the least show and inclination of our affection and will'.[19] Since, as Bright explained, melancholy 'persuadeth of misery where there is no cause', melancholics were peculiarly susceptible to such demonic temptation, melancholy here acting 'like a weapon [put] into Satan's hand' to be 'used to all advantage of our hurt and destruction'.[20]

On the one hand, Bright was at pains to insist that 'the affliction of the soul through conscience of sin is quite another thing than melancholy' and that those who sought to conflate the two states, or to collapse the former into the latter, were not merely mistaken, but 'the profane ones of this world . . . laboring by all means to benumb the sense of that sting which sin ever carrieth in the tail'.[21] Indeed, they were tantamount to atheists, people who judged 'more basely of the soul than agreeth with piety or nature and have accounted all manner of affection thereof to be subject to the physician's hand, not considering herein anything divine and above the ordinary events and natural course of things'. On the other hand, having undertaken to expound 'what the different is betwixt natural melancholy and that heavy hand of God upon the afflicted conscience, tormented with remorse of sin and fear of his judgement', Bright also conceded that the two states could, and often did, feed off one another, and thus took as his subject 'how the body and corporal things affect the soul and how the body is affected of it again'. Thus, he explained to the notional addressee of his discourse, one Master M, that he was to esteem his 'estate' as 'mixed of the melancholic humour and that terror of God, which as it is upon the wicked an entrance into eternal destruction, so unto you it is . . . a fatherly frowning only for a time'.[22]

Viewed in that light, at least for the godly, appalling though it was, such a spiritual crisis was, or at least could be, an entirely good thing, leading the person afflicted to a proper appreciation of his or her spiritual condition, and thus acting as the starting point either for a true conversion or for a return to a sense of assurance with 'more strength than ever it had before'.[23] Handled properly, such a state could be a part of its own cure. Thus, on the one hand, melancholy was a medical condition, with treatable causes and identifiable effects, and whenever and wherever it was detected it should be treated as such.[24] But on the other hand, because melancholy and true spiritual despair were so similar, and very often found together, there was a real danger that the two states could be confused. Thus, as Jeremy Schmidt has shown, myriad

> evangelically minded divines in the Elizabethan and Jacobean Church concerned
> with the health of the soul often complained that persons suffering from the terrors
> of their conscience themselves used the notion of melancholy, as Hamlet does – to
> avoid facing certain uncomfortable moral and spiritual demands.

Except, of course, despite Schmidt's almost reflexive reference in that passage to 'Hamlet', at no point in the play is it clear, either to Hamlet or to us, that that is what he is doing; and it is far from clear by play's end that that is what he has actually done.

Rather, Hamlet is shown trapped on the horns of this very dilemma – 'caught', as Schmidt puts it, 'between the world of his experience of religious despair and the medical diagnosis used by others to explain the "truth" of his feelings'. For

on the strength of the popularization of Renaissance medical theories of melancholy, those who suffered acute fear and sorrow in a religious form were often thought to be merely melancholy, or even mad. The refusal to accept the naturalistic interpretation merely confirmed the presence of a stubborn delusion.[25]

Thus, as we have seen, Hamlet finds himself confronted by the need to decide whether he is indeed 'mad' – that is to say, deluded by his own melancholy: a state perhaps exploited by the hostile attentions of the devil, or perhaps merely produced by the operations of his own melancholic imagination. Or was he rather the recipient of God's grace, called to act upon a (miraculously) revealed truth? And, of course, what was an urgent existential problem for Hamlet confronted Claudius as a no less urgent political conundrum. Hamlet's, then, was a case of conscience with pressing political consequences.

But even that apparently stark choice did not exhaust the possibilities; for again, as Schmidt points out, here echoing Bright and many other godly divines, even if Hamlet were 'mad', or at least suffering from an extreme case of melancholy, that did not ensure that the insights gleaned from and through that state were simply false. Even maladies and afflictions like these came ultimately from God, and thus had to be viewed providentially. 'It was to be understood that melancholy' – and indeed even the malign ministrations of Satan himself – were themselves 'a means of providence'.[26] Richard Greenham warned 'a gentlewoman troubled in mind' that she should

beware that you do not often alter your judgement of your estate: as saying sometimes it is God's work, sometimes melancholy, sometimes your weakness and simplicity, sometimes witchery, sometimes Satan: you may think melancholy to be an occasion, but no cause, and so of the rest. Therefore, look steadfastly to the hand of God, surely trusting on this, that he not only knoweth thereof, but that whatsoever is done directly, or indirectly, by no means or immediately; all is done and governed (by his divine providence) for your good.[27]

On one reading of the play, there could scarcely be a more accurate account of just what Hamlet finds himself struggling to do – and by play's end, successfully doing.

Either way, it seems clear that Hamlet's struggles with the linked spectres of melancholic self-delusion and the devil, his feverish attempts to discern and then comprehend and respond to the serpentine operations of God's providence and grace, spoke directly to a nexus of contemporary concern that was, at this very point, through pulpit and performance, and through the circulation of rumour, manuscript and print, entering the forefront of public attention.

As Weimann and de Grazia have observed, there are aspects of the Vice hanging around Hamlet's stage persona; and up through the theatre of Shakespeare's time, it was the fate of the Vice figure to be dragged off to hell by the devil. The play might thus be thought to be associating the most traditional of theatrical effects with the most up-to-the-minute, even *avant-garde*, religious imagery and concern.[28]

Despite the fact that very many of the activities and texts outlined above were associated with puritan divines or the godly laity, these sorts of concern were scarcely distinctive of – or peculiar to – Protestants, let alone puritans. On the contrary, if anything, certain sorts of Catholic were regarded as the experts in the religious subjectivity, doctor-of-the-soul stakes. The Jesuits, in particular, were renowned for their skills as spiritual counsellors and casuists, not to mention exorcists. One of the more remarkable religious bestsellers of the age was the edition of the Jesuit Robert Parsons' *Christian Directory* put out for Protestant use by the puritan minister Edmund Bunny. With only minor corrections and elisions, the book was launched onto the market as a source of spiritual counsel fit for the most pious Protestants.[29] The Jesuit John Gerard's famous memoir of his time on the mission in England is full of accounts of emotion-drenched and tear-stained conversions, most from church popery or a merely formal profession of true religion, but sometimes also from heresy itself: conversions effected, during precisely this period, through his application to his chosen targets of the *Spiritual Exercises*. Conversion, and its attendant emotions of melancholy and despair, was, therefore, a phenomenon of precisely this moment.

We have here, then, a nexus of immediately contemporary concerns, of emergent genres, practices and narrative tropes, all organized around questions of conversion, the control of spiritual experience; of melancholy, seen or experienced both as a condition and as an excuse; of despair, demonic possession, the threat of religious doubt, so great as to approach apostasy or atheism; of an all-encompassing sense of sin; and of spiritual impotence – all of which are central features of Hamlet's spiritual condition and travails.

Thus, when I use the term conversion narrative below, I use it in two senses. First, I will be referring to the incipient narrative structure of the ideal conversion, with its progression from the hammer of the law to the salve of the gospel; from despair to faith, and thence to repentance and amendment of life and a burgeoning sense of assurance. Secondly, and far more loosely, I will use the term to refer to the nexus of affective states and spiritual experiences outlined above, and to the terms and narrative strategies being developed and disseminated not only in the pulpit and press, but also in circulating anecdote and manuscript, to name and control those experiences.

Defined thus, I think we can add the conversion narrative, the soteriologically charged case of conscience, to the three other genres – the revenge tragedy, the history play and the murder pamphlet – against which I am arguing that *Hamlet* can profitably be read. Indeed, I am arguing that the play can be seen appropriating themes and narrative devices central to all four genres, not only in order to frame its own thematic and narrative structures, but also to elicit from its audience a series of associations, patterned reactions and expectations. Expecting a revenge tragedy, the audience was confronted with materials and themes, with snatches of narrative or action, taken from these other genres. Much of the energy of the play is, then, derived from the question of how all these divergent, seemingly incompatible, materials could, in fact, be satisfactorily combined; and, in particular, how the various narrative expectations, the conventional endings appropriate to each genre, could be brought together and reconciled at the end of the play.

6

⤝⤜⤠⤟

The (providential) purposes of playing

'The purpose of playing' anatomized

The play adverts directly to its own generic mixedness, its hybridity – and it does so twice: first through Polonius' famous commendation of the players; and second through Hamlet's disquisition on 'the purpose of playing'. Polonius famously describes the players as 'the best actors in the world, either for tragedy, comedy, history, pastoral, pastoral-comical, historical-pastoral, tragical-historical, tragical-comical-historical-pastoral, scene individable, or poem unlimited' [F, II, ii, 394–398; Q2, II, ii, 333–336]. There could scarcely be a clearer statement about the generic oddness of the play that the audience is watching, or a more obvious reference to the differences between it and the earlier version of *Hamlet* that had presumably primed their expectations of this one.

The point is driven home by the extended speech describing Pyrrhus' revenge upon Priam – given, at Hamlet's request, by the first player – which is a parody of a quite different sort of play. First of all, the language of this speech reproduces and parodies that of a certain sort of Senecan tragedy, and is thus quite unlike anything else to be found in the play.[1] Jonathan Bate notes the echoes of what he terms the 'Virgilian style' of Marlowe and Nashe's play *Dido and Aeneas*, and speculates that Shakespeare may even have been 'teasing his dead rival over the excessive length and poetic elaboration of his speeches'. Certainly, that style was now 'distinctly old fashioned', and here Shakespeare

> deliberately brackets out the epic voice by giving it to the player, contrasting it with the more subtle style that switches between stretches of every day prose and subtle blank verse that moves with the rhythm of thought and the beat of conversational speech.[2]

110

Secondly, while the speech might, at first sight, be thought to parallel and prefigure the action of *Hamlet* itself, it in fact evokes an entirely different sort of 'delay' and revenge. In the actor's speech, Pyrrhus personifies bloody revenge exacted at the height of passion. The only delay is the moment in which

> his sword
> Which was declining on the milky head
> Of reverend Priam seemed i' th' air to stick.
> So as a painted tyrant Pyrrhus stood
> Like a neutral to his will and matter,
> Did nothing.

But then

> a roused revenge sets him new a-work
> And never did the Cyclops' hammers fall
> On Mars's armour, forged for proof eterne
> With less remorse than Pyrrhus' bleeding sword
> now falls on Priam.

Fast forwarding to Hecuba's lament over the fate of her husband, the speech ends with Pyrrhus making 'malicious sport / In mincing with his sword her husband's limbs' [Q2, II, ii, 415–420, 426–430, 451–452]. This is a sight described in the sort of heightened language that one might find in a Senecan revenge tragedy, a play by Marlowe, or indeed in *Titus Andronicus*. But it bears no relation to what is actually happening in *Hamlet*. For what we are watching there is most definitely not the momentary delay in a bloody revenge that was always going to reach its consummation in a fit of annihilating violence delivered by a revenger lost in a *furor* of passion. Hamlet's delay is very different from this; indeed, as we have seen, it represents not so much a delay at all, but rather an extended diversion through an altogether different sort of activity, from which the revenger emerges a changed man, and his revenge an altogether different sort of action from that being attributed here to Pyrrhus.[3]

Moreover, as Richard Halpern observes, 'apart from a few moments of fatal sword play, *Hamlet* avoids violence, much less the grotesque blood-letting of plays like [Seneca's] *Thyestes* and *Titus Andronicus*',[4] the latter of which, with its cannibalism, child murder and gruesome violence, had directly recalled both the tragedies of Seneca himself, and earlier English revenge tragedies written on that model, most notably, of course, Kyd's *Spanish Tragedy*.

Indeed, as a number of scholars have pointed out, in addition to the scene in which Tamora is induced to eat her own sons baked in a pie – which recalls a similarly disgusting banquet in Seneca's *Thyestes* – in *Titus Andronicus* there are two, more or less direct, Latin quotations recycled from Seneca's play *Hippolytus*. In act I, Demetrius exits with the lament that '*Per Styga, per manes vehor*' ('I am dragged through Stygian regions, through hell') [II, I, 236]; and in act IV, Titus exclaims '*Magni Dominator poli / Tam lentus audis scelera, tam lentus vides*' ('O ruler of the great heaven, how can you be slow to hear crimes and so to see them?') [IV, I, 81–82]. The quotations are not exact and, according to Colin Burrow, the second combines '*Hippolytus* 671–2, with a passage of Seneca's *epistolae morales*'.[5]

All this sets up Shakespeare's as a play which starts out by aligning itself with Senecan models and prototypes. But the point here was surely not, as Richard Halpern suggests, simply 'to out Seneca, Seneca'. Clearly there was some of that going on. But if Halpern is right and 'the essential logic' of Senecan revenge tragedy is contained in Atreus' lines: '*scelera non ulcisceris / nisi vincis*' ('You do not avenge crimes unless you surpass them'),[6] then, with its intense concern with what Crosbie has called 'proportionality' (and at least a form of 'moderation' and justice), Shakespeare's *Titus* does not fit that bill at all. *Hamlet* thus repeats and extends a process begun in *Titus* itself – one that involves the citation and invocation of Senecan precedents and models, while at the same time seeking not merely to emulate them, but also to transform and critique them.

And, of course, by the time *Hamlet* saw the light of day in 1599/1600, *Titus Andronicus* itself had come to figure prominently among the plays whose tone and structure had generated a range of audience expectations which Shakespeare's new version of *Hamlet* was designed almost simultaneously to elicit and frustrate, and perhaps finally to transcend, even as it sought, by play's end, in some sense, to satisfy them.

Throughout the play, in a series of soliloquies, Hamlet has been taunting himself with his failure to be or become a properly Senecan revenger, in what proves to be an entirely fruitless attempt to force himself to act in the way assigned him in the sort of revenge tragedy that this version of *Hamlet* is not. As Colin Burrow puts it, 'a simple Senecan style of bloody revenge in *Hamlet* is at once a temptation and a kind of delusion. "If only I could be more like Medea or Atreus" is part of Hamlet's ambition' – and, we might add, of his Satanic temptation. In short, Hamlet admires and feels himself to be trapped in an outmoded sort of play, one entirely different from the play which bears his own name.

As though to drive that point home, the scene with the actors is followed by the famous soliloquy in which Hamlet tries to use the passion evinced by the actor over Priam's slaughter to force himself to exact a similarly summary revenge upon Claudius as that inflicted on Priam by Pyrrhus. As Colin Burrow points out, that speech echoes one given to Atreus in Seneca's play *Thyestes*. According to Burrow, 'the allusion to Atreus would to many of Shakespeare's audience have been absolutely unmissable', since 'many of the "wiser sort", whom Gabriel Harvey said *Hamlet* pleased, would have underlined Atreus' speech at school, and probably a few of them had it by heart'. All of which could only have served to underline that this was a very different sort of revenge play, and Hamlet was a very different (and, as we shall see, Christian) sort of revenger from those depicted both in Seneca's plays and in other earlier English revenge tragedies based thereon (up to and including Shakespeare's own *Titus Andronicus*). As Burrow observes, there was something 'insinuatingly audacious' about the ways in which Shakespeare was here appropriating, mimicking and even parodying Senecan models in a play whose appeal, and certainly whose grip on its first audiences, surely turned on its being a very different sort of play from Seneca's, with a revenging hero whose 'heroic' status stems not merely from his failure, but ultimately from his refusal, to play the role ascribed to him in the traditional 'Senecan-style' revenge tragedy.[7]

In precisely the same spirit, Hamlet's instructions to the actors on how he wants *his* play acted are framed against a satiric account of how not to do it, which almost certainly doubles as a denunciation of a style of acting with which the audience would have been familiar, and in which many of them may well have seen the earlier *Hamlet* (or plays very like it) bellowed out, to considerable popular applause. Against this negative image, Hamlet proceeds to outline what he wants [Q2, III, ii, 17–24; F, III, ii, 17–24]. The audience, then, has been put on notice that it is not going to get the sort of play that the old *Hamlet* – and the style of acting in which it would almost certainly have been presented – might have led them to expect. Rather than a fly-blown repetition of *The Spanish Tragedy*, the first version of *Hamlet* or indeed *Titus Andronicus*, they are getting a new sort of play altogether – one being played in a very different style, and with a pressingly contemporary purpose. After all, as Hamlet famously tells Polonius, the players are 'the abstract and brief chronicles of the time' [Q2, II, ii, 462–463; F, II, ii, 520] – a time identified at the close of act I by Hamlet as being definitively 'out of joint'. If that did not get the audience's attention, alerting it (and us) to the play's 'purpose' in providing something like a pointed and direct commentary on 'the time', then surely nothing would.

Burrow tends to see all this in essentially literary terms:

Learned Hamlet is haunted not just by the ghost under the stage but by a whole range of classical actions and modes of speech which threaten to absorb him, and which keep on coming out of his mouth, sounding like allusions to earlier works or parodies of them.

This is a brilliant insight, but, as I intend to argue below, the stakes raised by the play were not merely literary – consequent upon a knowing satire directed at earlier modes of play writing, acting or feeling; they were also ideological and existential, drawing directly from the immediate circumstances and issues within which the play was written and to which it was directed.[8]

As any number of commentators have observed, the seeming transparency of Hamlet's (humanist) theory of, and justification for, theatrical representation – 'Suit the action to the word, the word to the action, with this special observance, – that you o'erstep not the modesty of nature' [Q2, III, ii, 17–19; F, III, ii, 17–19] – is at complete variance with the complexity of the play's actual treatment, indeed performance, of performance and playing. After all, Hamlet enters the action decrying the falsity of 'playing'. The outward signs of his grief – 'my inky cloak', 'customary suits of solemn black', all the 'forms, moods, shapes of grief' – cannot, he tells his mother, 'denote me truly' precisely because 'they are actions that a man might play' [Q2, I, ii, 76–84; F, I, ii, 74–84]. Hamlet's grief is genuine, he famously claims, because he has 'that within which passes show'. But the ease of that distinction between outward show – that which 'a man might play' – and inner truth or reality, is then systematically broken down. From his meeting with the ghost onwards, Hamlet is caught in a world of playing, where the need to tell the real from the merely performed is crucial both to his and the other characters' purposes and fate. His life, and indeed his soul, depend on his capacity to tell whether his uncle and the ghost are what they seem; and, indeed, whether he himself is sane or mad, suffering from a reality-distorting melancholy or from a reality-heightening religious despair, or from some (either saving or damning) combination of the two. As we have seen, the extraordinarily dangerous knowledge which the ghost imparts to him puts him at odds with the entire social world – a world which immediately becomes a series of performances or pretences: Claudius playing the role of a legitimate and virtuous ruler; Gertrude that of a loving mother and virtuous queen; Rosencrantz and Guildenstern that of Hamlet's friends and well-wishers.

All of which rendered not merely useless, but positively dangerous, the humanist theory of social identity and ethical action in which Hamlet had almost certainly been reared and of which Polonius is such a verbose exponent in the play. To quote Rhodri Lewis, the aim here was 'to regulate self and civic existence in a manner that was "comly" (that is agreeable and respectable) in virtue of conforming to the natural condition of human social life.' The key virtues were *decorum* and *honestas*, and they, along with the appropriate self-knowledge that enabled their practice, were to be acquired by recognizing

> the likeness of oneself as reflected by others; directly from interpersonal observation; indirectly, by studying examples from the historical record. Virtues were to be explored and imitated, while vices were no less instructive in revealing the kinds of behavior that were to be avoided.

According to Lewis, this Ciceronian ideal represented an adaptation of 'the Aristotelian idea' that 'one's friends enable one to discern the image of oneself in a sort of morally exemplary mirror'.[9]

Self-evidently, the situation in which the ghost has put Hamlet renders all this received humanist wisdom not merely useless, but dangerous; and if, up to this point, as the play implies, Hamlet has indeed viewed himself in such terms, the consequent overturning of his received assumptions and habitual mental and social practices might go a long way towards explaining the state of discombobulation that he inhabits during the central sections of the play. It certainly renders it more than explicable why he fails throughout to observe the canons of bog-standard (Ciceronian) humanist ethical theory, as explicated by Lewis. After all, to have done so in the political and social world into which he has been thrust by the ghost's revelations would have been a form of political (and therefore, of personal) suicide.

If he is to survive, Hamlet must now navigate his way through – and penetrate to the truth or falsehood beneath – all of the (now by definition) false and threatening performances with which his social world confronts him. And he does so at first by himself playing a role, by putting on an 'antic disposition' – in effect, by feigning madness. Except that, as we have seen, in allowing him to act out an inner mental and emotional torment, that madness is itself more than an act. Indeed, just as Timothy Bright had warned it might, his melancholy in itself becomes a temptation, something through which Hamlet himself must see – or at least get to the bottom of. For, if his melancholy is more than an act, if it is a genuine malady, then his conversations with the ghost are likely to have been a mere chimera, an illusion, very likely induced not merely by his own affliction, but also by the interventions of Satan. If, however, he is not 'mad', then the ghost does exist, and he may need to take rather radical action, both spiritual and political. Starting out by positing a clear divide between that 'within which passes show' and outward forms, moods and shapes – all of which 'a man might play' [Q2, ii, 84–85; F, I, ii, 82–83] both in his relations with the outer, social and political world, the world of the court, but also in relation to his own inner life and consciousness – Hamlet ends up caught in a world of performance and appearance.

In this, once again, he unites the world of the conversion narrative with that of the history play and the revenge tragedy. For contemporaries had increasingly come to see the court as a place of delusory outward appearances, of performance and charade; a place where people played roles, performed emotions, and staged commitments and qualities that they did not necessarily possess or feel. The court, on this account, was an intensely competitive cockpit of rivalry and envy, characterized by illusion and playing. Many historians have seen the consequent shifts in perception as in part prompting, and in part being caused by, a shift away from an old-fashioned Ciceronian humanism to a more modish Tacitean one, better suited to existence, indeed survival, within the world of the court and both national and international politics. Traditionally located in the 1590s, the origins of that shift can, in fact, be traced back to the late 1560s and early 1570s.

There is, therefore, nothing particularly novel – certainly not anywhere near as novel as Rhodri Lewis clearly takes it to be – in observing that the values of a traditionally Ciceronian civic humanism were not merely looking somewhat dog-eared by the century's end, but were widely regarded as entirely unable to handle the political (and confessional) realities of the age. *Hamlet* might usefully be thought of as staging the existential, moral, spiritual and political consequences of that shift – consequences played out in a political emergency, a state of exception, that was not a mere reflection, but rather an intense evocation, achieved through the staging of essentially historical materials, of pressing contemporary events, concerns and anxieties.

For this, of course, is precisely the sort of environment into which the ghost's story of murder, regicide and usurpation plunges Hamlet. But again, the conversion narrative, and the methods of soul-doctoring and self-examination attendant upon it, pictured the individual consciousness as precisely the same sort of treacherous territory, a place where the soul, in desperate search of assurance, remained subject to all sorts of self-delusions and (sometimes demonically induced) illusions. As Bright informed his readers, it was crucial for the individual in distress to be able to tell real melancholy from a genuine spiritual crisis; and, as many a doctor of the soul would tell you, it was equally crucial for the Christian in search of a true (rather than a false) faith to be able to tell real assurance apart from mere security and presumption.

The stakes in this respect had been raised by William Perkins' assertion that the temporary faith experienced by the reprobate could replicate all but perfectly the true faith experienced by the elect. Such claims were made, Michael Winship has argued, in the face of the frustratingly complacent capacity of many an ordinary Christian to parrot the central claims of orthodox Protestant faith and to reproduce many of the outward forms of orthodox Protestant practice or profession. Perkins' insight very considerably raised the stakes and was intended to force the wannabe true believer into a personalized exercise in the discernment of spirits, designed to produce an upward spiral of ever greater spiritual and ethical exertion and self-examination.[10]

It was similarly essential to be able to see through the illusions of the devil. As we have seen, the Christian's entirely appropriate conviction of his or her own sinful impotence before the justice of God was, or certainly could be, entirely beneficial – the first step on the road to a true faith and a proper assurance of salvation. The devil, however, often tried to persuade tormented Christians otherwise in order to turn their sense of sin into a soul-destroying desperation, a conviction that their sins were too great ever to be forgiven, thus inducing them to believe that they were reprobates, doomed to hell – a conviction that might well lead them to the ultimate sin of self-murder. In both the realms of court and of conscience, therefore, it was crucial to be able to tell appearance from reality, to see through the performances and pretences both of others and of one's own self, if one's life, and indeed eternal soul, were to be preserved. In the play, Hamlet's political circumstances – his relation to the world of the court – become the occasion for just such a spiritual crisis, with his political dilemma compounding his spiritual predicament in a situation where both his life and his soul depend on his capacity to tell the difference between performance and reality. That the way out of this labyrinth is provided by theatrical performance is, of course, in itself remarkable. For in the performance of *The Murder of Gonzago*, the acting-out of a fiction becomes the way to reach within to that which really does pass show – i.e. to that which cannot be disguised by any amount of outward performance: the operation of the conscience, in this case of the conscience of a murderer, Claudius. In the context of contemporary debates about the moral depravity of the theatre and its corrupting effects on its audience, this is to make a remarkable claim for the potency, the moral power, of theatrical representation. On this account, the theatre – the most self-consciously and overtly fictive set of illusions and performances imaginable – becomes the way in which Hamlet starts to see through the false surfaces, the mere appearances, the playing and performance, that characterize both the outer world of the court, and indeed the inner world of his own consciousness.

In the scene of the play within the play, we are shown *The Murder of Gonzago* being performed before an audience. But there is, of course, another play being performed here – the play that, when asked by Claudius for the title of the performance they are watching, Hamlet terms 'the mousetrap'. In that play, Claudius is not a part of the audience, but is rather a part (indeed the central part) of the action, with Hamlet and Horatio providing the audience for the king's reaction to the play he is watching. Hamlet's jokey commentary upon the action, directed to the queen, to Ophelia and indeed to Claudius himself, adverts to this aspect of the scene, inserting a very considerable element of threat into the action – a threat which reaches its height, of course, in his identification of the king-killer in the play, Lucianus, not as the king's brother, but as his nephew. For with that gloss, the play becomes a reference not merely to Claudius' crime in killing a king, but also to Claudius' threatened or likely fate at the hands of his revenging nephew, Hamlet. It is, of course, because all that is involved here is a mere play that Hamlet is able to raise the stakes and the pressure to this height, even as he denies that there is any 'offence' in the argument of the play: 'No offence i'th'world . . . Your majesty and we that have free souls – it touches us not. Let the galled jade wince, our withers are unwrung' [Q2, III, ii, 228–236; F, III, ii, 227–234].

All of which adverts to the relationship between a mere play – 'a knavish piece of work' [Q2, III, ii, 234; F, III, ii, 232] written 'in jest' – 'they do but jest. Poison in jest' [Q2, III, ii, 228; F, III, ii, 226] – and directly current events. On one view of the matter, there can indeed be no offence in the world in a play, precisely because plays are indeed 'knavish' pieces of work, mere 'jests'. But as such, they remain far from 'the purpose of playing', as Hamlet has outlined it earlier to the players. However, for those in the audience who can (or do) recognize either themselves or 'the time' in the action being played out on stage, their consciences, as well as their attention, may very well be engaged, and the wider moral purposes of playing, as Hamlet has outlined them, might thereby be served. For, after all, there is a third play being staged here. Not only is *The Murder of Gonzago* being watched by the court, and not only are Hamlet and Horatio watching Claudius and the others watch that play in another play called *The Mousetrap*, but the audience ('we') are also watching Hamlet watch Claudius in *The Mousetrap* watching *The Murder of Gonzago*, in yet another play called *Hamlet*.

What is being staged here is the play's own relation to its 'time' – that is to say, to the immediate political moment or conjuncture in which it was written and performed, and to which it was very precisely addressed: a 'time' which, on certain contemporary views, was easily as out of joint as anything being acted out on stage. But at the very moment when the play is adverting most directly to that relation, it is simultaneously staging or articulating its own defence against giving 'offence' in that regard. Just as with Claudius and *The Murder of Gonzago*, the relevant connections are not being made on stage at all, but elsewhere, in the consciousness and the consciences of the audience. To those 'that have free souls', the play will remain just that, a play; in the estimation of many contemporaries – even of many avid theatre-going contemporaries – it will

1. Henry III of France, murdered in August 1589 by a Dominican friar; one of the most notorious assassinations in an age of political assassination. Whether this was a legitimate, God-prompted act of resistance, or a crime and a sin depended entirely on your religious and political convictions.

2. The Tudor succession represented. A protestant (Edward) followed by a catholic (Mary) and then another protestant (Elizabeth), attended by a reversionary Catholic interest centred on Mary Queen of Scots, framed the politics of Elizabeth's reign as an 'exclusion crisis', and fuelled the anxieties at the centre of many of Shakespeare's plays.

3. The face of a tyrant? This is an image of the ageing Elizabeth, whose last years, with death imminent and the succession unsettled, set up the end of her reign as a succession crisis waiting to happen.

4. The death of Elizabeth did not precipitate the political meltdown that, during previous decades, many Catholics had eagerly anticipated, all protestants had desperately tried to stave off, and many on all sides, both at home and abroad, had hoped to exploit for their own interests.

5. The accession of James I, while greeted with relief, also unleashed mutually incompatible hopes and fears amongst different sorts of Catholics and puritans, and various ambitious or desperate seekers after office. The result was an accession crisis that arguably did not end until the gunpowder plot in 1605.

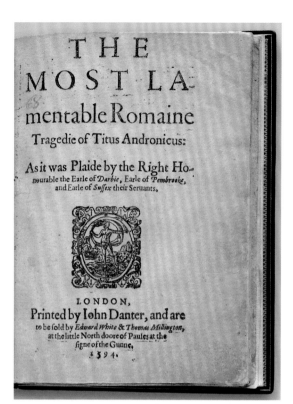

6. The title page of the first edition of *Titus Andronicus*.

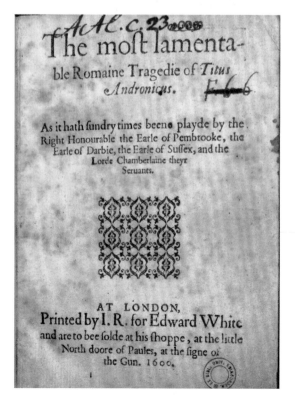

7. The title page of the 1600 edition of *Titus Andronicus*.

8. *Romanitas* realised. A drawing by Thomas Peacham of an early performance of *Titus Andronicus*, complete with Roman costumes.

9. A Catholic representation of the execution of Edmund Campion. Following his brief but in-your-face mission to England with Robert Parsons, Campion became perhaps the most famous Catholic victim of the Elizabethan state; for Catholics, the poster child for that state's status as a persecuting tyranny.

A. Edmundus Campianus focietatis Iefu fub patibulo concionatur, ftatimq̃ cum Alexandro Brianto Rhemenfis, et Rodulpho Sheruiño huius Collegij alumno fufpenditur.
B. Illis adhuc tepentibus cor et uifcera extrahuntur, et in ignem proijciuntur.
C. Eorundem membra feruenti aqua elixantur, tum a durbis turres et portas appenduntur, regnante Elizabetha Anno M.D.LXXXI die prima Decẽbris Horum conftanti morte aliquot hominum millia ad Romanam Ecclefiam conuerfa funt.

33

Persecutiones aduersus Catholicos à Proteſtanti-
bus Caluiniſtis excitæ in Anglia.

Sanguinis effuſi firmamus pignore Chriſti
Maiorumǭ fidem, magni fundamina Petri,
Et tantum Latijs apicem veneramur in oris.
At gregis electi custodia non cadet vnquam
In caput, ô Regina, tuum, regéſque profanos,
Et minus in vilem fidei myſteria ſexum.

L 2   MARIA

10. 'The lopping time hath come': an image encompassing the various forms of physical torment inflicted on Catholics executed for treason under Elizabeth I; dismemberments, eviscerations and beheadings at least the equal of anything portrayed in *Titus Andronicus*.

Persecutiones aduersus Catholicos à Prote-
ſtantibus Caluiniſtis excitæ in Anglia.

Poſt varias clades miſerorum, & cædis aceruos
Inſontum, comes exornat ſpectacula mater
Supplicio, & regum ſoror & fidiſſima coniux.
Illa Caledonijs diademate claruit oris,
Sed micat in cælo fulgentior, inde corona
Sanguinis, infandǭ manet vindicta ſecuris.

11. The execution of Mary Queen of Scots: justice or regicide? For certain Catholics Mary was a martyr who died for her faith rather than any sort of traitor. If, for them, her death cried out for revenge, for many Protestants Mary was as guilty as sin, her death long overdue.

12. The Jesuit Robert Southwell, poet, pamphleteer and devotional writer, executed in 1595. His *Humble Supplication*, a reply to the notorious anti-Catholic proclamation of 1591, circulated widely in manuscript. For Southwell, just like other Catholics, and indeed the Andronici, Mary Stuart was an innocent victim of persecuting tyranny.

THE
Tragicall Historie of
HAMLET

Prince of Denmarke

By William Shake-speare.

As it hath beene diuerse times acted by his Highnesse ser-
uants in the Cittie of London : as also in the two V-
niuersities of Cambridge and Oxford, and else-where

At London printed for N.L. and Iohn Trundell.
1603.

13. The title page of the first quarto of Shakespeare's *Hamlet*.

14. 'This thing that I have seen / May be a devil', or what Romanticism did with (or to) Shakespeare.

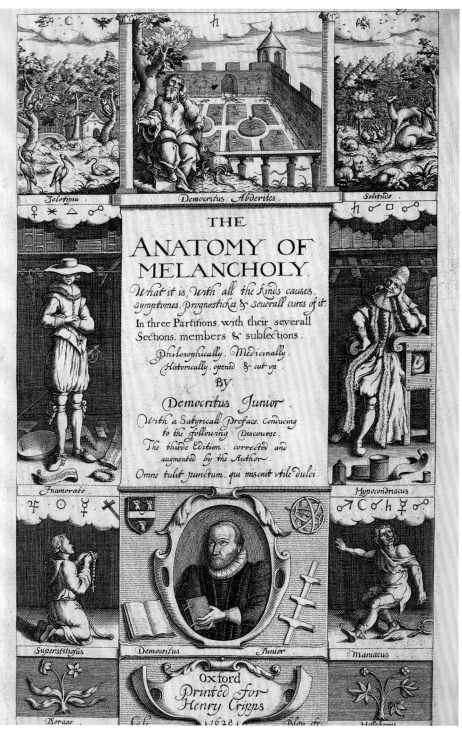

15. The title page to Robert Burton's *Anatomy of Melancholy,* a virtual *summa* on the topic of melancholy. Written in the 1620s, Burton's book arguably summed up the obsession with the melancholy of the previous decades.

16. Portrait of a young man standing under a tree; probably Sir Robert Sidney, possibly Sir Thomas Knollys.

17. 'The glass of fashion and the mould of form'? Two miniatures; one of a fashionable young man about the court, the other of another modishly melancholic man in black. If this is what Hamlet looked like before and immediately after he met the ghost, might we conceive the young man in flames on the cover of this book as a picture of him in the midst of his distraction?

18. Not Hamlet standing over Claudius at prayer, but rather a sixteenth-century representation of the murder of Thomas Becket; an event rendered newly controversial by the breach with Rome. For Catholics, Becket remained a saint and a martyr, but for Protestants he was a sinister agent of papal power.

remain 'a knavish piece of work', a mere 'jest'; and viewed thus, there can indeed be 'no offence i'th'world' to be taken from it. But to others – in this respect far more like Hamlet and Claudius than the other unknowing members of the audience for *The Murder of Gonzago* – who do indeed recognize the parallels between what is being acted in front of them and the events through which they are living, that will not be the case. For them, at least, the moral purpose of playing will have been fulfilled.

Here is vindication both of Hamlet's description of the players to Polonius as 'the abstract and brief chronicles of the time' and of his later claim made to Ophelia that 'the players cannot keep council – they'll tell all' [Q2, II, ii, 462–463; III, ii, 134–135; F, II, ii, 520; III, ii,137–138].

7

◄--►-

The politics of conscience

Talking like an atheist and acting like a Christian

Let us turn now to the action of the play, to see in detail how these various concerns, points of reference and sets of narrative expectation are brought together and resolved. Let us start with the depiction of Hamlet's spiritual crisis. The play, of course, shows us Hamlet obsessing over the prospect of suicide: puzzling over the extent, and the spiritual and epistemological consequences, of his own madness or melancholy, and wondering whether he is, in fact, the subject of demonically induced delusions and lies, or the providentially selected instrument, not merely of his father's revenge, but of divine justice. Even before he meets the ghost, he is to be found wishing for death and lamenting 'that the Everlasting had not fixed his canon ''gainst self slaughter' [Q2, I, ii, 131–132; F, I, ii, 129–130]. He returns again to the subject in the 'to be or not to be' soliloquy, where he locates fears about the nature of the afterlife and the fate to be suffered there by self-slaughterers as the reason why men in fact choose 'to grunt and sweat under a weary life', to suffer 'the whips and scorns of time', 'the slings and arrows of outrageous fortune', and all 'the heart ache and the thousand natural shocks that flesh is heir to', rather than their 'quietus make with a bare bodkin' [Q2, III, i, 55–87; F, III, i, 56–88].

As we have seen, from the outset the ghost has been associated with the devil. Horatio warns Hamlet of the danger that it might 'deprive your sovereignty of reason and draw you into madness', leading him to a place 'that puts toys of desperation / Without more motive, into every brain' and inducing him to commit suicide there by flinging himself off the cliff [Q2, I, iv, 73–76; F, I, iv, 52–53]. Despite the enthusiasm of his initial reaction to the ghost and its message, by the next act Hamlet has himself adopted something of Horatio's perspective, making the same associations between ghost as potential devil, the perceptual weakness consequent upon his own melancholy and the threat of damnation:

The spirit that I have seen
May be a devil, and the devil hath power
T'assume a pleasing shape. Yea, and perhaps,
Out of my weakness and my melancholy,
As he is very potent with such spirits,
Abuses me to damn me. [Q2, II, ii, 533–538; F, II, ii, 593–598]

But what appears to Hamlet in that scene to be a necessary and salutary circumspection in the face of his own melancholy, and the wiles and stratagems of Satan, has, by the next, become something more like a cause for self-laceration and contempt. As he discourses, in general rather than personal terms, on the subject of self-murder, in the midst of the 'to be or not to be' soliloquy, Hamlet reaches the famous conclusion 'thus conscience does make cowards of us all'. What 'conscience' seems to mean here is attention to the likely consequences of this-worldly action in the next life. He then shifts the subject of his meditation away from the issue of suicide [Q2, III, i, 83–87; F, III, I, 84–88]. Here, as throughout this speech, Hamlet's concerns are couched in general rather than in particular terms. It is a disquisition, as it were, on the human condition in general rather than on Hamlet's own circumstances in particular; but it seems reasonable to assume that the 'enterprise of great pith and moment' most likely to be on the audience's (and indeed on Hamlet's) mind at this juncture is his as yet unformulated purpose to kill Claudius. And the 'regard' that deprives such plans of 'the name of action' seems, again, to be concern for the consequences in the next life of actions undertaken in this.

This, of course, recalls Hamlet's earlier disquisition on suicide in act I. The general purport of these remarks seems to be that it is 'noble' to be able to choose whether to live or die, whether to break divine law ('the canon of the everlasting') and risk thereby whatever the consequences of such actions might be in the next life. By the same token, it is 'cowardice' to obsess about such things in a way that prevents the pursuit of 'enterprises of great pith and moment' – enterprises, that is, like Hamlet's purpose to revenge his father. Stayed here by what we might want to call 'religious' considerations about the afterlife – what Hamlet calls considerations of 'conscience' and assimilates to cowardice – elsewhere, in other soliloquies, Hamlet tries to force himself to act by invoking other, entirely secular or this-worldly, codes of conduct centred on notions of honour and nobility.

Immediately following the first scene with the actors, he uses an argument from 'passion' and honour. Having observed real tears in the eyes of an actor, as he spoke his lines about the death of Hecuba, Hamlet compares the emotion betrayed by a mere player with his own lack of passion in the cause of his father. The initial argument here is about 'passion', the affective force that should move Hamlet to his revenge, but hitherto has not. His failure so to do then prompts him to ask 'Am I a coward?' – an enquiry that prompts direct recourse to the binary opposition between honour and shame, around which the cult of the man of honour was organized:

> Who calls me villain? Breaks my pate across?
> Plucks off my beard, and blows it in my face,
> Tweaks me by the nose, gives me the lie i' th' throat
> As deep as to the lungs? Who does me this?
> Ha! Why, I should take it. For it cannot be
> But I am pigeon-livered, and lack gall
> To make oppression bitter, or ere this
> I should have fatted all the region kites
> With this slave's offal, bloody – a bawdy villain!
> [F, II, ii, 566–575; Q2, II, ii, 507–515]

It is as though his failure to kill Claudius has revealed him to be such a coward that, given the lie by any Tom, Dick or Harry, Hamlet would simply turn the other cheek, instead of responding with the instant reproof and revenge that should mark him out as a gentleman. There could scarcely be a clearer demonstration of the extent to which revenge is a matter of honour rather than of justice. Hamlet's honour, his masculinity, his social identity as his father's son, what Polonius describes to Laertes as his 'self', is at stake here; and in failing to act, Hamlet has called all those things into question. This thought, combined with the mere mention of Claudius and his crime, does indeed move Hamlet to the sort of passionate outburst that he had so admired in the actor – 'Remorseless, treacherous, lecherous, kindless villain! / O vengeance!/Whoa!'; but that, too, now becomes a source of shame, as, instead of taking real revenge like a gentleman, he finds himself reduced to cursing and emoting like a woman, a whore – or indeed an actor [Q2, II, ii, 495–522; F, II, ii, 553–582].

The speech then ends with his determination, before he does act, 'to have grounds more relative' [Q2, II, ii, 537–539; F, II, ii, 598–599] than the mere say-so of the ghost, who, after all, may well be a devil, sent to tempt him to hell. Here his attempts to use secular arguments – arguments based upon his emotional attachment to his father's memory, his natural rage and disgust at his uncle's conduct, his own standing, indeed his very identity as a man of honour – have again failed to move him to action, and they have done so (again) because of his supervening concern for the condition and salvation of his soul.

After Claudius' response to the play within a play has, both for Hamlet and for us, finally established his guilt beyond any reasonable doubt, Hamlet tries again to seek to use arguments about honour and reputation to force himself to act. Here the catalyst is provided by the example of Fortinbras, who is about to risk his own life and those of thousands of troops, in order to conquer from the Poles 'a little patch of ground / That hath in it no profit but the name' [Q2, IV, iv, 17–18]. The contrast between the martial virtue and valour, the true sense of honour, being displayed by Fortinbras and his own inaction provokes another outburst [Q2, IV, iv, 42–65].

Again, then, we have recourse to 'honour' and another version of the brittle honour and shame culture against which, in that earlier soliloquy, Hamlet had measured his own performance in avenging his father's death. When a man's honour is engaged, the merest trifle becomes a just occasion for the most extreme and dangerous action. On this account, 'true greatness' – or as Hamlet puts it, 'rightly to be great' [Q2, IV, iv, 52] – is a function not of the inherent worth or virtue of the cause defended, or of the end pursued, but rather of the 'ambition' and 'spirit', the valour and mettle, being displayed and asserted in pursuit of it. These, of course, are (again) entirely secular, this-worldly, un-Christian values. 'Honour', 'spirit' and 'ambition' are being defined in purely social and secular terms, and pursued with no thought to their spiritual consequences, either here or in the next world. Such attitudes were entirely typical of the culture of at least certain elements within the Elizabethan elite. They were sentiments that a whole range of courtiers and noblemen, caught up in an intensely competitive quest for 'honour' in the service of the queen at court and on the field of battle, would have found entirely recognizable.

These are also values which, when he is articulating them, Hamlet appears entirely to endorse. Except, of course, that in his conduct he does the very opposite. Indeed, his enthusiastic espousal in these speeches of the standards of personal and martial 'spirit' and 'ambition', demanded by the pursuit of true 'nobility', 'greatness' and 'honour', is predicated upon his own signal failure, under the terms that he is here setting himself, to observe that code and those ideals. Indeed, in the speeches quoted above, he is endorsing those values with such enthusiasm, so that, by exposing his own complete failure to live up to their demands, he can force himself to act. The resultant shame at his own 'cowardice' is what is supposed then to coerce him into action. For, in this mode, Hamlet can only attribute his failure to live up to the demands of 'honour' or 'passion' to 'cowardice'. Insofar as 'conscience' is involved in any of these explanations of his own conduct, it is discussed under that rubric.

Thus, in the last of these soliloquies, Hamlet goes some way to explaining how this moral calculus works, blaming his failure to act on 'some craven scruple / Of thinking too precisely on th'event – / A thought which quarter'd hath but one part wisdom / And ever three parts coward' [Q2, IV, iv, 39–42]. That word again. But what, we might ask, is the precise nature of the event or outcome about which he has been thinking too much? At no point in the play does Hamlet ever betray any tendency to calculate political advantage, to frame or control his conduct according to the likely secular or political effects of his actions. Indeed, as we shall see below, he does rather the opposite. The event or outcome about which he *has* been thinking too much is, in fact, a spiritual matter, concerned with the next world, rather than with this one. It is, in short, a question of 'conscience'; a question about the condition and salvation not only of his own soul, but also (as we see below) of the souls of others.

Using the term 'atheist' in its Elizabethan sense – as someone who is acting, or trying to act, as though God, the soul and the afterlife do not exist[1] – what we are being shown in Hamlet's soliloquies is someone talking like an atheist (or thinking back to Shakespeare's preceding play, *Julius Caesar*, like a pagan Roman), but acting like a Christian. On the one hand, we have an attempt, and a presumed obligation, to act according to entirely this-worldly codes of conduct – codes centred on the assertion and defence of honour, with honour being defined in terms of Hamlet's duty to revenge the murder of his father and the sexual dishonour of his mother. On the other hand, we have a persistent concern with the dictates of conscience, with the spiritual consequences in the afterlife of his actions in the here and now. It is the tension, indeed the contradiction, between these two imperatives that produces Hamlet's dilemma – what, in certain moods, he sees as his cowardly refusal, despite, as he says, having 'the cause, and will, and strength and means / To do't' [Q2, IV, iv, 44–45], to actually revenge himself on Claudius.

The extent of the disjunction between what he says in his soliloquies – between the self he tries to construct there – and his actions is made apparent throughout the central acts of the play. At one level, what Hamlet says about himself is perfectly accurate. At no point are we shown Hamlet making any practical political plans or calculations about how, when or where to kill Claudius, still less about how to handle the inevitable fall-out from such an act in ways that might preserve either his own life or indeed the stability of the state and the course of the succession once Claudius has been removed. Trapped by the ghost's revelation within an inherently political situation – a situation that, as we have seen, spoke directly to a number of contemporary political dilemmas and concerns – Hamlet's response is utterly apolitical, entirely devoid of the practical measures, the popular insurrections and court conspiracies that, in act V, characterize Laertes' response to his precisely parallel situation.[2]

Much of the action in the central acts of the play is not in that sense action at all, but rather the staging of Hamlet's internal affective states – his internal debate, as he struggles to convince himself both that he *should* act and then *to* act. Here the suspense established by the play in and for its first audiences revolves not so much around the issue of revenge – when and how will revenge happen? – but rather around the spiritual state and fate of Hamlet. In the soliloquies that we have just been discussing, a contemporary audience would have been all too aware that they were watching someone on the very edge of spiritual despair and atheism, and hence of damnation. The issue, then, was not only (or even mainly) whether Hamlet would take revenge – after all, as Empson observes, this was a revenge tragedy, and everybody in the theatre, and every reader of the play, knew that revenge would come. Rather the real question was: *could* he take revenge without either talking or acting like an atheist, and thus dooming himself to eternal perdition?[3]

Putting religion before politics: Hamlet as minister, not scourge

Thus, when Hamlet does act, his actions are directed not so much at immediate political objectives, but rather at the resolution of questions of conscience and belief through what are essentially appeals to, or tests of, conscience – not, in this (first) instance, his own, but rather the consciences of the notional felons, Claudius and Gertrude. The only time we see him planning or plotting is when he frames his scheme to use the actors and the play within the play to ascertain the truth of the matter. In so doing, Hamlet is operating within the structuring assumptions of many a murder pamphlet, and the play is appropriating a central element from those stories to drive along its own plot. For central to the contemporary assumption that murder will out was the idea that, confronted with the scene of the crime, the sight of the victim's body or an account of the crime, the conscience of the perpetrator would, in spite of itself (as it were), cry out, either prompting a full confession or at least some sort of tell-tale sign that would betray the murderer's identity and guilt. Like any common-or-garden reader of the murder pamphlets of the day, Hamlet has heard tell of such instances, and purposes to make just such a supposedly fool-proof appeal to Claudius' conscience through a carefully staged theatrical performance:

> I have heard
> That guilty creatures sitting at a play
> Have by the very cunning of the scene
> Been struck so to the soul that presently
> They have proclaimed their malefactions.
> For murder, though it have no tongue, will speak

With most miraculous organ. I'll have the players
Play something like the murder of my father
Before mine uncle. I'll observe his looks,
I'll tent him to the quick. If 'a do blench,
I know my course . . .
. . . the play's the thing
Wherein I'll catch the conscience of the King. [Q2, II, ii, 523–540; F, II, ii, 583–600]

Here, a question of conscience – rather than making cowards of us all by acting not as the grounds for, but rather as a disincentive to action – becomes the enabling condition for daring and decisive action. Seeking assurance, wanting to test the truth claims and ontological status of the ghost, and, in Rosendale's phrase, desperate to find a way to determine 'whether revenge is a devilish theological trap (in which action is a violation of the divine sovereignty and a sin) or the very will of God',[4] Hamlet turns to the testimony not of his own, but of Claudius' conscience, sure that, under the burden of its own sins and the supervening influence of divine providence, it will speak 'with most miraculous organ', if not to everyone, then at least to those in the know.[5]

And that is a group whose membership has now doubled. For it now becomes clear that at some point between the end of act I and the end of act III, Hamlet has let Horatio into his awful secret. He has done so not, it seems, to enlist Horatio as an accomplice in some conspiracy to murder Claudius, but rather because, under the influence of his own melancholy and the ghost's suggestions, he does not trust his own eyes and instincts, and wants an independent observer of Claudius' reactions to the play. Thus, he exhorts Horatio to look on 'his face, / And after we will both our judgements join / In censure of his seeming' [Q2, III, ii, 71–83; F, III, 73–83; F, I, ii, 73–84].

For all Hamlet's high spirits, when the play does in fact lead to the outcome he predicts – 'I'll take the Ghost's word for a thousand pound', 'Come, some music! Come, the recorders. / For if the King like not the comedy, / Why then belike he likes it not, perdie' [Q2, III, ii, 278–279; 283–286; F, III, ii, 277–278] – his newly established certainty still does not lead him to kill Claudius. It prompts action all right – swift, decisive, daring action – but it is action still contained within the spiritual realm, the domain of conscience, and aimed at achieving ends or outcomes in the next life rather than in this one. In short, Hamlet is continuing to act in what we might, in short-hand terms, refer to as the realm of 'religion' rather than 'politics'. For it is immediately after the scene with the play, that, for the first and only time, we are shown Hamlet offered, as it were, a clear shot at Claudius. Rushing off to see his mother, he finds the king alone in prayer. It is the perfect opportunity to finish him off, and Hamlet refuses to take it.

The incident is a crucial one for the case being made here, and we will return to it on several occasions. The play within the play's import has not, of course, been lost on the king. Aimed at his conscience – which, as we have already been shown at the start of act III, is 'smarting' under the 'heavy burden' of 'my deed' [Q2, III, i, 49–53; F, III, i, 49–54] – the play has hit home. However, it has not (yet) prompted thoughts about Claudius' own immediate political security, or about the threat posed to that security by Hamlet, or indeed about how best to meet that threat. On the contrary, it has led the king to an attempt at repentance. In the soliloquy that follows [Q2, III, iii, 36–72; F, III, iii, 36–72], we are shown the soul of someone sunk in sin, offered – through the operation of conscience – a chance to acknowledge its own corruption and to repent. Claudius' is a soul on the very tipping point between salvation and damnation. The king sees his predicament with extreme clarity, offering a finely tuned structural account of why, even though he would repent, he cannot.

It is an account straight out of the mental, theological and moral world of the murder pamphlets. There it was crucial, if the convicted felon were to be brought to true repentance, that he or she should be convinced that they were facing certain death and thus their maker. The condemned should be deprived of all hope of pardon or reprieve, since only then, having given up all hope of security or felicity in this world, would they be able to concentrate solely on their fate in the next. With their minds thus focused, staring death and God in the face, only then would they acknowledge the full force of their sin, the desperate nature of their current spiritual condition, and thence be led to a full and sincere repentance. And only then could they be induced or enabled to throw themselves on the mercy of God in Christ as the sole means available to save them – not, of course, from death, but from eternal torment.

Viewed from this perspective, Claudius' goose is cooked and he knows it. Still in possession of his throne and queen, Claudius is subject to no higher human authority; in this world, he has been always already pardoned by the relevant human power – himself. He has, therefore, always the fatal hope of escape, of immunity and impunity, before him. However much he may wish to repent, to win God's pardon, there is always the residual (albeit utterly false) hope that 'all may be well' in this world, and then perhaps even in the next. Thus, having comprehensively failed to escape his (spiritually, but not politically) desperate circumstances through spiritual means (repentance and prayer), Claudius then seeks to do so politically, through further (criminal) action.

It is in this remorseful state that Hamlet comes upon the king, alone praying. Again, Hamlet's thoughts dwell not on this life, but on the next [Q2, III, iii, 73–95; F,

III, iii, 73–95]. Taking his uncle's repentance as genuine, Hamlet refuses to kill Claudius now, for fear that, if he does so, he will send his soul to heaven, rather than to hell, where it belongs. While killing a man at prayer, perhaps even on the point of genuine repentance for his sins, might well send the party thus murdered to heaven, it was surely certain also to send his killer to hell. If so, that is a fate that Hamlet avoids here, but only for the worst of all motives – his desire definitively to consign his uncle to eternal torment.[6] This sets up perhaps the central paradox in the play: the fact that Hamlet is saved from the most obviously damning aspects of his role as a revenger only by his most deeply sinful – indeed, as de Grazia has observed, his most positively diabolic – impulse. If, therefore, Hamlet is saved, here is the play showing us God's providence using Hamlet's deepest sins and his most shockingly malign impulses to effect that salvation.[7]

The spiritual calculus upon which Hamlet has made this decision – one again based on a concern for outcomes in the next world rather than in this – proves, moreover, to be entirely erroneous. At the point that Hamlet leaves the stage, Claudius reports back on the utter failure of his attempts to repent: 'My words fly up, my thoughts remain below. / Words without thoughts never to heaven go' [Q2, III, iii, 97–98; F, III, iii, 97–98]. We have here the very picture of a reprobate soul. There is, moreover, a very significant change in the way that condition is characterized between Q1 and Q2. In Q1, that speech ends 'my words fly up, my sins remain below. / No King on earth is safe if God his foe' [Q1, 10, 33–34], which emphasizes the objective distance between God and the reprobate, centring God's enmity towards them on the basis of their sin. The version in Q2, however, emphasizes his incapacity truly to repent as the distinguishing characteristic, perhaps even the cause, of Claudius' reprobate state.[8]

Having been offered the chance to repent by the providential revelation of his crime, a revelation orchestrated by Hamlet for purposes altogether distinct from the salvation of Claudius' soul, Claudius – precisely because he is the king – still finds himself unable to do so. Still mired in the pleasures and structures of the world ('my crown, mine own ambition') and of the flesh ('my queen') [Q2, III, iii, 55; F, III, iii, 55], Claudius' thoughts return to where hitherto they have always been: the fabrication of schemes and plots to conceal his crime and to make good his hold on power. While Claudius remains caught in the world of politics, the contrivance of increasingly deceitful and violent schemes to maintain his own power and achieve his entirely this-worldly ends, Hamlet remains caught in the realm of religion and of conscience.[9] He leaves Claudius praying in order to rush off on an altogether different mission – a desperate attempt, before events reach the crisis point, to save his mother's soul.

The interview between mother and son towards which Hamlet is going, is, of course, a trap set by Claudius and Polonius, in the hope of finding out both what Hamlet knows and what he intends to do about it. Polonius has no idea what the real stakes are here – only Claudius and Hamlet know that; and the old councillor, intelligencer and now spy pays a very heavy price for his ignorance.

But if the interview with his mother is a trap set to make Hamlet betray himself, it is one into which he rushes without a second thought. Typically, his intentions are not in the least political. There is no excessive 'thinking . . . precisely on th'event' at work here. As he sets off, Hamlet's intentions towards his mother are neither very precise nor very charitable [Q2, III, ii, 378–389; F, III, ii, 378–389]. A part of Hamlet wants to take revenge on Gertrude almost as much as he wants to send Claudius to hell. His mental note to himself to avoid the fate of the mother-slaying Nero – not to mention his admission that, in resisting that impulse, his tongue and soul will be acting as hypocrites – reveals the intensity of his desire to do his mother violence and the extent of his continued addiction to the luridly violent language of 'revenge'. But when he comes into her closet, not only is his violence merely verbal, but it is designed to fulfil what can only be described as an evangelical purpose – one pursued, as we shall see, at very considerable personal and political risk. Hamlet has come to see his mother (and indeed has passed up the chance to kill Claudius) perhaps to save her life, but more particularly to save her soul.

As he has promised himself, Hamlet does indeed speak daggers; but, as he explains, he is being 'cruel only to be kind' [Q2, III, iv, 176; F, III, iv, 162]. He comes, he tells her,

> to wring your heart. For so I shall
> If it be made of penetrable stuff,
> If damned custom have not brazed it so
> That it be proof and bulwark against sense. [Q2, III, iv, 33–36; F, III, iv, 35–38]

Hamlet, then, has come to bring his mother to a saving sense of, and repentance for, her sins. However, throughout their subsequent exchange, it is never clear either to Gertrude or to us (and perhaps not even to Hamlet himself) in what precisely those sins consist. In marked contrast to Claudius, her entirely oblivious response to the *Murder of Gonzago* might, in itself, have been enough to clear her of any involvement in the murder. But Hamlet, his attention concentrated obsessively on Claudius, is still not convinced. Consequently, he tests her again, by introducing, at the very start of their exchange, the suggestion that she was implicated in the murder of his father and her husband. The sheer incredulity of her response – 'as kill a king?' [Q2, III, iv, 27; F, III, iv, 29] is all she can blurt out at Hamlet's introduction of the topic – clears her of that charge once and for all. But Hamlet proceeds on the assumption that she is indeed guilty of the foulest sins. He accuses her of

> such an act
> That blurs the grace and blush of modesty,
> Calls virtue hypocrite, takes off the rose
> From the fair forehead of an innocent love
> And sets a blister there, makes marriage vows
> As false as dicers' oaths – O, such a deed
> As from the body of contraction plucks
> The very soul, and sweet religion makes
> A rhapsody of words. Heaven's face doth glow
> O'er this solidity and compound mass
> With tristful visage, as against the doom,
> Is thought-sick at the act. [Q2, III, iv, 38–49; F, III, iv, 40–51]

This, in effect, is to accuse her of adultery, and then of incest. But, as Hamlet's subsequent rant reveals, what it amounts to is the accusation that Gertrude has slept with her new husband, Claudius, and by so doing in effect preferred him over his dead predecessor. The issue here is not crime, so much as sin – the sin of concupiscence, to be exact. As John Gillies concludes, 'Gertrude's "black and grained spots" speak the language of sin not crime'.[10]

On one level, it is, of course, entirely fitting that Gertrude's sins should remain nebulous and nameless. For her real fault – what makes her both repugnant and potentially fatal to Hamlet – is precisely the closeness of her relationship with Claudius. She is quite literally sleeping with the enemy. Her marriage to Claudius has made her one with his person and his rule. The fact that, ignorant of Claudius' murder of old Hamlet, she cannot know the nature or extent of her fault or crime thus conceived, is scarcely the point, since the extent of her ignorance does not, and cannot, alter the facts of the matter. Claudius is a murderer and a usurper and, as his wife and queen, she is his accomplice and ally: 'Man and wife is one flesh' [Q2, IV, iii, 49–50; F, III, vi, 47–48]. More even than the other (silent) protagonist in this scene, Polonius, Gertrude is utterly implicated in Claudius' purposes – purposes which, if realized, are (despite her best intentions) likely to prove fatal to Hamlet.

Whatever exactly Gertrude has done, and however much or little she knows, the sheer force of Hamlet's onslaught begins to wring from her the first signs of a confession of, and repentance for, sin:

O Hamlet, speak no more.

Thou turn'st my very eyes into my very soul,

And there I see such black and grained spots

As will not leave their tinct . . .

O speak to me no more.

These words like daggers enter in my ears.

No more, sweet Hamlet! . . .

O Hamlet, thou hast cleft my heart in twain. [Q2, III, iv, 87–94; Q2, III, iv, 154; F, III, iv, 79–87; F, III, iv, 147]

At this point, however, the ghost enters; apparent to Hamlet, it remains invisible to his mother. This prompts her to see his appalled reaction to what (to her) is vacant space ('vacancy') as confirmation that he is indeed as mad as general opinion would have him. Seeing the effect that his words have begun to work on Gertrude being dispelled by her renewed conviction of his 'madness', Hamlet urgently insists that

. . . it is not madness

That I have uttered. Bring me to the test

And I the matter will reword, which madness

Would gambol from. Mother, for love of grace,

Lay not that flattering unction to your soul

That not your trespass but my madness speaks.

It will but skim and film the ulcerous place,

Whiles rank corruption mining all within

Infects unseen. Confess yourself to heaven,

Repent what's past, avoid what is to come,

And do not spread the compost o'er the weeds

To make them ranker. Forgive me this my virtue,

For in the fatness of these pursy times

Virtue itself of Vice must pardon beg,

Yea, curb and woo leave to do him good. [Q2, III, iv, 139–153; F, III, iv, 132–146]

This speech, with all its talk of 'grace', its injunctions to 'repent', its imagery of unacknowledged sin secretly undermining and corrupting the soul of the sinner, is full of the discourse of evangelical religion. It is as though in this scene we, and Hamlet, have stepped out of a revenge tragedy and into a murder pamphlet – indeed, into a pietistic tract or sermon by William Perkins or even Robert Parsons. Hamlet is no longer playing the role of revenger; instead of acting, as it were, as a secular magistrate, whose function it was to administer justice by punishing the body of the offender, he is now playing the role of a minister of the word, determined to bring the felon to a soul-shattering, and therefore saving, repentance.

The point emerges the more starkly when we remember that this speech is largely omitted from Q1, in which, while Hamlet does exhort his mother to repent – threatening to 'make your eyes look down into your heart, / And see how horrid there and black it shows' [Q1, 11, 21–22] – a much shortened scene is dominated by his attempts to enlist her in his plan to exact revenge on Claudius: 'assist me in revenge / And in his death your infamy shall die' [Q1, 11, 95–96].

In Q2, however, throughout the course of his interview with his mother, he is seeking to play the role of the minister of God's word, struggling, through the force of his denunciation of her sins and the evocation of the power of repentance, to bring a sinner on the point of damnation to a full recognition of, and a saving repentance for, her sins.[11] This, of course, is precisely the same role that, despite his best intentions to the contrary, through his staging of the *Murder of Gonzago*, Hamlet has already played in relation to Claudius, who, through Hamlet's activities as a theatrical impresario, has been given (and has refused) one last chance to repent.

Of course, Hamlet's evangelical efforts, both involuntary and voluntary, fail. Claudius can be read as a figure for a reprobate soul, who, having heard the full force of the minister's evangelical call and the voice of conscience, has been rendered fully aware of the nature and extent of his own sins (and indeed of his crying need for repentance), but who remains unable to repent, choosing instead to plunge headlong towards spiritual destruction.

Gertrude, however, is a far more ambiguous figure. For John Gillies, she is the quintessential 'hypocrite', 'hypocrisy' being the default position of the averagely sinful (and therefore doomed) sinner in thrall to original sin. 'Hypocrisy,' he says, ventriloquizing Calvin, 'comes from knowing oneself before men, rather than before God . . . it is the ethical signature of original sin, a perpetual veto of the natural law originally inscribed in the human heart.' And in Gertrude, he opines, 'Shakespeare has taken the radically normalized category of hypocrisy of the Reformers seriously as a premise of characterization.'[12]

We might perhaps see her as a type of secure professor, a group defined by Timothy Bright as those who, unless 'some vengeance of God lay hold upon them, or some horrible fact gnaw their wounded conscience', pass 'their time in blind security, careless of God, and empty of all sense and hope of a better life or fear of that eternal destruction' and thus 'pass their days and finish their course as the calf passeth to the shambles not knowing their end to be slaughter by the butcher's knife'.[13] In its account of the structural nature of her complicity in evil, and of her total ignorance of the existence of that evil, and thus of the extent of her own implication in it, the play provides a wonderfully economical encapsulation of the effects of original sin, and of the condition of the unregenerate sinner. Always already guilty of sins the nature and extent of which they can neither readily comprehend nor fully acknowledge, such people never come to a properly soul-shaking repentance, but instead sleep-walk their way through life to a deserved damnation. Thus, if not exactly sure of her own virtue, then fatally imprecise in her apprehension of her own sin, and if not oblivious to all Hamlet's warnings, then certainly ultimately impervious to them, Gertrude goes to her end without ever having quite realized the nature and extent of her own sins, and thus without ever having appreciated either the spiritual danger she is in or her urgent need to repent.

The delicacy of the balance being struck here emerges clearly if the treatment of Gertrede[14] in Q1 is compared to that of Gertrude in Q2 and the Folio. In this, the most substantive divergence between the plots of the different versions of the play, in Q1 Gertrede is converted by Hamlet into a true believer in Claudius' guilt, and is thus recruited as a co-conspirator in his (still) entirely inchoate plans to bring her husband to book. In this version, Hamlet's mere mention of his uncle's fell deed in killing the king simply and immediately convinces his mother of Claudius' guilt. She even makes this admission after the appearance of the ghost has confirmed her in her opinion of 'the weakness of thy brain', conceding one line later that 'as I have a soul, I swear by heaven / I never knew of this most horrid murder' [Q1, 11, 83–86]. Having, as it were, conceded the main point to Hamlet, she then pleads with him that, because 'this is only fantasy', he should 'forget these idle fits' about his father's ghost [Q1, 11, 87–88]. However, fantasy or not, she then pledges herself to Hamlet's revenging cause: 'Hamlet, I vow by that Majesty / That knows our thoughts and looks into our hearts / I will conceal, consent and do my best – / What stratagem so'er thou shalt devise' [Q1, 11, 97–100]. Later in Q1, it is to the queen that Horatio imparts the story of Hamlet's ship-board discovery of Claudius' plot against him, whereupon she repeats her commitment to further her son's purposes:

Then I perceive there's treason in his looks
That seemed to sugar o'er his villainy.
But I will soothe and please him for a time
(For murderous minds are always jealous.) [Q1, 14, 10–13]

That this move to (re)locate Gertrude explicitly on the side of the angels is omitted in the longer versions of the play suggests a choice to render her a more darkly ambiguous, fully tragic figure. Certainly, it confirms a version of Gertrude as someone committed, almost despite herself, to a sinful course of action, the precise nature of which is never made clear to the audience – or perhaps even to herself. In these versions, the first glimmerings of conversion worked by Hamlet are all but completely dispelled by the (malign?) intervention of the ghost, which confirms her in her conviction that 'alas, he's mad' [Q2, III, iv, 106] 'mad as the sea and wind when both contend / Which is the mightier' [Q2, IV, i, 7–8; F, III, iv, 197–198]. In Q1, those words represent an attempt to protect Hamlet from Claudius' suspicions; but in Q2 and F they express the queen's sincere belief. Thus, in these versions Gertrude is left with not, as in Q1, a conviction of Claudius' identity as a murderer and a usurper, but rather an altogether more inchoate sense of guilt and sin. In both Q2 and the Folio (but not in Q1) Gertrude is found, subsequent to the scene in her closet with Hamlet, expressing a doom-laden sense of foreboding about her own (and others') nameless sins: 'To my sick soul, as sin's true nature is, / Each toy seems prologue to some great amiss, / So full of artless jealousy is guilt / It spills itself in fearing to be spilt' [Q2, IV, v, 17–20; F, IV, i, 17–20].

However salvifically ineffectual his impact on Claudius, and even (in Q2 and F, if not in Q1) on Gertrude, the fact remains that (in all three versions of the play) in his relations with both Hamlet is fulfilling one of the crucial functions of the minister of the gospel, one purpose of whose efforts in preaching the word was to vindicate the justice of God in damning the reprobate, by making sure that they have been informed, in general, of the terms and conditions upon which salvation is available to fallen humanity, and in particular, of their own spiritual condition, of the nature and extent of their sins and of their desperate need for true repentance and a saving faith. If, after all that, they still fail to respond to this proffered grace, their damnation is on their own head rather than on that of God (or indeed of the minister).[15]

In his rush to convince and convert his mother, Hamlet tells her a number of things that, up until this point, he has gone to considerable lengths to conceal. First, he informs her of his conviction that Claudius is a 'murderer and a villain / . . . A cutpurse of the empire and the rule / That from a shelf the precious diadem stole / And put it in his pocket' [Q2, III, iv, 94–99; F, III, iv, 88–90]. For good measure, he then tells her that he is not really mad at all, but only feigning for political purposes – 'I essentially am not in madness, / But mad in craft' [Q2, III, iv, 185–186; F, III, iv, 171–172]. He does this despite her conviction to the contrary, confirmed by his frantic behaviour towards the ghost, and in so doing deprives himself of the last shred of cover for his actions – a cover carefully built up over the period since his first interview with the ghost. It might be thought – and the understandably terrified Gertrude certainly takes this line – that Hamlet is doing all this because he is, if not mad, then certainly completely out of control. But there is also surely a method to his madness. As he himself explains at some length to his mother, he is acutely aware that his last desperate efforts to save her soul, and perhaps even her life, depend upon her coming to see the true character and malign purposes of the man she has married. But she will only do that if she takes everything that Hamlet has said to heart; and, of course, she will only do that if she believes her son is sane. Having spilt the beans in the furtherance of his evangelical intentions towards his mother, only as an afterthought does Hamlet attempt to repair the damage done to his political situation by asking her to keep his secret safe by not telling the king.

Gertrude does keep Hamlet's secret, but only because she is by now utterly convinced of his madness; but by this point, of course, Claudius needs no intelligence from his wife to tell him how immediate is the danger presented to him by his nephew, mad or sane. Act III ends with Hamlet about to be sent off to his doom by a triumphant Claudius, who has been enabled – more by the political ineptitude of his adversary than by any particular skill or cunning of his own – to preserve his hold on power and destroy the only remaining threat to it, without anyone being the wiser (except, of course, the soon-to-be-dead Hamlet). At this point, it appears that the result of Hamlet's obsession with questions of conscience – his propensity to think too much about, if not spiritual, then at least other-worldly ends or outcomes, is utter political and personal failure. Certainly, judged by the criteria of the revenge tragedy – criteria by which Hamlet has thus far tended to judge himself – Hamlet is a bust.

Delaying to do what, exactly?

Famously, this has led generations of critics to see Hamlet's delay, his fatal failure at this point to act, as the central problem – the organizing conundrum of the play. On the current reading, this is a mistake.[16] If we cease to view *Hamlet* only (or even) in its central sections primarily as a revenge tragedy, but instead conceive of it as staging the central concerns and themes – and following the central narrative structures – of the conversion narrative and the murder pamphlet, things start to look rather different. Put differently, if we return to the formulation coined above, we need to spend as much time and attention analysing the ways in which Hamlet acts (or tries to act) like a Christian, as we do poring over the famous soliloquies in which he talks to himself (for much of the time) like an atheist.

For, what looks like delay when viewed from the perspective of the revenge tragedy is, when viewed from that of the conversion narrative, in fact a form of action – a process of self-examination, whereby Hamlet, refusing to dismiss his condition as the product of mere melancholy, struggles to come to grips with his own spiritual state and with the real questions of conscience and belief that confront him. This first phase of his crisis is relatively rapidly brought to a close, when he manages to reduce or distil his dilemma into a single case of conscience framed around what seems to be a straightforward either/or question: either the ghost was his father's shade or it was a devil; either it was telling the truth or it was lying. Once his perplexities have formed themselves into that single question, Hamlet does the opposite of prevaricate: recruiting both Horatio and the players as his co-conspirators, he rapidly conceives and executes a daring and entirely effective plan.

Thereafter, rendered certain of Claudius' guilt by the brilliant success of his own stratagem, Hamlet rushes off again to act. His actions, however, remain directed towards ends and outcomes in the next world rather than in this. Newly enlightened and empowered by the certain evidence of Claudius' guilt secured through *The Mousetrap*, Hamlet is, in fact, in the grip of a false certainty, an exaggerated sense of his own righteousness, insight and power. It is in this state that he starts trying to usurp God's role as the ultimate judge of salvation and damnation. As Timothy Rosendale puts it, at this point Hamlet is 'acting as though he, not God, is setting the terms of revenge'. The result is 'the worst of all possible worlds; soteriological determinism and rigorous justice without the slightest hint of the grace that for Paul and Augustine and Calvin made it all worthwhile'.[17] Consequently, Hamlet falls into desperate sin, with predictably (both politically and spiritually) disastrous results.

The political situation is easily dealt with. For while, on one (as it were) spiritual or epistemological level, the ruse with the play has achieved its stated purpose perfectly, on another (practical, political) level, it has been a compete bust. While Hamlet may now, for the first time, know for certain that Claudius is guilty, Claudius (also for the first time) knows for certain that Hamlet is on to him. That, of course, puts Hamlet in extreme danger. He has now lost any element of surprise. Any advantage, any cover for his own plots or plans that his pose of madness might have earned him, has been entirely dissipated. The political initiative is now with Claudius, who is, after all, not only the king, but surrounded by people – up to and including Hamlet's own mother – who know nothing of what Hamlet knows, and anyway think that he is mad.

But even in this newly desperate and dangerous situation, given the opportunity to get Claudius before the king can get him, Hamlet refuses to act. That decision not only flies in the face of the demands of honour and passion, but rather more pressingly it utterly ignores the dictates of political prudence. Here is another example of the triumph of conscience, taking 'conscience' (as it has been defined in the 'to be or not to be' soliloquy) as a supervening concern with one's fate (and the fate of others) in the afterlife. For, taken in the context in which it happens – his frantic rush to confront Gertrude with her sins – Hamlet's decision not to kill Claudius can be seen as a function not only of his desire to consign the king to hell, but also of his equally fervent desire to send his mother (and perhaps even himself) to the other place. It is surely that imperative that leads him, in the very next scene, to compound the situation by telling Gertrude that he believes Claudius to be a regicide and a usurper. He also manages, albeit accidentally, to kill the 'innocent' Polonius, an act which serves greatly to increase Claudius' room for manoeuvre, while reducing his own almost to nothing.

And yet, as de Grazia has pointed out, so great is the grip of the problem of Hamlet's 'delay', and so complete the dominance of the agenda of 'the revenge tragedy', that generations of critics have failed to take Hamlet's stated purpose in refusing to kill Claudius in the prayer scene seriously. Rather it has been interpreted as a mere excuse, an exercise in self-deception, designed to enable Hamlet to continue to procrastinate. As she observes, for many critics, 'Hamlet's excuse for sparing Claudius at prayer becomes one among many stalling tactics. Procrastination becomes his salient, indeed his defining, trait.'[18] Of course, if Hamlet is taken to be the protagonist in a certain sort of revenge play – and for a good part of the play, that is indeed how he at least tries to see himself – then he is delaying, and, for instance, Patrick Gray is quite right to observe that 'the question of delay is not extrinsic, as de Grazia suggests, a latter day creation of misguided critics, but instead prompted, indeed explicitly foregrounded, by the play itself' – that is, *insofar* as that play is being experienced as a revenge tragedy of a certain sub-Senecan sort, and nothing else.[19]

But, in fact, *Hamlet* is not that sort of play, and there are other narratives, and other roles, at work here, of which contemporaries would have been a good deal more aware than (mostly secular-minded) modern critics have been. And in terms of those other narratives and roles, Hamlet is not delaying at all. Most importantly, delay is precisely not what Hamlet is shown doing in the action of the play. He might *talk* a lot about delay, because he is not acting as a revenger; but he is acting in other, dynamic and courageous, albeit often heedless and desperate, ways. There is, in short, astonishingly little delay going on in the play; indeed, through much of it Hamlet is hyperactive. And here de Grazia is quite right to point out how extraordinary it is that the strength of their obsession with Hamlet's delay should have prevented generations of critics from noticing what is happening, in front of their very eyes, both on the page and on the stage.[20]

Certainly, when the play is construed as a conversion narrative and a murder pamphlet, as well as a revenge tragedy, the prayer scene emerges not as an interruption or forestalling of what de Grazia terms the 'climactic action' of the play (i.e. revenge), but rather as an integral part of that action – indeed, perhaps as the axial point on which the whole of the play turns. The death of Polonius is, of course, the moment when the political and spiritual consequences of Hamlet's attempt, in effect, 'to play God' – to punish the sins and save or damn the souls of others – meet. For in rushing to punish the sins of others, Hamlet falls into dreadful sins of his own. First, we have the small matter of his attempt or desire to consign Claudius to hell; and second we have his slaughter of the 'innocent' Polonius. This latter act is an accident, of sorts. Tormented by murderous thoughts towards his mother, and about to have a potentially life- and indeed soul-threatening conversation with her, Hamlet finds himself being spied upon and takes desperate action. Asked by his mother 'what hast thou done', he answers at first truthfully enough 'I know not', only to follow that admission with the question 'Is it the king?' Later he tells the corpse 'I took thee for thy better'. But in fact, as the nature of these responses reveals, what Hamlet had thought he was doing at the moment of action was to kill an unknown figure caught spying on his conversation with his mother. The notion that it might be the king is an afterthought; indeed, a delusory hope that, in a moment of passion and of self-defence (much like the fit in which he later does indeed kill Claudius), he might actually have managed to do the deed that hours of self-examination, of casuistical exertion and self-laceration, have not yet enabled him to do.

We are confronting here the organizing paradoxes, the linked set of conundrums, that animate the central portions of the play; and they have little to do with delay, hesitation or failure to act. For, on the account given above, it is simply not true that Hamlet hesitates or refuses to act: he merely hesitates to kill Claudius and refuses to plan or use what we might term practical political means towards that end. But he certainly does not refuse to act in order to address the central cases of conscience with which his encounter with the ghost has confronted him. On the contrary, he does so with expedition, effectiveness and nerveless – indeed reckless – courage. Acting on the level of what he terms conscience, Hamlet is positively heroic. And that heroism is not merely (or even mainly) intellectual or emotional: he takes decisive and dangerous action to resolve what (erroneously, as it turns out) he takes to be the central question of conscience confronting him. It is just that the heroism of his actions planned, directed and executed at the level of conscience is entirely incompatible with – indeed runs completely counter to – the realization at the practical, political level of his fate or intentions as a revenger. Put differently, it is as though, in trying to play his part in a revenge tragedy, Hamlet has suddenly started to act according to the demands and expectations of a murder pamphlet and a conversion narrative. The result, of course, is a mess, with none of the central needs of any of these narratives having been fully or successfully met, and with Hamlet, by the end of act III, facing apparently certain death, and quite possibly damnation.

For by that stage, it is not only in terms of the narrative expectations and moral demands of the revenge tragedy that Hamlet is a bust. Viewed from the perspectives provided by our other three genres – the history play, the murder pamphlet and the conversion narrative – by the end of act III things look grim indeed. Hamlet's little burst of conscience-based action has left his soul in mortal danger and his person at the mercy of an apparently triumphant Claudius; sin has been neither publicly exposed nor punished; no one, not even Hamlet, has been converted to a true saving repentance; revenge has not been achieved; a regicide and usurper remains in unchallenged possession of the throne; and the agent through whom these various outcomes were to have been achieved is himself facing defeat, death and perhaps even damnation. As Hamlet sails off to what seems like certain death in England, Claudius remains on the Danish throne, still married to Gertrude, who, for all Hamlet's desperate attempts to tell her what he now knows to be the truth, still has no idea of the realities of her situation, of the nature of the man to whom she is married or of the regime over which, as queen, she is presiding.

In short, the play has used a number of different sets of expectations and concerns, culled from different sorts of narrative, in order to mess with the orderly presentation of any of the narrative structures that it is feeding off or appropriating. Frustrated and confused with the play's mixing and matching of these disparate materials, as they might well be, at the end of act III the audience is confronted by what appears to be an impasse – a situation from which it is seemingly impossible for any (still less all) of the conventional, morally appropriate or expected endings of the four genres with which we started to emerge. This, of course, is a set-up. We are only in act III; there are two more acts to go, and the central question, the hook upon which the audience's attention is to be caught and held, is, of course, how are such disparate materials and concerns finally to be reconciled and brought together to create a satisfying ending or conclusion?

Providence

The foundations of that satisfying end are, of course, laid in the final scenes of act III. The crucial exchange takes place between Hamlet and his mother over the corpse of Polonius:

For this same lord
I do repent, but heaven hath pleased it so
To punish me with this, and this with me,
That I must be their scourge and minister.
I will bestow him and will answer well
The death I gave him. [Q2, III, iv, 170–175; F, III, iv, 156–161]

In this speech, we see the beginning of Hamlet's acknowledgement of his real situation.

On the one hand, we have here Hamlet's first conscious articulation of the fact that there might be something more at stake in the killing of Claudius than 'revenge'. Rather than a private act, performed on his father's say-so and out of his own passion, designed to assert or defend his honour, what is at stake now is an issue of divine justice. For the first time, Hamlet sees himself as both the scourge and the minister of heaven. The distinction drawn here between the roles of scourge and minister delineates perfectly the division between the roles of the secular and the spiritual arms – of the magistrate and the minister – in bringing felons to book: that is to say, both to punishment and to at least the chance of a saving repentance. As we have seen, these are roles which, in his dealings with both Claudius and Gertrude, unwittingly and sometimes in spite of himself, Hamlet has already been discharging for some time. But now, in this speech, he is starting to come to a conscious realization of just what he has been trying (and failing) to do up to this point, and of what he must successfully accomplish in the future. In short, at this moment Hamlet can be seen consciously leaving the moral universe of the revenge tragedy and moving into that of the murder pamphlet.

On the other hand, the speech also represents the first time that Hamlet begins to recognize the full extent of his own, personal sin. As we have seen, he has had, almost from the outset, a developed sense of human depravity; but since the play within a play, that has only served to feed his own sense of spiritual superiority and self-righteousness, his entirely presumptuous, indeed blasphemous, belief that, now armed with a knowledge of the truth – that is to say of Claudius' guilt – he can act to determine the fates in this life and the next of a whole range of people. But now he, too, has killed a man, a deed for which he must 'repent' and indeed 'answer well'. He must do so before man, where, as the son of a prince and heir to the throne, he might be thought likely to get off rather lightly. But he also has to answer to God (a forum where his royal status will cut no more ice for him than it would for Claudius). In seeing his killing of Polonius – which was accidental, done on impulse, in some sense in self-defence and out of a mixture of intense emotions – as the work of 'providence', Hamlet might be thought to be trying to slough off his guilt by seeing himself (again) as merely the agent of forces greater than himself. That, however, seems not to be the case.

Certainly, the play has, throughout, presented Hamlet (and Hamlet has sometimes presented himself) as the subject, even the victim, of a set of contradictory obligations and impulses, of forces and demands not of his own choosing or making. Now, again for the first time, we see him interpreting that situation in terms of his relationship with God's supervening providence and purposes. He is here mixing and merging the organizing tropes and narrative dynamics of the murder pamphlet with those of the conversion narrative; and then, through the trope of providence, moving on to the history play. For it is precisely the providence of God that not only punishes sin and saves souls, but also restores kingdoms to legitimate government.

But even as Hamlet is starting to conceive of himself as the instrument (or, as he puts it, 'the scourge and minister') of heaven, he is also coming to the realization that this is a role from which, in his present circumstances, as a newly minted murderer, he can take no pleasure or relief. Far from freeing him from blame, his (if not unwitting, then, to this point, only partly conscious and deeply misguided) discharge of that role has now plunged him into a sin – the killing of Polonius – which, for all that it forms part of God's purposes (indeed, for all that it may help to vindicate both God's justice and mercy), may yet still condemn the doer of that deed to hell.

At this moment, we see Hamlet starting to grasp that the certainty, the sense of self-righteousness and spiritual insight, the frenetic, almost hysterical zeal, that have characterized his behaviour since the moment he realized that Claudius really was guilty, have all been an illusion. There may be a considerable irony in the fact that Hamlet's lament that in these 'pursy times' his own 'virtue' must 'pardon beg' of his mother's 'vice' [Q2, III, iv, 151–153; F, III, iv, 144–146] takes place in full view of the corpse of the man whom he has just killed. But it is an irony or contradiction that, by the scene's end, Hamlet is beginning to realize. He cannot, through his own moral exertions, however fervent, hope to avoid sin and merit salvation. Just like Claudius, he is a sinner; indeed he, too, is now a murderer. Unaided, he cannot save even himself, let alone others. Now he is in a position, at last, to realize that the case of conscience, the either/or choice, into which he had distilled the spiritual crisis set off by the ghost's injunction to revenge has itself been an illusion. It was just not true that either the ghost was lying and therefore a devil, or that it was telling the truth and was therefore benign. The ghost might well be a devil and still be telling him the truth, hoping, by so doing, to lure Hamlet into actions that would damn him to hell. Now, Hamlet realizes, it might well be that, just as with the death of Polonius, so with that of Claudius, 'heaven' might well be 'pleased' to 'punish me with this and this with me'. After all, in a fallen world, presided over by an omnipotent God, both the devil and even the direst of sinners could only obey God's will and serve his (ultimately beneficent) purposes.

What we are watching here is Hamlet coming to an emergent realization of the sheer difficulty of reconciling the demands of human and divine justice (and indeed mercy); of the extraordinary spiritual (as well as the obvious temporal) dangers attendant upon the discharge of his ascribed role as the revenger of his father's death and agent of divine justice; and of the labyrinthine complexity of the relations between human will and divine omnipotence, between the workings of God's providence and the all-too-human and sinful purposes even of those whom God has chosen to be the agents and ministers of his will.

In coming to this realization, Hamlet is discovering a whole range of things that the audience already knows. He may, for the first time, have consciously stepped out of the revenge tragedy in which, up to now, he has been acting (or rather trying and failing to act), to embrace his starring roles in the murder and conversion narratives that the play also contains; but the more attentive or astute members of the audience are likely to have been long aware that there is more at stake in the play that they are watching than revenge. Now, however, both Hamlet and the audience are on track to move towards the resolution of the impasse in which, by the end of act III, the play has placed them both.

What extricates Hamlet from the predicament into which his own folly, as much as the cunning and malignity of his enemy, Claudius, has plunged him, is, of course, a mixture of accident, coincidence, inexplicable impulse and unintended consequence. The extraordinary means which the play uses to get Hamlet off the ship to England and back to Denmark – the discovery of the sealed instructions, the fake commission, the pirate raid – taken together constitute precisely the sort of wildly improbable events and outcomes that were habitually described both in the pamphlet press and on the popular stage as the work of providence, and it is as such – in Q2 and the Folio, albeit not in Q1 – that Hamlet describes them to Horatio.[21]

Even the aspect of these events that owed most to his own planning and artifice – his spying upon Rosencrantz and Guildenstern and forging of a new commission – Hamlet attributes to the workings of a force greater than himself:

> In my heart there was a kind of fighting
> That would not let me sleep . . .
> . . . Rashly,

And praised be rashness for it, let us know,

Our indiscretion sometimes serves us well,

When our deep plots do fall: and that should learn us

There's a divinity that shapes our ends,

Rough-hew them how we will. [Q2, V, ii, 4–11; F, V, ii, 4–11]

Indeed, he sees the workings of divine providence even in the smallest detail of these events. He describes his plan to forge a new commission as a spontaneous, almost instinctive, reaction to the circumstances in which he found himself rather than as the result of any conscious thought or planning:

Being thus be-netted round with villainies,

Ere I could make a prologue to my brains,

They had begun the play. I sat me down,

Devised a new commission, wrote it fair. [Q2, V, ii, 29–32; F, V, ii, 29–32]

But what enabled him to pull off the coup of forging a new commission was the presence in his purse of 'my father's signet, / Which was the model of that Danish seal'. His comment on this happenstance is typical of his attitude to these events in general – 'even in that was heaven ordinant' [Q2, V, ii, 48–50; F, V, ii, 48–50].

Hamlet's hermeneutic instincts are likely to have paralleled exactly those of the audience. Here we see the structuring assumptions of the murder pamphlet and of at least some of the history plays (of, say, *Richard III*, if not the *Henry VI* and *Henry IV* plays) being confirmed both by the action of the play itself and by Hamlet's commentary upon that action. After the disruptions and doubts, the contradictions and tensions, of the first three acts, these passages are surely a signal that the determinations and interventions of providence are at last going to swing into proper alignment with the actions and purposes of the protagonist of the play and lead us to resolution – and that Hamlet has himself started to acknowledge as much.[22]

It is a commonplace that the Hamlet who returns from his voyage with Guildenstern and Rosencrantz and his run-in with the pirates – that is to say, the Hamlet of act V – is very different from the Hamlet of the first three acts. When he leaps back into the world of the court, he announces himself unequivocally as 'Hamlet the Dane'. In the first three acts, he is presented as a youth, someone barely out of his undergraduate studies at the university. Now the play goes out of its way to inform us that (magically) he is 30, on the edge of full maturity. In the scene with the gravedigger, he is able to contemplate with relative equanimity not merely the inevitability, but the grotesque physical details, of death and decay. After his return, his first public act is to own his love for Ophelia. Both these actions look back to earlier statements made, and emotions expressed, by the young Hamlet.

In a brutal speech dominated by a visceral disgust at the thought of sexual passion or desire, and horror at the physical presence of his beloved, Hamlet had denied ever having loved Ophelia. Now he can take pride in the public declaration of how much he had indeed loved her. In an earlier scene with Claudius, he had discoursed bitterly and threateningly upon the physical facts of death. Asked 'where's Polonius?' he replies

> At supper . . .
> Not where he eats, but where he is eaten: a certain
> convocation of politic worms are e'en at him. Your
> worm is your only emperor for diet: we fat all
> creatures else to fat us, and we fat ourselves for
> maggots: your fat king and your lean beggar is but
> variable service, two dishes, but to one table:
> that's the end . . .
> A man may fish with the worm that hath eat of a
> king, and eat of the fish that hath fed of that worm.

Asked, by an increasingly irritated Claudius, 'What dost thou mean by this?', Hamlet replies threateningly 'Nothing but to show you how a king may go a / Progress through the guts of a beggar' [Q2, IV, iii, 17–30; F, III, vi, 18–28]. As Prosser remarks here, 'Hamlet is not meditating on the meaning of his own death; he is sardonically dismissing the death of the man he has killed' and darkly threatening the man he wants to kill next.[23]

Now in the graveyard scene, Hamlet returns to the same subject and produces another disquisition on the inevitability of death and decay: 'To what base uses we may return, Horatio! Why may not imagination trace the noble dust of Alexander till 'a find it stopping a bung hole?' To Horatio's objection that "Twere to consider too curiously to consider so', Hamlet replies:

> No, faith, not a jot. But to follow him thither with
> modesty enough and likelihood to lead it: as
> thus: Alexander died, Alexander was buried,
> Alexander returneth to dust, the dust is earth, of
> earth we make loam, and why of that loam whereto he

was converted might they not stop a beer-barrel?

Imperious Caesar, dead and turned to clay,

Might stop a hole to keep the wind away.

O, that that earth which kept the world in awe

Should patch a wall t'expel the winter's flaw. [Q2, V, i, 192–205; F, V, i, 200–213]

The two passages rework almost exactly the same material and sentiments: a sense of the disgusting physical effects of death and decay, and of death as the great leveller, a figure and a fate before whom all distinctions of status or wealth mean nothing. But while the subject of the two speeches is almost identical, there is a crucial difference of tone and indeed, by the end of the second speech, of form, as the staccato back and forth of the prose used in the scene with Claudius is replaced by the controlled, positively artificial, rhyming verse with which Hamlet's exchange with Horatio ends.

In the former interaction, there is an almost hysterical levity and lack of control, as well as a sense of threat directed by Hamlet (who has, after all, just killed a man) against Claudius. Hamlet is in the thick of his antic disposition, and uses the subject of Polonius' corpse, in the words of Michael Bristol, to disrupt, indeed to invert, 'the basic distinctions of social life: between food and corrupt, decaying flesh, between human and animal, between king and beggar. Temporal authority and indeed all political structures of difference are turned inside out.'[24] Hamlet is here displaying 'the habit of insulting those to whom he should be deferential, including the Ghost of his father . . . the King, . . . his mother . . . [and] the old counselor' that, de Grazia observes, in his antic mode he had picked up 'from the professional clown', or Vice, a figure which, as she also observes, was replete with positively demonic overtones and associations.[25]

In the later scene with Horatio and the gravediggers, however, the tone is completely different. As Bridget Gellert has shown, the whole graveyard scene is suffused with the iconography of melancholia.[26] A man lost in the contemplation of a skull or death's head was, of course, a very common image or personification of 'melancholy'; and the actor playing Hamlet holding, indeed addressing, Yorick's skull would surely have appeared to the more educated members of the audience as a mimed or staged version of that image. And yet that sight – that pose – does not provoke in Hamlet a return to his old malady, but rather provides him with the occasion for a perfectly balanced and conventionally Christian *memento mori*.[27]

The exchanges between Hamlet and the two gravediggers feature precisely the sort of word play, the punning associational games, that had characterized Hamlet's speech. When 'mad', he had used such techniques to undercut, render foolish and threaten both Polonius and the king. Now such speech is an attribute of the gravedigger and his mate, and Hamlet takes part in the resulting banter only as an amused outsider, a patrician visitor beamed down into the carnivalesque word play of the lower orders.[28] In his reclaimed persona as Hamlet the Dane, a Renaissance prince, returned to claim his place in the world, he has no use for a carnivalesque discourse that, in Bristol's phrase, turns all social or political hierarchy 'inside out' – or indeed upside down.[29]

The contrast between the scene in the graveyard and his earlier exchanges on the subject of death and decay with Claudius are thus redolent not only of a major shift in Hamlet's relationship with his own mortality, and indeed with his old malady, but also with his sense of himself and his place in the world. Confronted by Laertes and moved by 'the bravery of his grief', Hamlet, as he later explains, is put 'into a tow'ring passion'. Now, when Hamlet loses control, it is passion – of precisely the sort to which he had earlier failed to move himself – that overtakes him rather than the antic humour that had previously characterized his performance of madness before the court. While the former is entirely appropriate to his status as a prince, the latter is anything but. Now 'passion' prompts Hamlet to leap into Ophelia's grave and provoke a confrontation with Laertes that threatens to degenerate into violence. But it does not prompt anything like a return to his former 'madness'. Rather, now it is Hamlet who controls himself. To Laertes' expostulation 'the devil take thy soul', Hamlet replies

> Thou pray'st not well.
> I prithee take thy fingers from my throat,
> For, though I am not splenative rash,
> Yet have I in me something dangerous
> Which let thy wisdom fear. Hold off thy hand. [Q2, V, i, 248–252; F, V, i, 256–260]

For Hamlet sees in Laertes not a rival, but an equal, 'a very noble youth', with whom he has no quarrel [Q2, V, i, 213; F, V, i, 221]. Indeed, he regrets 'That to Laertes I forgot myself' and reassures Horatio that thereafter 'I'll court his favours' [F, V, ii, 75–80].

In act V, then, we are confronted with a Hamlet of a very different sort from the character we have come to know during the first three and a half acts of the play. No longer mad, Hamlet can now not only acknowledge and apologize for his madness, as he does to Laertes [Q2, V, ii, 204–215; F, V, ii, 173–184],[30] but he can parody it, too, as, in his comic interlude with Osric, he forces the courtier to humour the 'madman' and the prince. Confronted in the graveyard with the emblems and outward forms of his old malady, he can contemplate them without danger, and indeed turn them into a subject for edifying speech. The earlier intemperance and extremity of his visions of the nature and effects of original sin have been tempered. He is now able to make his peace with the world and the flesh. As his response to Ophelia's death and the 'bravery' of Laertes' 'grief' show, he is capable of passion; but, as his immediate efforts to control himself and then to compose his differences with Laertes also reveal, he is no longer either passion's or honour's slave. Sure of his identity as 'Hamlet the Dane', he is able both to know and to take his true place in the world. Once at war, an almost entirely honour-based sense of self, and – one founded on conscience and the claims of the immortal soul, have been reconciled and brought back into something like equilibrium. The sharp, as it were, perfect Protestant antinomies, the contrasts and contradictions between 'grace' and (an utterly fallen) 'nature' that characterized the early stages of his spiritual crisis, and indeed of his 'conversion', have been overcome, synthesized now into something like a stable sense of self, based on the true nobility of stoic virtue, on lineage (as Hamlet the Dane, he is his father's son) and on Christian faith.[31]

What we are surely being shown here are the effects of a successfully completed process of conversion (albeit not one of a 'puritan' or even a 'Calvinist' complexion). The central act or transitional moment of that process has taken place off stage, apparently at sea. There two things have happened: Hamlet has come to realize that there is indeed a 'divinity that shapes our ends' and that that shaping process takes place often in spite of our own best intentions or plans. Hamlet's general observation on his shipboard experiences that 'our indiscretion sometimes serves us well / When our deep plots do pall' [Q2, V, ii, 8–9; F, V, ii, 8–9] could stand as a comment on his whole career to this point. Previously, as Perry Curtis puts it, Hamlet had been intermittently 'obsessed with the plotting and *mise en scene* of his own play'.[32] Now, recognizing the futility of such efforts, he puts such concerns aside. Ceasing to plan, Hamlet has come to accept his fate as the product not of his own will and intentions, but of an interaction between his own puny and often counterproductive ethical exertions and the workings of divine providence. That repudiation of human means and purposes, and the consequent subordination of his own intentions and ends to the will of God, has been hard won. Indeed, it could be said that Hamlet's progress towards such a condition constitutes the real action of the play, that to which all Hamlet's previous efforts had been tending, despite the determination with which he has been trying to force himself to take on the persona – to simply become – the revenger that the expectations inherent in the genre would have him be. All of which speaks to the extent to which Shakespeare's *Hamlet* is a reaction against Senecan drama, playing with and off it in order to establish its own credentials as a different kind of (Christian) revenge tragedy altogether. Again, Shakespeare's play is working against the assumption of its audience that what they are watching is an older, more conventional, 'Senecan' version of the revenge drama.

With the realization of his utter dependence upon the will and providence of God comes a moral certainty about the rightness of his course in killing Claudius – a certainty that stands in absolute contrast to the labyrinthine reasonings, the moral and spiritual convulsions, of the first three acts of the play. This new assurance comes, just like his new-found reliance on providence, from his time on board ship. Confronting Horatio with his own experience of, and with the physical evidence for, Claudius' murderous duplicity, Hamlet asks his friend what turns out to be a wholly rhetorical question: 'is't not perfect conscience / *To quit him with this arm? And is't not to be damned, / To let this canker of our nature come / In further evil?'* [Q2, V, ii, 62–66; F, V, ii, 63–70].[33]

As James Shapiro points out, unlike the Folio, Q2 breaks off at 'perfect conscience'. (The lines in italics above are to be found only in the Folio.) It may be something of an exaggeration to claim, as Shapiro does, that this change serves to 'activate something that has been dormant in the play', since on the current reading, in any and all of the versions of the play, such considerations have been anything but dormant. However, Shapiro is absolutely right to observe that the added lines *do* work very considerably to emphasize the play's insistence on issues of salvation and damnation, and on the role of providence in shaping 'our ends' – and, indeed, in shaping the end of the play. In particular, in these lines, Hamlet might be taken to be asserting that, in becoming a matter of 'perfect conscience', killing Claudius – that is to say, killing a regnant king – has ceased to be a private matter, a question of revenge, a matter of honour and passion, something which he must force himself to undertake through the adoption of the most desperate atheistical reasoning. Rather, dispatching the tyrant has become something more like the doing of public justice: an action, the righteousness of which is beyond question. Here, at last, is 'conscience' not making a 'coward' of Hamlet, but instead prompting him not merely to act – it had done that before – but to act against Claudius. For the first time in the play, his obsessive concern with salvation and damnation is confirming him in his determination, indeed in his obligation both to God and to man, to kill Claudius. Here, remarkably, revenger and Christian seem to be becoming one. Thus, in answer to the question 'how then can Hamlet claim a "perfect" conscience in the imponderable case of regicide?', John Gillies responds that, in so doing, Hamlet is 'gesturing toward a specifically Reformed discussion of both the nature and discretion of conscience'; claiming, in effect, that in this case 'his conscience is founded on faith and guided by it'.[34]

One notable effect of his new-found moral certainty is to free Hamlet once and for all from the spectre of the ghost and from the nagging questions about what the ghost was and what its purposes might have been in urging him to revenge. For now, none of that matters. Hamlet is no longer acting as the surrogate of his father: he has his own evidence of Claudius' guilt and his own – personal *and* political, honour- *and* justice-centred – reasons for revenge against him. In short, Hamlet has emerged as his own man, and his aims in moving against Claudius now transcend mere revenge.[35] Thus Rhodri Lewis' comment that, at the death, Hamlet 'forgets to mention that he is avenging old Hamlet's murder'[36] seems peculiarly inapposite, since, at this point, avenging old Hamlet is precisely not what Hamlet is doing. As for the ghost, even if it is a devil intent on luring Hamlet to damnation, that no longer signifies. Hamlet's faith in, and reliance upon, providence has, in effect, relegated the ghost/devil to the role which, in a universe controlled by an omnipotent God, he must always already play – that of a mere instrument, a second-order cause, activated or empowered in order only to realize God's providential control over the world and his inscrutably beneficent purposes in saving the elect and damning the reprobate.

Hamlet's other half: Laertes and the resort to politics

The extent of Hamlet's transformation from the person we have observed in the first three acts into the person we encounter in the last is further demonstrated by a comparison between his condition in act V and that of his two moral and spiritual doppelgangers, Ophelia and Laertes. It is, of course, a commonplace that Hamlet is twinned with both those characters. After he has killed Polonius, they are placed in essentially the same structural and moral relationship with him as he is with Claudius. Indeed, Hamlet famously observes to Horatio of Laertes that 'by the image of my cause I see / The portraiture of his' [F, V, ii, 77–78]. As Eric Dodson-Robinson observes, 'both return from abroad to seek revenge, both profess their love to Ophelia in passionate terms and both revolt against Claudius. Both are also accomplished swordsmen' – and courtiers.[37] With Laertes thus paired with Hamlet, their conduct and fate in acts IV and V provide a gloss on Hamlet's moral and spiritual condition, the state in which he will meet his end.

Confronted by her father's death at the hands of the man she had once hoped to marry, Ophelia succumbs to madness and suicide. In the first three acts of the play, Hamlet had been sorely tormented (and tempted) by both; but by act V, he has definitively overcome them. Laertes, on the other hand, succumbs to a different set of temptations – temptations also experienced by Hamlet in the first half of the play.[38] He gives in to the pursuit of revenge at any price, prompted thereto by precisely the same considerations of passion, honour and lineage that Hamlet, in atheist mode, had (unsuccessfully) used to goad himself into action against Claudius. On his first encounter with Claudius, told to calm down, Laertes responds:

> That drop of blood that's calm proclaims me bastard,
> Cries Cuckold! to my father, brands the harlot
> Even here, between the chaste unsmirched brow
> Of my true mother. [Q2, IV, v, 116–119; F, IV, i, 116–119]

Here, then, the demands of passion and revenge are identified with the honour of the household and lineage. Laertes' status as a true son of his father (rather than as a bastard) is made to depend on the passion he displays in seeking to revenge his father. Notions of sexual pollution and the dishonour of women serve as markers of the dishonour inherent in the failure to exact revenge, just as they had in Hamlet's earlier diatribes about his mother's lost honour and his need to wreak revenge on Claudius for that, too. Central to Laertes' rage for revenge are questions of status, and the absence of due respect for his father and his house:

> His means of death, his obscure funeral –
> No trophy, sword nor hatchment o'er his bones,
> No noble rite, nor formal ostentation –
> Cry to be heard as 'twere from heaven to earth. [Q2, IV, v, 205–208; F, IV, i, 208–212]

Laertes' wrongs admit of no other outcome than Hamlet's death, at Laertes own hand [Q2, IV, vii, 26–30; F, IV, iii, 26–30]. 'It warms the very sickness in my heart / That I shall live and tell him to his teeth / "Thus didst thou" ' [Q2, IV, vii, 35–55; F, IV, iii, 54–56].

Such extremity of language and emotion has, of course, its parallels in Hamlet's earlier speeches figuring the wrong done to him by Claudius and evoking the gloriousness and violence of the revenge he will exact. But unlike Hamlet, Laertes explicitly states that his pursuit of revenge will not merely ignore, but, if necessary, trample upon, the constraints of conscience or religion. At the start of his first interview with Claudius, he rants that

> I'll not be juggled with.
> To hell allegiance, vows to the blackest devil,
> Conscience and grace to the profoundest pit.
> I dare damnation. To this point I stand –

That both the worlds I give to negligence,

Let come what comes, only I'll be revenged

Most thoroughly for my father. [Q2, IV, v, 129–135; F, IV, i, 128–134]

Later, he even expresses his readiness 'to cut his throat i' th' church' [Q2, IV, vii, 124; F, IV, iii, 99].

Having, like the atheist that Hamlet had only aspired to be, set revenge as the defining project of his existence, Laertes then pursues it using the conventional range of political means. First, he returns 'in secret' from France and exploits what Claudius describes as 'the people muddied, / Thick and unwholesome in their thoughts and whispers / For good Polonius' death' [Q2, IV, v, 81–83; F, IV, i, 78–80]. On that basis, he raises a popular insurrection or rebellion. As a messenger informs Claudius and Gertrude, cowering in their palace,

young Laertes in a riotous head

O'erbears your officers. The rabble call him lord,

. . . They cry, 'Choose we! Laertes shall be king!' –

Caps, hands and tongues applaud it to the clouds –

'Laertes shall be king! Laertes king!' [Q2, IV, v, 101–108; F, IV, i, 100–10]

Having forced his way into the royal presence, Laertes, no match for the faux majesty and political cunning of Claudius, resorts to a second mode of political manoeuvre – the court conspiracy.

Throughout, he is encouraged in these dreadful threats and imprecations by the now entirely villainous Claudius, who is, of course, anxious first to divert Laertes' rage against Hamlet, and then to use that rage as the means to rid himself of the only person who knows what he has done. The untempered nature of Laertes' determination to revenge himself on Hamlet has sent him over entirely to the dark side, embroiling a nature ostensibly motivated by honour in the utterly dishonourable treacheries of a murderer and a usurper. Indeed, as P.K. Ayers points out, by the end, Laertes' villainy seems even to exceed that of Claudius himself: 'The murder-disguised-as-sporting-accident, originally proposed by Claudius, is treacherous enough', but 'Laertes' refinement with the poison' leads to the 'further reduction of his own status from warrior, to duelist, to assassin' – and finally to that by-word for cowardice and deceit, poisoner.[39]

All this is, of course, in marked contrast to Hamlet, who had precisely not 'dared damnation' and, given the chance, had refused (albeit for the worst, quintessentially un-Christian of reasons) to cut Claudius' throat, if not in the church, then certainly at prayer. If the ghost was, in fact, a devil bent on luring him, through the intensity of his desire for revenge, to damnation, Hamlet has resisted those temptations. In direct contrast, Laertes – who, just like Hamlet, is desperate 'to know the certainty / Of your dear father's death' [Q2, IV, v, 139–140; F, IV, i, 138–139] – falls hook, line and sinker for the blandishments of that other demonic creature, Claudius, who, just as the ghost had done to Hamlet, offers to tell him the truth of the matter and help him to his revenge – and in so doing, lead him to damnation.

The play goes out of its way to emphasize that Hamlet could have taken the course pursued by Laertes. After all, he had a plausible claim to the throne and a popular following – one so great that Claudius claims any move he might have made against Hamlet would simply have rebounded on his own head [Q2, IV, vii, 10–25; F, IV, iii, 10–25] – and could easily have led the sort of insurrection staged by Laertes. Similarly, an insider at court, protected (as Claudius again explains to Laertes) from the ire of the king by his mother's favour, all manner of conspiracy was available to him, as indeed his little plot with Horatio and the players showed rather well. Hamlet, however, had eschewed such means, preferring, as we have seen, to act in the realm of conscience and obsess about, rather than 'dare', 'damnation'. In all this, he was the exact opposite of Laertes.

There is a case to be made that, in behaving as he does, Laertes is in many ways merely doing what Polonius had told him to do in the advice that he had conferred on his son as Laertes was preparing to return to France. Famously Polonius had instructed him then 'to thine own self be true', and proceeded to describe what that process of moral constancy would look like. As he did so, he outlined the behaviour of the averagely sinful, wholly secular nobleman about court whom he clearly wanted his son to be. The advice was conventional in the extreme, melding classicizing moral theory – the impulse towards the mean and temperance – with the necessity of behaving as a member of the noble class should when his honour or standing was called into question [Q1, I, iii, 54–80; F, I, iii, 55–80]. As Polonius' subsequent conversation with his agent and spy Reynaldo shows, included in the modes of conduct that he expected – indeed, in effect wanted – to find his son displaying was a certain leavening of the averagely sinful debauchery – 'drinking, fencing, swearing, / Quarrelling, drabbing' [Q2, II, i, 25–26; F, II, i, 25–6] – regarded as appropriate for a young man of his age and class. Prudential, calculating Polonius' advice called on Laertes to behave as his standing in the world and his lineage demanded that he should, while pursuing his own interests and advancement.

In seeking, at all costs, to revenge his dead father, Laertes can be seen as merely obeying Polonius' instructions. For the view of the 'self' to which Polonius had enjoined him to be true was a wholly secular one, defined by his relation to his house and father, and dominated by the need to maintain his own honour and that of his lineage. Having, in the unpunished death and secret burial of his father, suffered the ultimate affront, Laertes can only be 'true' to a 'self' thus defined by seeking to revenge himself on Hamlet. On this view, the savagery of Laertes' urge for revenge is a function of an identity, a sense of 'self', entirely defined by his 'nobility' and honour – that is to say, by his lineage and his very expensively acquired mastery of the arts and attributes of 'gentry'. In that sense, his desperate pursuit of revenge for his father is, in effect, a desperate attempt to preserve himself. In that respect, he is, as Rhodri Lewis observes, 'typical' of 'the late Elizabethan stage revenger'.[40] As such, for all the similarities between them, he is typical of that which Hamlet is not.

Hamlet, too, has been seen trying to be true to himself; but the 'self' to which he has been struggling to be 'true' is not one defined solely by his standing in the pecking order of honour – that is to say, by his relationship to his father, and his status in the world as simply his father's son. The ghost's instructions to him to take revenge on Claudius are predicated on such a view and, as we have seen, throughout the first three acts, Hamlet is tempted – and, in part at least, defined – by such a sense of self. But throughout, and increasingly as the play goes on, the sense of 'self' to which he has been trying to be 'true' has owed a good deal to the operations of conscience and to his sense of himself as a being with an immortal soul to save, as well as a socially defined honour or name to preserve. The first three acts found Hamlet torn between the demands of what the play presents as two radically opposed senses of 'self' – the one secular, this-worldly, honour- and lineage-based; the other spiritual, founded on 'conscience' and on Hamlet's possession of an immortal soul. Act V sees the emergence of a new Hamlet, in whom these two hitherto opposed principles have been brought into some sort of equilibrium. He is now both 'Hamlet the Dane' – a Renaissance prince with a proper sense of his standing and worth in the world – and a Christian with a soul to save and a divinely conferred calling to fulfil.

The same contrast between the two men persists into the play's last scenes. Hamlet continues to eschew political planning or conspiracy. He must be intending to formulate some plan of action, for, when Horatio opines that 'it must be shortly known to him from England / What is the issue of the business there', Hamlet replies that 'it will be short. The interim's mine. / And a man's life's no more than to say "one"' [F, V, ii, 71–74]. But at precisely that moment, Osric arrives to set up the fencing match that is intended to see Hamlet off once and for all. Denied by events any chance to plan, Hamlet goes off, as politically unwitting as ever, to confront his fate. Famously, before he does so, he tells Horatio that 'thou wouldst not think how ill all's here about my heart – but it is no matter'. When Horatio responds by advising him that 'if your mind dislike of anything, obey it. I will forestall their repair hither and say you are not fit', Hamlet will have none of it:

> Not a whit. We defy augury. There is a special
> providence in the fall of a sparrow. If it be now,
> 'tis not to come; if it be not to come, it will be
> now. If it be not now, yet it will come. The
> readiness is all, since no man of aught he
> leaves knows what is't to leave betimes. Let be. [Q2, V, ii, 190–202; F, V, ii, 160–171]

Perhaps tellingly, Q1 has 'there's a predestinate providence in the fall of a sparrow' [Q1, 17, 45–46]. There could, of course, scarcely be a clearer indication of Hamlet's faith in providence or preparedness for death than that speech.

Resolution(s)

This sets up a final denouement that, according to the conventions of revenge tragedy, the history play and, one might add, the murder pamphlet, is quintessentially providential. For the conspirators are hoist with their own petard. The queen drinks the poisoned draught and Laertes is fatally wounded by his own poisoned rapier, both of which were, of course, intended for Hamlet. While the death of his mother alerts Hamlet to the fact that there is 'treason' afoot, it is again conscience that comes to his aid: this time that of Laertes, who, confronting his own death, spills the beans [Q2, V, ii, 298–305; F, V, ii, 268–275]. At that point, Hamlet finally has his revenge on Claudius, first wounding the king with the poisoned sword designed for himself, and then forcing him to 'Follow my mother' [Q2, V, ii, 311; F, V, ii, 281] by drinking of the poisoned cup that has already finished off the queen. With that, Laertes and Hamlet reconcile [Q2, V, ii, 314–316; F, V, ii, 284–286].

At this point, the proceedings are interrupted by the advent of ambassadors from England and Fortinbras, and the play switches from the register of the revenge tragedy to that of the history play, associating the work of providence not with the doing of justice or the salvation or damnation of individuals, but rather with the settling of the state. Thus, Hamlet's last speech concerns neither himself nor his fate, but rather the future of the crown of Denmark: 'I cannot live to hear the news from England, / But I do prophesy th' election lights / On Fortinbras: he has my dying voice' [Q2, V, ii, 338–340; F, V, ii, 308–310]. Horatio's response to this is to consign the dying prince to heaven: 'Good night, sweet prince, / And flights of angels sing thee to thy rest' [Q2, V, ii, 343–344; F, V, ii, 314–315]. On this (admittedly partial) account, at least, Hamlet has succeeded in saving his soul. But he has also preserved his honour, telling Horatio to survive him and 'tell my story', lest 'things standing thus unknown' he shall leave behind him 'a wounded name' [Q2, V, ii, 326–333; F, V, ii, 297–303].

This is a task that Horatio undertakes with a will, arranging with the new power in the land, Fortinbras, to have the dead bodies 'high on a stage be placed to the view,/ And let me speak to th'yet unknowing world / How these things came about' [Q2, V, ii, 362–364; F, V, ii, 333–335]. As for Fortinbras, as Hamlet has predicted, he makes a play for the crown – 'I have some rights of memory in this kingdom / Which now to claim my vantage doth invite me' [Q2, V, ii, 373–374; F, V, ii, 344–345] – and he marks the transition of power by granting to Hamlet (who would, of course – almost certainly along with Laertes – have been his rival for the throne) the honour of a full military burial [Q2, V, ii, 400–405; F, V, ii, 350–358]. At the end, at least according to Horatio and Fortinbras, Hamlet has squared the circle: he has satisfied the demands of conscience and of honour; he has had his revenge; served the purposes of both human and divine justice; and, if Horatio is to be believed, saved his soul, his reputation and the state.

The tale that Horatio will tell is, he says, one

of carnal, bloody and unnatural acts,
Of accidental judgments, casual slaughters,
Of deaths put on by cunning, and forced cause,
And in this upshot purposes mistook
Fall'n on th'inventors heads. [Q2, V, ii, 365–369; F, V, ii, 336–340]

If Horatio's trailer for the full account that he is about to give 'the people' is anything to go by, his recounting of the events will be entirely tragic – that is to say, devoid of any feel-good, providential take-home message.

But, of course, the audience has seen more and knows more than Horatio does, and is, therefore, in a position to provide precisely just such a gloss on proceedings. Much turns here on the narrative expectations implicit in the various genres and narratives upon which the play has drawn throughout, and on the audience's familiarity on which it is even now drawing. Certainly, the expectations implicit in the belief that one has been watching a revenge tragedy have been met. Surveying the pile of bodies now littering the stage, Fortinbras observes that, while it might become 'the field', such a sight 'here shows much amiss' [Q2, V, ii, 385; F, V, ii, 357]. Except that 'here' – that is to say, at the end of a revenge tragedy – such a sight is anything but amiss. Rather it is precisely what the customers have paid (and expect) to see: the revenger has had his revenge; the revengee has met his fate; both the main protagonists, as well as a variety of their accomplices, are dead; and the stage is littered with their corpses. Honour and audience expectation have both been satisfied. There can be no doubting the 'woe' and 'wonder' of the scene with which the play ends: 'This quarry cries on havoc. O proud Death, / What feast is toward in thine eternal cell / That thou so many princes at a shot / So bloodily hast struck?' [Q2, V, ii, 348–351; F, V, ii, 317–322] is Fortinbras' editorializing reply. Those members of the audience who turned up to see a revenge tragedy have, in short, had more than their money's worth.

But what of the history play which the play also might be taken to be? There, too, audience expectations have been met. The usurper has been removed from power, and the succession settled. The salvation of the state by the arrival of a foreign-born claimant from the north, after an abortive coup, may not have been altogether devoid of immediately contemporary resonance in 1599, 1600, 1601 or indeed thereafter, when the two quartos were printed in 1603 and 1604. More than that, however, the transition has been made with a minimum of political disturbance or civil strife. Impressive though the body count on stage is at the end of proceedings, and tragic though the outcome undoubtedly is, civil war, disruptive political change, popular insurrection and the breakdown of order have all been averted. We need only refer ourselves to earlier history plays to see a worked example of what the ruthless pursuit, by every available means, of ambition and revenge could do to a kingdom. Hamlet, of course, had considerably more urgent, ethically pressing and emotionally charged reasons to act against Claudius than ever the duke of York had to move against Henry VI. Moreover, in his speech using the example of Fortinbras to drive himself to act, Hamlet can, in effect, be seen urging himself to emulate York, in risking all for 'ambition' and 'honour'. But Hamlet resists that temptation and, in so doing, arguably saves Denmark from the fate visited on England by the Wars of the Roses.

Essentially the same point emerges with even greater force if *Hamlet* is compared to its companion piece, *Julius Caesar*. There Brutus' decision, in the face of incipient usurpation, tyranny and political change, to resort to the overtly political means of conspiracy, assassination and coup had led to the descent of the Roman world into popular insurrection and civil war, and the transformation of the Roman state from the republic that, under Caesar's dominant influence, it was perhaps ceasing to be, into the overt tyranny which that same dominance had yet to visit upon it. The course taken by the conspirators in *Julius Caesar* – recourse, at the promptings of honour, to the politics of popularity, conspiracy and assassination – is precisely that followed by Laertes in

Hamlet. As we have seen, in Laertes' case, and in the overtly Christian context of Hamlet's Denmark, this is also the politics of atheism: a path taken by Laertes, until, quite literally at the death, his conscience gets the better of him. Throughout, of course, such a course of action remains an option for Hamlet. Hamlet, however, never gives in to that temptation. By refusing to act like an atheist, by refusing the temptations of 'ambition', of 'honour' and 'revenge', of what Claudius, confronting Laertes, calls accurately enough 'rebellion', Hamlet, guided by his conscience and relying on providence, sets up the final showdown that, in one fell swoop, clears the political stage in Denmark of rival claimants to the throne and leaves the way clear for the unopposed and peaceful accession of a claimant to whose legitimacy all can accede.

Whatever we think of the military hero Fortinbras, estimations and accounts of whose character fluctuate considerably during the play, judged by the standards set by the other history plays – or indeed by *Julius Caesar* – this is a distinctly 'happy', indeed an entirely providential, ending – one which sees Denmark saved from the corrupting rule of a regicide and incipient tyrant, a *de facto* (if not a *de jure*) usurper, and safely entrusted to a new king, untainted by the bitter passions and conflicts of the recent past, imported from the north. And all this without popular insurrection, civil war or the transformation of the polity into a tyranny waiting to happen. Now that really would have been an unhappy ending; and, by those standards, judged at the political level, and regarded as a history play, the end of *Hamlet* is a feel-good story of disaster averted, stability preserved and legitimacy restored. In the play's own terms, 'the time' has truly been put back into 'joint' by the person not merely 'born' but chosen by providence – and, finally, by himself – to do just that. Here, then, *Hamlet* as history play reaches its final resolution.

If we apply the narrative expectations and demands of the murder pamphlet to *Hamlet*, we see a similarly satisfying closure being effected. After all, by play's end we have seen the providential revelation of a hitherto unknown, indeed unsuspected, crime bring the perpetrator to justice. Along the way, both he and his moll (Gertrude) have been confronted with their crimes and offered the opportunity to repent. Only after that have they faced punishment. The agent behind both processes has been Hamlet. Judging his conduct in terms of what he has actually done under the guiding hand of providence – rather than in terms of what he has at times been intending to do – Hamlet has managed to distinguish between, coordinate and discharge the linked functions of both the spiritual and the temporal arms, of both minister and magistrate, with punctilious attention to the approved script. As magistrate, having been alerted by the ghost to an alleged (and hitherto unsuspected) crime, he has gone to considerable lengths to establish the nature and extent of both Claudius' and Gertrude's guilt. He has then suspended the execution of punishment long enough for both of them to be offered, through the efforts of the minister of God's mercy (a role he plays himself), a chance to acknowledge their guilt and repent of their sin – and through repentance to save their souls. He does this for Claudius by setting up the play, and then by refusing to kill the king as he kneels in prayer, desperately trying (and, as it turns out, failing) to repent. And he does it for Gertrude by restraining his (very strong) impulse to rush to judgement and punishment by doing her physical violence, and instead proceeding, in the closet scene, first to test the depth and nature of her guilt and then to appeal to her to repent. Only after this does Hamlet discharge his role as scourge or magistrate by exacting this-worldly punishment (revenge) on Claudius for his crimes.

Thus are the demands of human and divine justice met, and those of divine justice and mercy squared or reconciled. While this outcome has clearly been brought about by Hamlet's actions, at almost no point has it been a direct product of his intentions. Rather, these results have been produced by providence bending and manipulating Hamlet's (often but not always) vengeful and corrupt purposes and his (often but not always) inadvertently just actions to its own broader (always already just and beneficent) purposes. On one level, this is entirely typical of Hamlet's condition – which might be taken to stand here for the condition of fallen humanity in general. For both the immediate, 'secular' or 'political', and the longer-term, 'spiritual' or 'religious' effects of his actions and intentions (whether in themselves virtuous or vicious, just or sinful) are very often the opposite of what he had at first intended or believed them to be. Hamlet is saved from the ultimate sin of killing a man at prayer not by any compunction on his part, but by his most overtly devilish impulse: the desire to have revenge not merely in this life, but also in the next. For all his efforts to do the right thing – whatever that was, and for the bulk of the play he has no real idea – there can be no question of merit here. He is saved from the worst effects of his own malign intentions by their very malignity. *Felix culpa* indeed.

Again, not only is Hamlet brought to the situation in which he can finally exact punishment on Claudius by a train of events that is anything but of his own making, but also he enters that scene intending not to kill Claudius at all, but rather to make up with Laertes. It is when his immediate impulses are at their most charitable that Hamlet at last gets to play the revenger. And here it is worth remembering that, even in extremity, he is reconciled to Laertes at the death. In very different senses, they are both victims of Claudius and both embrace their fate with acceptance and mutual forgiveness. In short, while Hamlet is the main instrument or agent whereby these various effects have been worked, he is shown as having acted throughout – as even he gradually comes to acknowledge – not in his own right, as the (failed) revenger of his father's death, but rather as the instrument or agent of providence; or, as he puts it himself, with a precision perhaps greater even than he realizes at the time, as both 'the scourge and minister' of heaven. Thus is the murder pamphlet contained within the play brought to its expected and ultimately happy ending.

Certainly the appropriateness of that ending (if not its happiness) does not depend on Hamlet's salvation. But it does depend upon his death. In this he is (almost) in the same boat as Claudius and Laertes. For, for all the differences between their crimes – those of Claudius and Laertes have been premeditated, treacherous and calculated while Hamlet's have been anything but, Hamlet still ends the play both a murderer and a regicide. As such, according to the demands of the murder pamphlet and the revenge tragedy (not to mention works of political theory, such as *The True Law of Free Monarchies*), he, too, must die the death.

Hamlet has discharged his functions; the demands of divine mercy have been met – both Claudius and Gertrude have been offered the chance to repent and be saved; justice has been done; and the state has been saved. All of this, of course, remains the case whether Hamlet ends up in heaven or in hell. However, insofar as the play is also a conversion narrative – and one of its central organizing questions or concerns is whether or not Hamlet can indeed discharge his functions as revenger, minister and scourge and still be saved – the final destination of his soul remains a pressing question. And here the play might be thought to have gone out of its way to engineer a very particular set of circumstances, which might well be taken to have enabled Hamlet to discharge his various roles as scourge and minister, revenger and regicide, and still to go to heaven. For in the end, Hamlet kills Claudius not in some premeditated, long-plotted and carefully executed act of revenge or justice, but spontaneously, according to the logic of a situation set up by his adversary to kill him.

We might, in fact, here employ the argument used by the gravedigger, as he tries to distinguish, for the benefit of his mate, between suicide and drowning:

Here lies the water – good. Here
stands the man – good. If the man go to this water
and drown himself, it is, will he, nill he, he
goes. Mark you that? But if the water come to him
and drown him, he drowns not himself. [Q2, V, i, 15–19; F, V, i, 15–19]

In these terms, Hamlet has precisely not come to the water, 'will he, nill he'; the water, in the shape of Claudius' and Laertes' conspiracy to murder him, has come to him.

I cannot, therefore, agree with Lander that 'the Clown's reasoning is deliriously confused and confusing', and 'works as an extended joke about the baffling scholasticism of the theology of grace'.[41] On the contrary, the passage encapsulates the central paradoxes at the heart both of contemporary debates about predestination and of the play's action. The play stages those paradoxes in ways that enable – indeed, that in many ways force – the audience to decide what they think about the play and its characters, and in particular what they think about Hamlet's fate, both in this life and the next, in effect to choose between the various versions of predestination. The play's impulse, therefore, is precisely not to induce the viewer or reader to distance him or herself from, but rather to engage intensively with, issues of providence and predestination, of divine foreknowledge, will and fate. The play thus does anything but avoid 'religious controversy' (as Jeffrey Knapp claims that all Shakespeare's plays always did), the better to realize their 'theatrical ministry' of effecting 'reconciliation' among everyone – except, of course, 'the puritans'.[42]

Here a comparison with the ending of *Titus Andronicus* might help to drive the point home. Both plays conclude with a carefully choreographed series of exchanges, which see the various parties to the crimes committed in the play come to fitting ends, and the way cleared for the accession of a new prince; but whereas in *Titus* that choreography is shown to have been the result of the careful plotting of Titus himself, the very opposite is true in *Hamlet*. Hamlet acts on the spur of the moment: were he not dying as he does the deed, one might almost say that he acts in self-defence. His mother is killed, but he has nothing to do with that. The man he kills has (albeit accidentally) killed his mother and (rather more on purpose) murdered his father, and in effect (with the poisoned sword which he has placed in Laertes' hand for exactly that purpose) has just killed him.[43] On the one hand, this is as close to 'killing no murder' as it is possible to get.[44] On the other hand, Hamlet is here inflicting on Claudius precisely the sort of death that he had not merely foreseen, but positively wished for him when he had stopped himself from dispatching the king while at prayer. Claudius has indeed been killed in the midst of the most dreadful and damning of sins – not merely drunk, swearing or *in flagrante delicto*, but attempting to commit the most treacherous, premeditated murder it is possible to imagine. In his last words – 'Oh, yet defend me friends, I am but hurt' [Q2, V, ii, 308; F, V, ii, 278] – there is no trace of repentance, but rather a futile attempt to keep up appearances to the end.

Had Hamlet killed Claudius while he prayed, he might not have sent Claudius to heaven, but he would almost certainly have consigned himself to hell. He had avoided that fate, if only for the worst of reasons. But avoid it he had. Now he gets his wish, with, as it were, no blame attached; except, of course, that by this point it is no longer his wish or intention, but rather providence's judgment. To quote Peter Ure, since Hamlet's is 'a kind of action where something is done without the doer's having to work himself up to it', Hamlet

> is able to achieve the act of revenge without ever really becoming a revenger . . . the identification of the self with the revenger, the coalescence of the two, is no longer enjoined upon him . . . Providence, or the storyteller, has . . . abolished the role.[45]

Thus, what we are left with is providence's judgment upon the unrepentant Claudius rather than Hamlet's revenge upon his uncle.

Greatly aided by providence, Hamlet has finally got the roles of minister and scourge straight. By fatally confusing them, he had once blasphemously sought to usurp God's role as final arbiter and judge of the spiritual state and fate of others. But now, in killing Claudius, he is acting only as God's scourge, killing the body of the felon, while leaving the judgment of the soul to a higher power. Claudius, of course, through the dreadful nature of his sins and his repeated refusal to repent, is damned; but he has, in effect, damned himself. Hamlet's hands are clean and God's justice and mercy vindicated. Or so, without perhaps finally clinching the matter, the play certainly enables us to conclude.

However, it is important to note here that while the play certainly does seem to lean towards such a happy conclusion about the final destination of Hamlet's soul, the question is never quite resolved. After all, both Fortinbras and Horatio have reasons – Fortinbras' political, Horatio's personal – to say nice things about Hamlet after he is dead. Hamlet's final words, his concern at the death with the future of the Danish throne, might be taken as the sign of a finally resolved conscience, and the expression of a charitable concern for the kingdom and commonwealth that he is leaving behind. But equally, given his complete failure to repent or, at the end, to express any opinion or hope about his fate in the next life, they might be taken to be the outward sign of an inward corruption – the final words of a man who, having struggled so long to reconcile the role of revenger and scourge with his own salvation, has gone to his death thinking only of events in this world. And here it is worth noting that while in Q1 Hamlet's final words – 'farewell, Horatio. Heaven receive my soul' [Q1, 17, 111] – do indeed seem to insist that Hamlet's thoughts have turned to heaven and that he is therefore saved, his last words in Q2 and the Folio – 'the rest is silence' [Q2, V, ii, 342; F, V, ii, 312] – do not. Of course, they do not insist upon the opposite conclusion, either; rather they leave the question of Hamlet's salvation or damnation open, for the audience to decide.

This is highly significant, not least because how we construe the political message of the play's final scenes is a function of how we construe Hamlet's fate in the next world. If we take Hamlet to be damned, then the play becomes merely a restatement – an intensely provocative and paradoxical restatement, it is true, but a restatement nonetheless – of one of the central orthodoxies of late-Elizabethan and Jacobean political theology. For if Hamlet is damned for his sin in killing Claudius, then all the play does is (on the one hand) show us the evils of tyranny and the inevitable consequences of those evils in revolt and regicide, and (on the other) demonstrate, through the fate of Hamlet in both this and the next life, the sinful nature of rebellion, and alert us once again to the fact that, both now and in the hereafter, the wages of sin is death. On this reading, having used Hamlet's sins of rebellion and regicide as a scourge to punish Claudius, God would have then committed both the primary object of his wrath (Claudius) and the scourge that he has used to punish him (Hamlet) to the annihilating fire of his judgment.

It is only if Hamlet is saved that the play becomes something rather more contentious – indeed, on certain views of the matter, rather more subversive. And, as we have seen, whether Hamlet is damned or saved is quite deliberately left an open question, to be decided by each and every member of the audience through the application to the scenes played out before them of the political and religious prejudices and presuppositions, the various narrative templates and tropes, which they have both brought with them to the playhouse and been provided with by the play itself. As ever with Shakespeare's plays, the really crucial, the actually or potentially subversive interpretative acts take place not on the stage or on the printed page, but rather between the ears of the viewer or reader.

Admittedly, even on the most optimistic view of Hamlet's ultimate fate, the aperture opened by the play for 'resistance' is very narrow indeed. When Hamlet kills Claudius, he is certain that he himself is dying. In this state, and for the first time in the play, there can be no chance that he could gain politically from the death of Claudius. About to pass from the world, he kills the king and then, with his dying breath, elects Fortinbras to the empty throne. Whatever else this is, it is as close to a politically selfless act as it is possible to get. Here, then, is an act of resistance that is not really resistance; of regicide that is not really regicide. As such, it sends a murderous tyrant and usurper to a deserved fate and his killer to heaven, while conferring the crown on a claimant of unimpeachable legitimacy – and all this without causing the slightest popular disorder, or even widespread political conflict, let alone the civil war, accompanied by fundamental political change or 'innovation', that concludes *Julius Caesar*.

And here it might be worth remarking that, if there is anything in Richard Dutton's ingenious and thoroughly plausible claim that Q2 was in fact a rewritten version of the play, produced for court performance before James I in 1603/04, then this aspect of the play becomes even more daring. After all, James might well be thrilled to see himself in Fortinbras, a claimant to the throne, newly arrived from a northern kingdom to restore order to a state riven with division and revolt; a ruler whom 'fate has made the right man in the right place; and he has an army to answer any doubters'. 'This,' Dutton comments, 'was surely what James I wanted to hear after his long wait in the wings.'[46] And here it is surely worth pursuing Dutton's thought experiment, for if James is Fortinbras, then his predecessor on the throne, Claudius, a regicide and a usurper, is none other than Elizabeth. Whether James would have enjoyed quite so much the picture of tyrannicide as a thoroughly justified act, the consummation of which might well send the perpetrator to heaven, is another matter. Of course, as we have seen, the play scarcely insists on such a reading; but it certainly makes it available, particularly for someone as well versed in reformed orthodoxy as James I.

What I have been trying to do in the last few paragraphs is to view the final scenes of *Hamlet* through the lenses provided by the narrative structures, the demands and expectations that animate the various genres, the different sorts of text and narrative, upon which the play draws and which it uses to elicit, manipulate, frustrate and ultimately satisfy the responses and desires of its audience. If we do that, then it becomes clear that by the end of the play the various sets of expectations, the different senses or sorts of ending inherent in those genres, have been brought together; indeed, they have been fitted inside one another like so many Chinese boxes, each one lending strength to the others to confirm a providential reading of the events that have been acted out on stage. Different levels of discourse and concern have been brought together in a complex dialogue or dialectic. The political has been fitted within the confessional and the spiritual, and vice versa. The 'inside' of religious despair and spiritual crisis has been fitted within and related to the 'outside' of court and succession politics. And through that process, what Horatio calls 'accidental judgments, casual slaughters' have been given a shape and meaning that we can only call 'providential'. Providence here offers another link between, on the one hand, the 'internal' and the 'religious' – the search for spiritual assurance, and the theological basis of that search in the doctrines of election and reprobation – and, on the other, the 'external' and the 'political' – the doings of the great and the good, the rise and fall of princes and of states, the fate of nations and of Churches, which contemporaries also took to be the subject of directly providential control. Moreover, in and through that 'providentializing' process, the events depicted on the stage have been made to speak to present and future circumstance and concern in myriad, complicated and rather daring ways.

8

⊰⊹⊹⊱

Contemporary resonances

Catholic/Protestant/Christian

I argued above that, through the figure of the ghost, Shakespeare deliberately inserted the issue of confessional politics into the play. If, as I have also argued, the play can be read as, in some sense, a conversion narrative, it seems reasonable to ask two questions: first, how, in the end, are we to conceive of the play's relation to Catholicism? And second, if Hamlet has by the end of the play been, in some sense, 'converted' or even 'saved', then what does the play allow us to say about the sort of Christianity to which he has been converted, and which has notionally saved him?

At first sight, the Denmark of the play appears to be an entirely Catholic country. Whatever the truth of the ghost's claim to be a soul on night release from purgatory, that claim is clearly made in order to make Hamlet believe him. It is in that sense a wholly Catholic claim, and Hamlet, as a loyal Catholic, initially accepts it at face value. The ghost is an 'honest ghost' [Q2, I, v, 136; F, I, v, 137]; if it looks like his father and talks like his father and claims to come from purgatory, where his dead father has almost certainly gone, then, for Hamlet, it is his father: 'I'll call thee Hamlet' [Q2, I, iv, 44; F, I, iv, 23]. Told by Horatio that 'there's no offence', Hamlet replies: 'yes, by Saint Patrick, but there is' [Q2, I, v, 134–135; F, I, v, 134–135]. As Stephen Greenblatt has pointed out, St Patrick had strong associations with purgatory through 'St Patrick's purgatory', a cave in Ireland reputed once to have provided the aperture or entrance for a legendary visit to purgatory. Into the sixteenth century and beyond, it was a sight much visited by pilgrims.[1]

As we have seen, Hamlet's sense of the dreadfulness of his father's death is confounded by the sense that he was consigned to his fate unprepared, 'unhousel'd, disappointed, unanel'd' [Q2, I, v, 77; F, I, v, 77]. Hamlet applies this same, distinctively Catholic, set of assumptions about the nature and consequences both of a good death and of its absence in his calculations surrounding the consequences of killing Claudius while at prayer, as opposed to in the midst of his sins. Laertes, too, is obsessed with the outward forms of a proper death and burial, railing at what Hamlet describes as 'the maimed rites' [Q2, V, i, 208; F, V, i, 216] that attend the funeral of Ophelia. Even as a suicide, the attending priest explains, she has been allowed 'her virgin rites, / Her maiden strewments, and the bringing home / Of bell and burial', and still Laertes demands 'must there no more be done' [Q2, V, i, 221–224; F, V, i, 229–232]. When the priest insists that indeed no more can be done, Laertes calls him 'a churlish priest'; 'a ministering angel shall my sister be / When thou liest howling' [Q2, V, i, 229–231; F, V, i, 237–239]. For all his bravado on the subject, Laertes is clearly afraid that his sister's salvation might be at stake if she is deprived of the full obsequies due to the dead.

We are here in what is, in late-Elizabethan terms, a distinctively and recognizably Catholic world. That impression is confirmed by Ophelia's scene with Claudius and Gertrude. As Alison Chapman has pointed out, the snatches of ballads that Ophelia sings there are suffused with the imagery of the old religion. The description of her lover in 'his cockle hat and sandal shoon' identifies him as dressed in the garb of a pilgrim to the shrine of St James at Compostela. Ophelia also refers to the old shrine at Walsingham and to St Valentine's day, and another snatch of song opens with the words 'by Gis and by St Charity' [Q2, IV, v, 25, 58; F, IV, i, 25, 58] – Gis is a compressed form for Jesus, and swearing by St Charity a peculiarly Catholic turn of phrase. Again, Ophelia's remark that 'they say the owl was a baker's daughter' [Q2, IV, v, 42–43; F, IV, v, 41–42] represents a glancing reference to a traditional miracle story about Christ. Entering a baker's shop, he asked for bread. The baker's daughter, thinking a small piece would suffice, placed a meagre lump of dough in the oven. When this started miraculously to swell and fill the oven, she emitted owl-like screeches of surprise. Because of this and her lack of charity, Jesus transformed her into an owl. Finally, as Ophelia met her end, floating 'mermaid-like' on the surface of the stream, she 'chanted snatches of old lauds' [Q2, IV, vii, 174–175; F, IV, iii, 148–149, where she is described as singing only 'old songs']. To quote Chapman,

> although 'laud' can be a generic noun denoting any song or hymn of praise, it was typically used in a religious context. Furthermore, it often carried specifically Catholic associations. Lauds referred to the morning service in the monastic divine office when participants sang praises to God . . .

Gertrude is quite specific that Ophelia is 'chanting' these lauds, and the 'religious and especially monastic associations of the verb' strengthen the view of Ophelia as voicing recognizably papist forms of piety. Indeed, Chapman continues by claiming that they 'raise a dark irony', since in act 3 Hamlet 'commands, "Get thee to a nunnery" (Q2, III, i, 120; F, III, i, 121) and Ophelia later dies intoning the very chants most associated with nunneries'.[2]

The play, then, is suffused more or less throughout with the language, practices and images of the old religion; but since it is set in a Catholic country, in itself that need not surprise us. However, we are dealing here with a play written for a largely Protestant audience, to be performed in a formally Protestant nation where such beliefs by now constituted a form of heresy or superstition. Moreover, it may not be entirely fanciful to imagine that, given the recent political and religious history of Elizabethan England, the sight of an avowedly Catholic entity enjoining someone to murder the reigning monarch, in order to avenge the death of a former incumbent would have set certain alarm bells ringing. The quite deliberate references made at crucial points to these Catholic materials and images thus set up a certain tension between text and audience.

Nevertheless, within the Catholic context evoked so carefully by the play, Hamlet himself comes across as anything but an orthodox believer. Not only do the ghost's injunctions to revenge, murder and regicide lead Hamlet into the depths of doubt and despair, as Anthony Low has pointed out, while Hamlet might have been transfixed by the appearance of his father's shade, the one thing this does not lead him to do, or even to think of doing, is to pray for it. Aside from avenging him, Hamlet seems to think that there is nothing he can do either to ameliorate his father's condition or alter his fate. 'As was the case with England, so in Hamlet's Denmark. Purgatory is not just abolished but effectively forgotten, as if it never were.'[3]

So little has Hamlet's belief in purgatory been confirmed or strengthened by his encounter with the ghost that when he experiences 'the dread of something after life', he does not know precisely what it is that he is afraid of. Death is now 'the undiscovered country, from whose bourn / No traveller returns', a place which 'puzzles the will' [Q2, III, i, 78–79; F, III, i, 79–80]. While he might no longer simply believe the ghost about purgatory, he does not yet know what else to believe about death or the afterlife. This is a soul trembling on the edge of 'atheism', despair or indeed unbelief – states associated by contemporaries not only with demonic possession, but also with the apostasy that resulted from a failure rightly to negotiate the process of religious change, or the transition from one confessional identity or ecclesial allegiance to another. As we have seen, the most infamous and archetypal example of this connection was Francis Spiera, a man caught between confessional identities and ecclesial allegiances, who had slipped inexorably into a damning despair and suicide. Hamlet, too, may be being portrayed in that sort of condition, trapped between Churches and professions.

At this point, it is worth remembering that nearly all of the cultural materials, the snatches of belief and practice, the almost reflex assumptions, the verbal forms and tics that conjure the old religion into the play are associated with dead fathers and with the claims of the dead on the living; with loss and regret; indeed with despair, madness and suicide. The claims exerted on Hamlet by his father – and whatever the ghost is, for most of the proceedings Hamlet certainly takes it to be his father – almost lead him to madness and suicide. The loss of her father (killed, of course, by her lover) does lead Ophelia to that state and fate. And before she goes, she gives voice to her madness, and the almost unutterable regret for the lost presence, and the linked senses of abandonment and betrayal that have caused it, in the series of ballads discussed by Professor Chapman. Suffused with references to a series of beliefs, practices and stories associated with the old religion, her snatches of song effectively associate the loss of her father and lover with the loss of the old religion.[4]

In thus staging the effects of religious change, one of the things that the play is allowing, perhaps even forcing, its (probably largely Protestant) audience to watch is the appalling, sanity- and soul-threatening effects, the emotional and spiritual shockwaves set off by the fracturing of the links between Elizabethan England and the old religion, and thus – with the loss of purgatory – of the links between the living and the dead. But it is also doing more than that: in its portrayal of Hamlet's progression from doubt and despair to something like assurance, it might also be taken to be staging the salvific benefits of forgetting – of letting the past, and the claims of the dead, go. How these elements in the play were received would, of course, have depended on the religious sensibilities, the different perspectives, personal histories and interpretative frameworks brought to the play by what must have been a religiously heterogeneous audience; an audience whose interpretative options the play keeps open to the very end.

Hamlet, at least on the current reading, is 'converted'. But that raises the question of just what he is converted to. Is his a distinctively 'Protestant' conversion, or even a conversion to Protestantism? If there is anything to the reading essayed above, it is certainly the case that Hamlet has undergone an evangelical conversion – a conversion from unregenerate sinfulness to true Christianity – and that the defining mark thereof is his complete faith in and acceptance of the providence of God. But to argue, on that basis, that this is a distinctively Protestant (still less a Calvinist) conversion might be going a good deal too far. After all, Catholics, as well as Protestants, believed in providence (and indeed predestination); Catholics, as well as Protestants, strove to effect the evangelical conversion of sinners, of merely formal or 'hypocritical' Christians, to a true saving faith, and saw the defining characteristic of such faith in a complete reliance on the grace and providence of God. But we can go further than this in characterizing the nature of Hamlet's conversion.

Predestination

Like no other play since *Richard III*, *Hamlet* not only stages the workings out of the doctrine of predestination, but even the experiences (certainly, in the case of Claudius) of reprobation and (arguably, in the case of Hamlet) of election. The revelation to the audience of the manner in which providence has worked its way through the tangled materials of the plot both to punish sin and to limit its destructive effects upon the world, while saving the elect and damning the reprobate, was central to the structure and workings of the play. Crucial, too, was the play's staging of Hamlet coming to rely completely upon the providence and grace of God. As in any play, the audience can see the general patterning of events, the overall workings and structure of the plot – things that the play presents as the workings of providence (rather, of course, than of the plotting skills of the playwright) – far better than can any of the characters. Given, as it were, a 'God's eye view' of the proceedings from the outside, through a series of soliloquies, the play also confers on the audience the illusion of being able, at crucial points, to see in and through the characters to the motions of the conscience, and indeed almost to the motions of divine grace within. The play is careful not to attempt to stage the moment of conversion, the climacteric point of Hamlet's spiritual development, which, of course, takes place off stage, at sea, under the direct operations of providence and grace.

In short, the play does its best to create the illusion that the audience is watching the interactions between, on the one hand, the workings of the will and purposes of fallen humanity, and, on the other, the prevenient operations of divine providence and divine grace. They can see how providence works its purposes through the sins (just as much as through the virtuous acts) of fallen humanity; working good ends through the unforeseen and wholly unintended effects of the evil impulses and acts not only of the reprobate (like Claudius), but also of the elect (if, that is, Hamlet is elect).

But if Claudius is the archetype of a reprobate soul, in the scene in which he tries and fails to repent, we are being shown such a soul at the tipping point between salvation and damnation. Indeed, if we adopt the (proto-Arminian) view, which held the double decree to be predicated as much upon divine foresight as upon divine sovereignty, what we are being shown here is a soul at the tipping point between election and reprobation.[5]

But what, then, of Hamlet? Can we see him as the balancing archetype of an elect saint, as Jacob to Claudius' Esau, as it were? Perhaps. But if that is the case, what are the grounds for Hamlet's election and salvation? At first sight, the contrast between him and Claudius seems clear enough. Unlike his uncle, Hamlet never puts the pursuit of this-worldly power or felicity before the demands of conscience. As the play makes clear, if he had wanted to do so, the means were readily available; but Hamlet never gets close to using them. Throughout, he is guided by the desire to do what he ought to do; guided by the dictates either of honour or of what he calls 'conscience'. It is just that, until act V, it is never entirely clear to him precisely what 'conscience' does dictate. But even so, in the interim, there can be no doubt that Hamlet struggles mightily against the siren songs of despair and suicide, and the equally destructive force of his own atheistical arguments for summary action. In short, the operation of Hamlet's conscience, his own ethical and spiritual exertions, plays a very large role in setting him apart from the sinner Claudius, and in opening up for him at least the chance of salvation.

However, even when following his conscience as best he can, Hamlet, as any fallen human inevitably must, stumbles into the most (potentially) damning of sins. After his undertaking to send Claudius to hell and his slaughter of Polonius, not only can there be no question of Hamlet meriting or earning salvation, but his own choices have left him confronted with seemingly certain failure, death and (very likely) damnation. As we have seen, the play goes out of its way to show that it is only the (entirely unlooked for and undeserved) intervention of providence that rescues him from a situation created almost entirely by his own folly and presumption, ignorance and sin.

Not only that, but God's providence turns his deepest sins into the occasion of his conversion, indeed of his salvation. For it is only his entirely delusory and blasphemous belief that he can determine Claudius' fate in the next world (as well as in this) that saves him from the potentially damning act of killing the king while he is prayerfully trying to repent. Moreover, it is his murder of Polonius in the next scene that gives him his first inkling of his real spiritual condition, and of the true nature of his calling – not as the ghost's surrogate, the revenger of his father's death, but rather as God's instrument, the 'scourge and minister' of heaven.

In these two scenes, we are being shown three characters – Claudius, Hamlet and Gertrude – poised between damnation and salvation. Refusing the proffered grace, unable or unwilling to take the opportunity to repent given by Hamlet to both of them (in Claudius' case quite inadvertently, and for the worst of reasons), Gertrude and Claudius lapse back into their sins. Hamlet, on the other hand, who, in the flurry of action following the play within a play, had seemed nowhere near a saving repentance, is in fact saved by his own sin – or, rather, his response to his sin in killing Polonius starts to alert him to his real spiritual condition and relationship with the overarching providential purposes of God. That response might be thought to have initiated the process of repentance and enlightenment that culminates not only in his providential rescue at sea, but also in his subsequent gloss upon that deliverance, and his application of that gloss to his own spiritual betterment.

As we have seen, the extraordinary concatenation of events through which his rescue is effected could all have been organized or interpreted under the signs of accident, fortune – or, indeed, of his own political insight or skill. That would have been the atheist's response; and had Hamlet chosen to take that view, he, too, would have refused the offer of grace and redemption. But he does not. Instead, alerted by his murder of Polonius and his currently desperate straits to his complete dependence for safety and salvation on the providence of God, he sees in his rescue an unmistakable sign of God's providential care.

What all these events stage is the inextricable connection – the constant interplay – between the prevenient grace and providence of God, on the one hand, and, on the other, the will, conscience and actions of sinful humanity, represented here in the persons of Claudius, Gertrude and Hamlet. Offered grace, Claudius and Gertrude, in effect, refuse it. Hamlet, on the other hand, continues his insistent (albeit deeply flawed) efforts to save his soul by the conscientious discharge of his obligations to God and man, and is rewarded for his efforts (although not for his achievements, still less for his merits) by the saving interventions of providence. On the one hand, God is shown responding to Hamlet's own exertions, strengthening them, sustaining them, and turning even his lapses – indeed his gravest sins – into further opportunities for spiritual growth and right action; on the other hand, we see Hamlet's dawning realization that he is helpless before his own sin – that even as he continues to strive with all his heart to do the right thing, he must acknowledge his complete dependence on the grace and providence of God. Thus, what distinguishes those two sinners (and murderers), Hamlet and Claudius, from one another is *both* the action of divine providence *and* their own choices and actions. The result is that there can be no doubt that the reprobate Claudius has deserved, indeed chosen, his fate. As for Hamlet, while the elect saint (if that, in fact, is what he turns out to be) might be said to have chosen salvation, he cannot be said to have achieved it by his own efforts (still less, in any obvious sense, to have merited or deserved it).

On this account, then, *Hamlet* can certainly be read and experienced not only as an intensely providentialist, but also as an intensely predestinarian play. But it is by no means clear that it contains an unproblematically Calvinist account of that doctrine. For the play's recounting of the relations between divine providence and the interventions of divine grace, on the one hand, and human free will, on the other, is at least as open to what we might term a proto-Arminian gloss as it is to a Calvinist one – that is to say, to a conditional, as well as to an absolute account of the workings of divine will and the operation of divine grace. Certainly, the play does not stage a version of the workings of divine sovereignty or of the double decree that privileges the entirely gratuitous exercise of divine will, the utter freedom of free grace, and the total perversity and corruption of human nature after the fall. On the contrary, while Hamlet espouses such a view of human nature, he remains mired in despair, tempted by both atheism and the direst and most sinful of acts. Moreover, throughout due place is given to the exercise of human free will, choice and ethical exertion both in Hamlet's case (in the process of conversion) and in Claudius' case (in the process whereby the reprobate come to be damned). As we have seen, the crucial change in Q2 in the last two lines of Claudius' soliloquy at the end of the prayer scene is designed to highlight precisely that fact. As for Hamlet, as Russell M. Hillier observes, he is far from 'a merely passive instrument. His rough hewing coalesces with the divinity shaping his ends.' Having quoted Calvin on the world as God's theatre, Hillier then pursues the metaphor, characterizing Hamlet as 'a player, collaborator and co-producer, as well as a spectator, in the climactic plot of God's theatre'. Whether such a view is entirely compatible with a genuinely Calvinist view of the matter must remain at best an open question.[6] Indeed, the play might be thought to give an account of these issues that stresses rather the cooperation between the workings of the human conscience and will, on the one hand, and the prevenient grace and providence of God, on the other, and thus perhaps to be rather more susceptible to a proto-Arminian gloss than to a Calvinist one.[7]

To see the play opening up the possibility of the sort of tension between the Calvinist and the anti-Calvinist, the absolute and conditional versions of predestination outlined above – indeed, exploiting this tension for its own dramatic purposes – is of course to locate it within an immediately contemporary set of concerns and debates. In 1595/96, Cambridge University had been rocked by a series of disputes on precisely these issues. The assault on Calvinist orthodoxy that began those disputes had, however, started not in the university, but in London and at court. At their height, these controversies had attracted the attention of major courtiers, and had indeed become part of the emergent rivalry between Essex and the Cecils. A central figure here was Lancelot Andrewes. Thanks to the researches of Peter McCullough and Nicholas Tyacke, we know that Andrewes was preaching precisely this sort of doctrine in London throughout the 1590s in a parish, St Andrew's, Holborn, next door to the one where Shakespeare was living for much of this period.[8] These, then, were live issues at the time; and both Shakespeare and the more theologically informed and sophisticated part of his audience may well have been very aware of them.[9] And here it might well be significant that on the title page of the first quarto it was claimed that the play had been recently performed not only in London, but in both the universities. Even if it was not actually written for the sophisticated and theologically informed audiences to be found there, they would certainly have been able to subject it to the sort of engaged theological reading suggested here.

Indeed, Jesse Lander has even suggested that the differences between Q1 and Q2 can be explained (at least partly) by a desire to produce, in Q2, a more elaborated text, likely to appeal to a self-consciously discerning readership, and as such distinct from the more stripped-down version offered in Q1, 'as it hath been diverse times acted by his highness' servants in the city of London'. And as Lander quite rightly observes, one central aspect of that elaboration was a far greater emphasis on things theological, indeed predestinarian. If, as Lander notes, 'Q2's structure centres on Hamlet's character, while Q1 is driven by plot', then 'Q2 spends considerably more time on the problems of providence' and, one might add, of predestination, 'presenting the reader with a topic of theological debate' of very considerable current interest.[10]

The conditional version of predestinarian doctrine that was at least enabled by the play was frequently associated by its critics with popery – and not without reason. It was used by many Catholic theologians as part of their critique of what they took to be the heresies and presumptions of orthodox Calvinism. But by the late 1590s, as the court and Cambridge disputes of 1595/96 showed, these were not (or certainly were no longer) exclusively Catholic doctrines. They were, however, inherently anti-puritan and anti-Calvinist ones, and as such they came to provide the basis for an assault on what the puritans' enemies took to be the spiritual presumption of the godly in asserting not only the certainty of their own salvation, but their capacity to make judgements about the moral condition, spiritual state and likely destination in the next life of others. On this account, the puritans' absolute doctrines of election and reprobation created an overwhelming spiritual arrogance or presumption. Not only did this constitute a blasphemous arrogation of the divine prerogative to tell the saved from the damned, but it represented a claim to insight and authority that was subversive of all pre-existing hierarchy in Church, state and society. From the height of their own purity, the puritans presumed to tell princes and magistrates what to do; to license resistance, even rebellion, against legitimate authority; and to stir up the people against their rulers and superiors of all sorts. That sort of critique of puritan subversion was commonplace among conformist opponents of Presbyterianism (the great majority of whom were themselves formally 'Calvinist'). As part of a broader condemnation of Calvinist doctrine, it was commonplace among Catholics. In the theological disputes of the 1590s, we can see such strains of anti-Calvinist polemic starting to be associated with established strains of anti-puritan polemic, with the resulting toxic mix being deployed for the first time in the conduct of intra-Protestant disputes about predestination.

Here it is worth noting that, in the play, having emerged from simple obedience to the dictates of paternal and Catholic authority (a stage that does not last much beyond the disappearance of the ghost from view), Hamlet passes through a dark night of the soul, obsessed by the pervasive effects of original sin, desperate of his own salvation, tortured by doubt and the temptations of suicide and atheism. As he emerges from this, his conscience apparently resolved by the success of his ploy with *The Murder of Gonzago*, he moves into a period of frenetic activity, during which his behaviour is marked by a fever pitch of (entirely misplaced) self-righteous confidence and zeal. As Rosendale puts it, act III scene iii 'shows our protagonist acting as though he, not God, is setting the terms of revenge' not only in this life, but in the next.[11] Might we discern in all this something like a critique of false (perhaps even of puritan) zeal?[12] With wonderful understatement, Timothy Rosendale writes of Hamlet at times personifying what he terms 'the grave potential danger of a misconstrued sense of commission or election'.[13] It may well not be an accident that, as de Grazia has pointed out, at some of his crucial moments in this mode, Hamlet is also acting out the role of the devil-tinged Antic-vice. It is only after he has passed through this stage and abandoned his antic-mode, brought to his senses by the death of Polonius and by his experience at sea, that Hamlet can achieve something resembling Christian resolution.[14]

Hamlet here is of a piece with Shakespeare's other portraits of puritan hypocrisy and false zeal in, say, *Twelfth Night* and *Measure for Measure*.[15] If – and it is a fairly large 'if' – Richard Dutton is right that Q2 was prepared for performance before King James in 1603/04, then that makes two plays – *Hamlet* and *Measure for Measure* – with a virulently anti-puritan and (in *Hamlet's* case, at least) potentially anti-Calvinist tinge and tone that were written (or rewritten) by Shakespeare for performance at court, at precisely the time when the newly arrived Calvinist king was thought, at least in some circles, to be about to reform the national Church in a decidedly pro-puritan direction.[16]

At this point, a comparison between *Hamlet* and *Julius Caesar* can come to our aid. *Caesar*, of course, is set in a carefully delineated pagan and republican context, and *Hamlet* in a Christian and monarchical one. In the former, we are presented with a picture of what the most ethically sophisticated – the noblest and most virtuous – of pagans could achieve when confronted by something that Brutus describes as incipient tyranny. Famously, the circle around Essex (although by no means only the members of that circle) had developed an interest in Tacitean and stoic thought, hoping to distil from classical (largely Roman republican) sources axioms and principles that could then be used as both an ethical and prudential guide to contemporary political action. If, as I have argued elsewhere,[17] *Caesar* can be read as a warning of the dangers inherent in such a classically inflected approach to contemporary Christian and monarchical politics, then *Hamlet* can be taken to develop that case by showing what adding a Christian dimension to the dictates of pagan philosophy will do.

Here the crucial points of comparison and contrast concern suicide; the Christian notions of an immutable, omnipotent, both perfectly just and perfectly merciful God; divine providence and the afterlife; and the impact on political action of a conscience informed by such beliefs. For even the noblest of Romans – devoid as they were of any idea of a Christian afterlife, their consciences uninformed by any sense of a (Christian) god presiding over events in the world, punishing sin and rewarding virtue – the highest ends and the greatest goods are to be found in this life. The only immortality that concerns such men is fame; and that, of course, is something conferred upon them by their fellow men – indeed, in a republic, by their fellow citizens – for deeds done for the common good. For such men, suicide might well be the noblest response to the slings and arrows of outrageous fortune. Indeed, such a conclusion to a life spent in pursuit of honour and the defence of the commonweal can only add to the immortal fame of the person concerned.[18]

Hamlet, of course, knows a good deal of what the likes of Brutus and Cassius know. His famous encomium on Horatio is also an encapsulation of stoic, Roman virtue [Q2, III, ii, 59–70; F, III, ii, 61–73]. Hamlet, like Brutus, is tempted by the promptings of honour and the political legacy and ethical obligations placed upon him by a noble ancestry. But because he is a Christian, Hamlet knows a good many other things as well. He knows that suicide is wrong, because the Christian God has told him so. Even in the depths of his religious despair, racked by doubt and tempted by atheism, he knows that he has a soul and that there is an afterlife and that he will have to answer there for his actions in this life.[19]

Of course, for a good deal of the play, he is entirely unsure about what that entails; and, as we have seen, in the opening acts, trying to force himself to act like an avenger, he spends rather a lot of time talking to himself like an atheist. However, it is that residual half-formed determination to do the right, Christian thing, to follow the inchoate promptings of 'conscience', that prevents him from having the easy recourse to conspiracy, assassination, popular insurrection, civil war and, indeed, when all else fails, to suicide; all of which come almost as second nature to Brutus and his fellow conspirators, not to mention Laertes. And that crucial restraint, that seemingly fatal hesitation, throws him into a maelstrom of events that are decisively not shaped by his will, intentions or virtues. Seemingly downed by fortune, Hamlet is in fact sustained by providence. This works a radical change in Hamlet, and in that sense he is surely 'converted'. But while there is, after all, a literal sea-change in his affect and demeanour between acts III and V, the play presents us with no definitive moment of choice or transformation. While in the prayer scene, we arguably do get to see the moment when Claudius definitively rejects – or perhaps we should say fails to accept – the offer of divine grace presented to him through the effect of the play within a play and his own afflicted conscience, Shakespeare draws back from identifying (still less from staging) the crucial operations of divine grace working in and on the soul of Hamlet. The play simply does not identify any precise, Paul-on-the-road-to-Damascus moment of conversion.

Thus, we get to watch the beginning of that change in Hamlet's words over the corpse of Polonius in act III, and then we get to see its effects in act V. We are not shown the autonomous action of an irresistible divine grace transforming Hamlet's interior life and persona, as it were, at a stroke. In short, Hamlet's conversion is presented as a process, a series of stages, the crucial moments of which (if such crucial moments there were) we do not see.

Ironically, when he had conferred the typical virtues of the stoic upon his friend in act III, Hamlet himself had lacked almost all of them himself. No one could describe his conduct or affect in the first three acts as that of someone who is not in some sense 'passion's slave' or who has accepted 'fortune's buffets and rewards' with 'equal thanks' [Q2 III, ii, 72, 66–67]. Indeed, we have seen him desperately trying to fit himself into the role of some Senecan revenger, given over wholly to a furor of revenge, and failing miserably in the attempt. But by act V, Hamlet has given up those attempts and thrown off his madness or melancholy. The result is that his character does conform a good deal better to that stoic ideal; but it does so only because he has undergone the Christian conversion outlined above. No longer either passion's or fortune's slave, he is rather providence's instrument. As Maynard Mack puts it, 'the point is not that Hamlet has suddenly become religious; he has been religious all through the play. The point is that he has now learned, and accepted, the boundaries within which human action, human judgement are enclosed.'[20] To quote Rosendale on the same topic:

as disorganized resistance and tension give way to more composed action upon Hamlet's new understanding, the action of obedience or cooperation with a transcendent and good deity proves more productive than the pseudo-action of paralytic self-assertion . . . In previous acts, Hamlet had thought of God as an unwanted commissioner, a frightening judge, a forbidding obstruction to desired oblivion, then as a rubber stamp to his own desires.

But now in the fifth act, 'divinity becomes . . . a saving and comforting ally to which he is at last able to entrust and subordinate his own actions'.[21]

Hamlet's is thus now something like a Christian stoicism; his real-enough human virtues – the sort of virtues to which, even without knowledge of the gospel, the best or noblest pagans (like Brutus) could aspire – have now been inflected, indeed animated and enabled, by a version of Christian resolution. Hamlet can now both accept and collaborate in his fate (or rather, in the role chosen for him by providence); and by so doing, he – in marked contrast to Brutus and Cassius – saves not only the Danish state, but also very probably his own soul as well.

As Alan Sinfield has observed, this is a version of Christianity devoid of (either Calvinist or puritan) zeal. Rather it is 'a state of grace' (if that indeed is what it is) that contains within itself many of the stoic virtues for which Hamlet had earlier praised Horatio (and which Brutus and Cassius attribute both to themselves and to one another with such unbecoming enthusiasm). To quote Sinfield,

> the intricate working out of events obliges Hamlet to recognize the precise control of the Protestant God but he does not find in himself the joyful response theologians anticipated. Calvin distinguished Stoic patience, which accepts what happens because 'so it must be', and Christian, which cheerfully embraces God's will 'with calm and grateful minds' . . . Hamlet contemplates God's intimate and pervasive direction of the universe with only stoic patience.[22]

Robert G. Armstrong was surely making what I take to be essentially the same point, when he observed that the 'state which Hamlet is in at the end of the play' – a state which Armstrong, for one, does want to call 'a state of grace' – 'bears little relationship to the psychological condition of the elect as it is usually imagined in Christian theology'. This is because 'repentance and faith, the two great clues to a Christian's spiritual condition', are all but absent from Hamlet's last scenes.[23] What we have here is a state of what we might term 'Christian resolution', decidedly different from puritan or Calvinist notions of zeal or assurance. Indeed, I would argue that we are confronted here with a decidedly a-confessional version of mere Christianity.

Starting out in a milieu that is wholly Catholic, Hamlet experiences a crisis of faith that is, in many ways, Protestant in its central features and feelings, and even becomes puritan in its excesses of false zeal and blasphemous spiritual presumption, before ending up with something like a model of true Christianity. In the process, many of the forms and feelings of the old religion have been sloughed off. But they have scarcely been repudiated or discarded in disgust. There is no trace of anti-popish denunciation or of iconoclastic revulsion here. Rather, as we have seen, the mood of Ophelia's evocation of the old religion is elegiac, filled with tenderness and regret; much like the feelings of many an audience or critic towards Ophelia herself, in fact. But, as Chapman has argued, Ophelia's songs and snatches, her old lauds, all serve to articulate a sense of unappeasable and irreversible (religious) loss. Again, the origins of Hamlet's own conscientious scruples lie in what a contemporary Protestant audience would surely have seen as superstitious, indeed popish, beliefs about purgatory and the nature and necessity of a good death. But if Hamlet starts off obsessed with his obligations to a dead father suffering the torments of purgatory, by act V, the ghost, along with its nexus of purgatorial and popish associations, has been lost from view, and the father is no longer the cynosure of action or identity.[24]

As in both *Titus* and *Julius Caesar*, the binary opposites in and through which the mere Christianity achieved by Hamlet at play's end is defined and justified are not those between one form of Christian profession or confessional identity and another, and certainly not those between Protestantism and Catholicism. Rather they are those between what we might term 'religion' and 'politics'; between, on the one hand, the pursuit of salvation in the next life and, on the other, the pursuit, through the conventional methods of political manoeuvre, of purely secular goods and ends in this; between the claims of 'conscience' and those of 'honour' and 'passion'. Offered such a set of starkly binary options, there was only one choice for an Elizabethan audience to make, only one side for early modern Christians of all stripes to be on.

The (relative) indeterminacy of the play's treatment of the old religion is reflected in the similar (relative) indeterminacy with which it surrounds its treatment of the topic of predestination. All of which, of course, parallels a similar (relative) indeterminacy left swirling around the question of Hamlet's salvation, or indeed the status of the ghost.[25] By giving the spectator or reader ample material with which to construct almost equally compelling accounts of the ghost as an agent of God or of the devil, of Hamlet as either saved or damned, and indeed of the interactions between human free will and divine grace through which his fate has been determined, the play opens itself up to a range of widely divergent readings.

Given the extremely delicate nature of the political, confessional and theological issues that the play was staging, one could argue that such studied indeterminacy might be thought to have been the price of doing this sort of business on the public stage at all. But since overtly Protestant and explicitly Calvinist answers to those questions would have run entirely with the grain of current orthodoxy, the fact that the play consistently refuses to explicitly endorse them must in itself be significant. Then again, such open-ended ambiguity was probably essential if the sympathies and attention of what would always already have been a religiously and politically, an ideologically and socially, mixed audience were to be effectively engaged. And insofar as the play was performing the ideological work that I am imputing to it here – that is to say, moving persons of a variety of different religious persuasions and religio-political outlooks or affiliations towards, in religion, an a-confessional version of 'mere Christianity' and, in politics, towards a particular view of the current conjuncture – of the very recent past, present and immediate future – then such indeterminacy, the availability of the play for a variety of widely divergent and mutually contradictory interpretations, was essential to its very being and purpose. For allowing people to come at the play from different perspectives, to engage with it at different levels and to enter into its processes from very different starting points, could be seen as but the beginning of a process of persuasion that the play hoped to work upon its audience.

Conclusion
Pagan/Catholic/Protestant/Christian

In conclusion, let us return to the comparison between *Hamlet* and *Titus* with which we started. As I argued above, *Titus* operated almost as an exercise in natural theology – a thought experiment set not in a state of nature, but in an elaborately evoked pre-Christian Rome. The play sets up a revenge-based primal scene, within which, through the dialectical interactions between the religion-based violence of the Andronici and the revenge-based violence of their enemies, the relations between revenge, religion and resistance are examined. An a-confessional version of mere Christianity emerges (at least in outline) as a sort of third term, produced out of the clash between the 'cruel, irreligious' and absurdly over-literal piety of the Andronici, and the sheer atheistical malignity of their enemies. The great confessional conflicts of the age are evoked through the annihilating religious violence and the attendant discourses of martyrdom and persecution at the heart of the action. However, the master division, the great contrast or divide, through which that play's moral argument is advanced is not that between Catholicism and Protestantism, but rather a triangulation between atheism, paganism and the outlines of an emergently proto-Christian position – a position embodied, with delicious irony, in the black, bastard child produced by the adulterous union between Tamora and Aaron, and saved from death by the combined forces of Lucius' inhumanly severe, Roman, indeed (as Aaron has it) 'popish' conscience and Aaron's atavistic drive to save the life of his infant son at (almost literally) any cost. As Nick Moschovakis has argued, the result is a moral lesson drawn from a barbaric and pre-Christian Rome that the new 'iron age' created by the confessional conflicts and religion- and revenge-based persecutions of the post-Reformation desperately needs.[1]

At this point, we might usefully compare the relationship between *Titus Andronicus* and *Richard III* to that between *Hamlet* and *Julius Caesar*. In both cases, Shakespeare was responding to the central issues of tyranny and resistance; and he was doing so by writing two plays: one set in a pagan Rome and the other in a Christian and monarchical polity (in the first case England, in the second Denmark). In the first instance, the English history play (*Richard III*) was suffused with the sorts of prophecies, omens, dreams and pseudo-miracles that contemporaries associated with the intervention in human affairs of divine providence, while the play set in pagan Rome was entirely devoid of such elements. Indeed, as we have seen, the audience's noses were positively rubbed in the absence of such signs: events and outcomes that, in other plays and tracts, would have cried out for providential interpretation were given elaborately secular explanations – 'natural causes', we might say.

While the two plays addressed essentially the same tyranny-centred problematic, and staged essentially the same sort of events – crudely the deposition of a tyrant through internal plotting, external invasion, regicide and usurpation – what takes place in *Richard III* under the umbrella of the providential is rerun, in *Titus*, as a self-conscious piece of human planning and self-help. The Roman setting allowed the most radical potentials, left implicit in the English history play, to be rendered explicit.

In the case of *Hamlet* and *Caesar*, the relation between the Roman play and the Christian is reversed. Now it is the Roman play that is suffused with the providential and the prophetic, and the point becomes the incapacity of its pagan protagonists to read the signs aright and to respond accordingly; as compared to the ability of the Christian protagonist of *Hamlet* to do precisely that and, in so doing, to avoid both political stratagems and the obsession with this-worldly means and ends that lead Brutus, Cassius and Laertes to their differently dreadful ends, and that bring ruin to the Roman, if not to the Danish, state.

In many ways, *Hamlet* can be read as a reworking and recombining of many of the central themes and tropes of *Titus* and of *Richard III*. Both *Hamlet* and *Titus* take place in elective monarchies. Both feature a central protagonist intent on revenge. Alerted to the existence of a primordial crime or sin at the centre of the political establishment, both Titus and Hamlet delay, waiting on events until they know the real truth of the matter. Both feign and/or experience madness, and use their supposed mental distress as a pretext to taunt and test their enemies with gnomic and anticly threatening statements. Both plays end in elaborately scripted tableaux, through which the tyrant and his party are hoist with their own petard, justice is meted out and the revenger achieves his revenge, before himself being killed. Both end with the murder of the king and the reintroduction of a new monarch from abroad at the head of a foreign army, who is immediately elected king. In both cases the transition to a new regime is eased by broadcasting the story of the secret crimes and tyrannies of the past regime to the people, emphasizing the wrongs visited upon the revenger, and therefore the justice of his revenge.

The affinities between the two plays are heightened by the ways in which, at the outset, *Hamlet* looks like just another bloody revenge tragedy: a play that is just like not only the lost earlier version of *Hamlet*, but also Shakespeare's own famously successful exercise in the same genre, *Titus Andronicus*.

But, as we have seen, having elicited and toyed with the narrative expectations attached to that genre, *Hamlet* turns out to be a very different sort of play. In the pagan Rome evoked in *Titus*, providence has no role, and revenge and resolution are worked entirely through the agency, the cunning and the virtue of human protagonists. In the Christian context of *Hamlet*, essentially the same outcomes are shown to be not the product of the plots and conspiracies of Hamlet (or indeed of any other human agent). Rather, they are worked through the interaction between Hamlet's (deeply imperfect) efforts to respond to the contrary promptings of conscience, honour and revenge and the (at times) irruptive interventions of providence into human affairs. The complex choreography whereby the last scene uses one sinful stratagem to punish another, leaving the stage littered with corpses and the state ripe for re-foundation, is the work not (as in *Titus*) of the ingenuity of the revenger, but rather of a series of coincidences, accidents and unintended consequences. Just like the bizarre series of events that rescued Hamlet from Claudius' plot to kill him, these radically unlikely contingencies are surely expressly designed to appear to an Elizabethan audience as the interventions of providence. Such a view, of course, immediately reduces Hamlet to the role, if not of innocent bystander, then at least of the unwitting (albeit not unwilling) agent or instrument of higher powers. Thus is the radicalism of *Titus*, with its apparent endorsement of elective monarchy and the right to resist, its apparent vindication of resistance and regicide as just and justifiable responses to tyranny and persecution, at least partially forsworn, in the heavily Christianized and providentialized treatment accorded to essentially the same themes, tropes and outcomes in *Hamlet*.

The point emerges still more clearly when we compare *Hamlet* with *Richard III*. In *2* and *3 Henry VI*, Shakespeare and his collaborators had produced an account of political and moral declination, of the loss – through weak rule, excessive female influence and noble faction – of the constraints and benefits of monarchical legitimacy. The consequence is the descent of the whole society not merely into civil war, but into moral and political chaos. The resulting narrative was largely secular in its account of cause and effect, its explanation of how things got from here to there. However, when, at the close of *3 Henry VI* and throughout *Richard III*, the time came to pull the rabbit of monarchical order and legitimacy out of the hat of civil war, usurpation and tyranny, Shakespeare had immediate recourse not merely to the irruptive influence of divine providence, but to the determining course of the pendant doctrine of predestination to drive the action and explain the outcome.

This was done primarily through the demonic figure of Richard III, a character presented as so evil that, for all that he was a regnant king (and after the death of his brother and his nephews, the obvious legitimate successor to the throne), his removal was an act, the legitimacy of which no one could doubt. Richard is presented as the epitome of the reprobate soul, a man so sunk in evil as to be unable to repent. From the outset, Richard is shown not merely tempted, but determined, to plunge down the chain of sins that will lead him to murder, usurpation and tyranny, and thence to death, damnation and hell. Having thus characterized Richard, the play then enlists the direct testimony of a series of prophecies, visions and ghostly visitations, which confirm the extent of Richard's evil and the righteousness and legitimacy of his removal from power – an outcome which is presented not so much as an accomplishment of human political virtue or military prowess, as a direct product of providence itself.

Just as in *Hamlet*, through a series of soliloquies, the inner workings of the central protagonist's (in Richard's case, reprobate) soul are revealed to the audience. They are also, of course, known to God; and by giving the audience such a 'God's eye view' of both the inside and the outside of the action, the play creates an irresistible sense that Richard's death at Bosworth, his deposition from the throne and replacement as king by Richmond, are not so much the human acts of rebellion and regime change that they in fact are, as the consummation of God's will and justice, the working-out, through events in the world, of his purposes, as reprobates like Richard are brought to their deserved end, sin is punished and order restored.

Hamlet does many of the same things. Again, the play presents its audience with the workings of God's providential and predestinarian purposes, working inexorably, through the punishment of sin and the preservation of order in a fallen world, towards the salvation of his elect and the damnation of the reprobate. Like Richard III, Hamlet retains many of the features of the vice and addresses the audience in lengthy soliloquies.[2] As Weimann observes, Richard 'is presented as the image of a royal person in history, but at the same time he remains the punning, self-expressive, ambidexter, directing, in continuous contact with the audience, his own murderous rise to the throne'.[3] Hamlet uses something of the same antic mode to 'release himself from his own role of the Prince of Denmark: with the help of popular proverb and aside he momentarily disassociates himself from the illusion of the world of the court and revives a late ritual capacity for reckless sport and social criticism' – and, one might add, for spiritually self-conscious comment upon the significance of his own actions and the operations of providence.[4]

Hamlet's soliloquies are anything but laudatory accounts of his own Machiavellian plotting, or commentaries upon the folly of his various dupes and victims. Rather they are either self-lacerating assaults upon his failure to either plot or act in what he takes to be the appropriately violent and political manner, or commentaries upon or expressions of what he takes to be his current spiritual condition. Of course, even Richard III had ended up in that mode and again, just like *Richard III*, through a series of soliloquies – Hamlet's, of course, but also Claudius' crucial lucubration on repentance – *Hamlet* shows the workings of the conscience, and perhaps even suggests (but does not attempt actively to stage) the internal motions of the spirit. Thus, Shakespeare uses what Weimann's analysis has revealed as long-standing elements in 'the popular tradition', centred on the figure of the Vice, to articulate modishly contemporary predestinarian concerns and tropes. As de Grazia has shown, he also used the demonic characteristics traditionally adhering to the figure of the Vice (who often ends the play being dragged off to hell by the devil) to alert the audience to, and to heighten the suspense surrounding, the question of Hamlet's ultimate destination in heaven or in hell.

As de Grazia points out, the status of this question as the central organizing concern of the play would have been far more pressingly obvious to Elizabethan readers and audiences than it has been subsequently to their more 'secular minded' modern counterparts. As she puts it, 'stage devils may have survived the Reformation, but not the closing of the theatres'. We might broaden the observation to include the religious concerns of the post-Reformation period, more generally construed – and more particularly, the preoccupation with predestination and the nature and experience of election and reprobation. All of which, by the early eighteenth century, had disappeared from the purview of both the drama and of literary criticism, to give way, as far as the interpretation of *Hamlet* is concerned, to what de Grazia terms first 'neo-classical judgement' and then 'psychological analysis'.[5]

While Richard's and Claudius' status as reprobates is no secret, the question of Hamlet's spiritual state and ultimate destiny hangs in the balance for far longer. At the close, however, the point being made is essentially the same: by coming to believe or accept that they have been watching the internal effects and operations of the divine decrees – in Richard's and Claudius' cases, certainly that of reprobation; perhaps rather less certainly, in Hamlet's that of election – the audience has been led to accede to the conclusion that the violent and intensely political acts with which both plays close – the killing of a king and the diversion of the succession to claimants (Richmond and Fortinbras) who enter the scene at the head of foreign armies, armed with dynastic claims of less than overwhelming strength – are, in fact, not what they might otherwise seem. Not subversive and sinful acts of regicide, rebellion and usurpation, but rather the providential ends of narratives plotted not by human political agents in pursuit of their own variously sinful, vengeful, this-worldly, purposes and interests, but rather by the will and providence of God himself. But while, at the end of *Richard III*, providence is being used to effect a sort of moral and political sleight of hand, to make events of one sort seem or signify as though they are events of an altogether different type, the same is not true of *Hamlet*, where it is precisely Hamlet's lack of agency, his total reliance on and faith in providence, that is shown enabling a resolution that is, in the end, brought about almost entirely by the hidden hand of God's providence rather than by any conscious intention or purposive act on Hamlet's part. All of which represents the sharpest of contrasts to *Titus*.

Whereas the confessional issue is necessarily altogether absent from *Julius Caesar*, and is only implicitly present in *Titus*, it is all over *Hamlet* – put there by the purgatorial pedigree claimed for itself by the ghost, and indeed by the Catholic imagery that clings to Ophelia, both in life and in death. As we have seen, religious despair, demonic possession and suicide were all topics linked both to predestinarian soteriological crisis and to the doubt and apostasy that could attend movement from one confessional identity to another. In explicitly raising those issues, and indeed in drawing a great deal of its emotional energy from their resolution, *Hamlet* certainly seems to move definitively from an intercessory, purgatory- and lineage-centred style of religion (and indeed notion of honour and the self) to a far more individualistic, providence- and predestination-centred view. The play thus stages the course of a quintessentially post-Reformation form of religious change and spiritual development. But, as I have been arguing here, whether that progression involved a move from Catholicism to Protestantism, or whether the view of predestination encoded in the play is a Calvinist or proto-Arminian one are questions that the play quite deliberately refuses to resolve.

The result, it seems to me, is a decidedly and distinctively post-Reformation style of Christianity, a heavily providential Christianized stoicism (or perhaps an equally providential stoicized Christianity) with an ideal of Christian 'resolution', rather than of Calvinist 'assurance', somewhere near its heart. Composed, but not equally, of classical pagan Roman and Christian elements, the synthesis offered in *Hamlet* attempts to transcend or contain the confessional divisions of the age within a vision of mere Christianity that is not a straightforward *via media* – a splitting of the difference between Protestantism and Catholicism – but is rather a self-consciously dialectical product of the clash between pagan and Christian values – or, in the terms set by Titus, between the over-literal legalism, the 'cruel and irreligious piety' of the Andronici and the atavistic, revenge-based malignity and atheism of Tamora and Aaron – applied to the experience and polarities of post-Reformation religious change and conflict.

Thus, Peter McCullough has concluded that 'the impulse to define the play as either broadly Catholic or broadly Protestant flies in the face of its own relentless effort to assert both possibilities in a dramatological process that cancels the signifying power of each'. That is, of course, true enough, and very nicely put; but then McCullough goes on to claim that 'discussions of religion in *Hamlet* have been disproportionately concerned with two things . . . the supernatural status of the ghost . . . and the degree and nature of the predestinarianism' implied in the play. It is quite true that, insofar as the attention given to those topics has been predicated on the assumption that, having raised certain questions about them, the play can then be expected – under the right sort of interrogation – to yield definitive answers, then that attention has indeed ended up leading all too many critics down a blind alley. But, given the importance and prominence at certain crucial points in the play of both the status and veracity of the ghost and of certain predestinarian and providential themes and language, not to mention the very obvious connection between those topics and questions of confessional allegiance and religious identity of the most pressingly contemporary sort, that attention can hardly be said to be simply 'disproportionate'. Since the play positively invites its audience and readers to ask those questions, subsequent critics can scarcely be blamed for responding to those very obvious – one might even say, rather heavy-handed – prompts. I think the play poses those questions because it wants its audiences and readers to confront a situation in which – in the play, certainly, and perhaps even in the world – none of them can be resolved definitively. Religious analyses of the play have to go through these topics, not around them.[6]

The Christianized *Romanitas* staged in *Hamlet* rules out of court the notions of political virtue and honour that animate the main protagonists of both *Titus* and *Caesar*. These are almost entirely secular and civic, laced (particularly in Titus' case) with lineage-based considerations of personal and family honour, and in both instances centred on service to the (Roman) state and, in the overtly republican setting of *Julius Caesar,* to the public or common good. The only notion of immortality on offer is that of an immortal fame won in the service of the state; and in both, suicide is a perfectly viable option for a truly honourable and virtuous man. In *Hamlet*, any civic humanist or 'republican' talk of service to the state or the common good is conspicuous by its total absence; and lineage-centred notions of honour, while intermittently prominent in the play – in the revenge talk of young Hamlet in the first half of the play, and of Laertes in its later stages – fall away by the end, revealed as so much soul-destroying detritus by the play's denouement.

In *Titus*, the Andronici's private pursuit of revenge against Tamora and her allies in effect doubles as, indeed morphs into, the rescue of the Roman state from tyranny.

The foreign invasion led by Lucius and the Goths combines with Titus' domestic insurrection and Lucius' act of tyrannicide to produce, in the election of the resonantly named Lucius as emperor, a fresh start for Rome. But while, in *Titus Andronicus*, the Andronici manage, after a fashion, to emulate the state-saving or state-founding achievements of Marcus Junius Brutus, in *Julius Caesar*, the efforts of a second Brutus to do the same fail ignominiously. In contrast, Hamlet, like the Andronici, succeeds in converting what starts out as an atavistic, essentially private, lineage-based impulse towards revenge into a search for – indeed, into the achievement of – a sort of state-saving doing of justice. In the process, both Titus and Hamlet die the death; but while the Christian Hamlet might well be thought to have achieved eternal salvation, even a contemporary with the most charitable of attitudes towards the spiritual fate of pious pagans would surely have found it hard to have entertained any such hopes for Titus.

While in *Titus*, justice is done (and is shown to be done) through the political planning and righteous political violence of the Andronici, in *Hamlet*, human planning and the recourse to the conventional political means of conspiracy, popular rising and foreign invasion that such planning usually involves have had nothing whatsoever to do with it. In *Hamlet*, the outcome is wholly providential: *both* because it has been brought about through the sorts of coincidence, happenstance and wholly unintended consequence that myriad tracts, sermons and treatises had taught contemporaries to regard as quintessentially providential, *and* because the central instrument used by providence to work its beneficent way has, throughout the play, been shown gradually coming to a full consciousness of his status as, in his own words, the 'scourge and minister' of God. In other words, quintessentially political ends have been achieved, but without recourse to anything remotely resembling conventional political means. The pursuit of private revenge has been transmuted into the doing of public justice and the salvation of the state – and perhaps (remarkably – and uniquely in the plays normally discussed under the rubric of revenge tragedies) that of the revenger himself. And all this has been achieved through the efforts of the main protagonist to follow the dictates of what he insistently refers to as 'conscience'.

I have argued elsewhere that the result may well represent a fantasy-happy (or indeed an admonitory-happy) ending to the political crisis that had just concluded in the tragic farce of the Essex rebellion.[7] On that reading, the differences between the two plays can, in part, be explained by the very different political conjunctures to which they were responding.[8] In the case of *Titus*, the structuring circumstances were provided by the notional succession crisis of the early 1590s, a crisis *in potentia* to which texts like Robert Parsons' *Philopater* tract, or, slightly later, his *Conference about the Next Succession* were a response and of which they formed a major constituent part. In the case of *Hamlet*, the circumstances were provided by the climacteric point of the Essex project. However, such political contingencies are pretty much completely incidental to the current analysis, which has been concerned with what we might term the intellectual and emotional substance of these plays, organized, as they were, around structurally almost identical, but substantively very different, treatments of the relations between revenge, resistance and religion.

Such an approach enables us to watch Shakespeare using the genre of the revenge tragedy to think through, to aggregate and disaggregate, combine and recombine the linked topics of religious change and confessional conflict, political and religious violence, usurpation and persecution, tyranny and resistance at a time when those issues were at their most pressing for his contemporaries.

But Shakespeare was doing more than that in these plays; he was, as it were, conducting a series of thought experiments about how a moral (and political) agent, faced with a very similarly structured political situation and politico-moral dilemma would respond – first, acting on the premises and beliefs available to a pagan Roman; and second, armed with certain basic assumptions about the immortal soul and an omnipotent God available only to a Christian, even one as mixed up as Hamlet appears to be in the early and middle stages of the play.

In both cases, out of the internal dynamics of the plot – in the first instance, one driven entirely by the intentions and perceptions of the characters, unaided by the intervention of either divine grace or providence; in the second, one shaped by the influences and inputs of both – the central protagonists find themselves in (or better yet, find their way to) a religio-political space very different from the one they were occupying at the beginning of the play. While, if there is anything to the preceding analysis, both plays gesture strongly at recent events and current religious and confessional divisions, changes and conflicts, the emergent positions reached at play's end are by no means the product of any sort of compromise between (or synthesis of) Catholicism and Protestantism. On the contrary, the dominant binary oppositions in play were those between religion and atheism, Christianity and various versions of Roman paganism. If both end with strong gestures towards an a-confessional 'mere Christianity', that vision is portrayed as the result of a life-and-death struggle between those opposing forces rather than between anything that resembles some sort of compromise or accommodation between Catholicism and Protestantism.

The result of those clashes is not, therefore, any sort of *via media*, some carefully calibrated middle ground between two extremes, but is rather a synthesis, created out of the violent clash between two mutually exclusive opposites. Admittedly, as with all true syntheses, the final position contained elements from both sides. In *Titus*, the final synthesis was composed in almost equal part of the Andronici's heartless obedience to the demands of conscience, as their style of 'cruel and irreligious piety' constructed it, and the human sympathy evidenced by Aaron's tigerish determination to preserve the life of his son at all costs. In *Hamlet*, the final synthesis was composed of a version of stoic virtue, with a distinctively Christian submission to the promptings and dictates of an omnipotent God; a subjection enacted by a human agent acutely aware of his own sinfulness and fallibility, of his possession of an immortal soul and of his complete dependence on a God who was both absolutely just and absolutely merciful.

The dialectical forces in play here emerge more clearly if we compare *Hamlet* not only with *Titus*, but with the other Roman play that immediately preceded it in Shakespeare's oeuvre, *Julius Caesar*. For there, a series of Romans, in possession of the highest forms of wisdom and virtue of which pagan republicans were capable, were confronted by a political dilemma not dissimilar to Hamlet's. Taking an entirely secular, political view of their situation, they threw themselves into precipitate, violent action – and failed disastrously. Not only did they not preserve the state, but they plunged the Roman world into civil war and an emergent tyranny. Moreover, as the (Christian) audience knew (but the (pagan) characters could not), in attempting to seal their immortal fame by choosing death rather than dishonour, Brutus and Cassius were, in fact, committing the damningly ignominious sin of self-murder. These, of course, were all outcomes and fates with which the emergently Christian Hamlet toyed, but in the end (triumphantly) managed to avoid. He did so by ignoring the siren song of direct, political action, prompted by the wholly secular (and pagan) ideals of honour, virtue, service to the state and just revenge, all of which had been staged with such effectiveness and force in *Titus* and *Julius Caesar*, and pursued in *Hamlet* with such disastrous consequences by Laertes. Instead, by following the initially inchoate and half-formed demands of conscience, Hamlet managed to arrive at the Christian stoicism which he embodies at play's end.

This enabled him, for the first time in the play, to combine a properly honourable sense of himself as Hamlet the Dane with submission to the dictates of his conscience and the purposes of an omnipotent, both perfectly just and perfectly merciful, Christian God.[9] He is rewarded with a revenge as comprehensively appropriate as that plotted with such ruthless attention to detail by Titus, without having to resort to any sort of plotting or purposive action. For at the end, as the gravedigger has already explained, Hamlet does not so much come to the water as the water comes to him: he does not act, but rather reacts to the malign plotting of Claudius and Laertes.

In this way, he is able to achieve a form of revenge quite as extreme as anything that he had pictured to himself as he stood over Claudius at prayer. At play's end, just as he had fantasized in the prayer scene, Hamlet is able to dispatch a wholly unrepentant usurper, regicide and now multiple murderer, in the midst of the foulest imaginable sin. He does so having given said sinner ample opportunity to confront his guilt and repent – something which we have seen Claudius (and to a lesser extent Gertrude) comprehensively failing (in effect, refusing) to do. Unlike Titus, Hamlet is enabled to do all this by circumstances that have nothing to do with the workings of his own will, and everything to do with the dynamics of divine providence and justice. Thus, Hamlet does not so much achieve a longed-for revenge, as do a form of justice, recognizable as such to God, man and, perhaps most importantly, the audience. He saves not only the state from usurpation and tyranny, but also (perhaps) his own soul from the damnation that would surely have awaited him had he achieved the sort of revenge that he has spent a good deal of the play trying to goad himself into exacting.

While the version of Christianity with which we are confronted at the end of the play is heavily providential and predestinarian, the precise ways in which we are supposed to see the workings of the divine decrees, and the autonomous action of divine grace, interacting with human agency and choice are left open. That is an issue which the audience – or at least its more theologically acute members – must decide for themselves. How they do so will determine a great deal of where they set themselves in the religious controversies, and among the contending religious identities, of the day.

For all the intensity (and, at least in the case of *Hamlet*, the tenderness) with which the two plays evoke the old faith, neither can be said (unequivocally) to regret, still less to resist, its passing. Admittedly, for most of the play the virtue and piety of the Andronici are the only versions of those qualities on offer. However, at the very outset their best efforts to satisfy both the gods and the shades of their ancestors are outed by Tamora as 'cruel and irreligious'. Subsequently, for all Tamora's unreliability as a witness, the play not only establishes the truth of that assertion, but also provides a sketch of the sort of piety and virtue that would be necessary if cycles of annihilating violence – of the sort that it has just set before its audience with such relish – are to be averted in the future. While undoubtedly Christian, Aaron's description of Lucius' conscience as defectively 'popish', leaves little doubt that the resulting value system is unlikely to be Catholic in any narrowly confessional sense of the term.

I have argued that these two plays are uniquely concerned with the troubled relations between revenge, resistance and religion; a nexus of concerns that lay at the heart of what one might term the post-Reformation dilemma: that is to say, during an era of religious war and political assassination, in which – for all contemporaries' fervent efforts to distinguish both practically and in theory between 'politics' and 'religion' – religious identity and allegiance, dynastic, 'geo-political' and confessional conflicts and tensions became inextricably mixed. While Elizabethan England was integrally connected to that explosive mix of forces, England itself was spared the sort of gut-wrenching violence, the moral and political meltdown, visited upon France and parts of the Low Countries throughout the latter half of the sixteenth century. While propagandists for, and supporters of, the Elizabethan regime trumpeted the (relative) peace enjoyed by England under the rule of Gloriana, Elizabethan Englishmen and women could never be sure that the exigencies of religious division, an unsettled succession and European war would not, at any moment, visit such a fate upon them. As I have argued elsewhere, throughout the 1590s, Shakespeare wrote a whole series of plays using both English and Roman history to stage those concerns and address the practical and theoretical issues raised by them.[10]

While the two plays under discussion here can be analysed within that same frame of reference, the matter at the centre of both of them transcends such a narrowly or exclusively political register. Here the crucial religious – we might say, existential – issues at the heart of the relation between resistance and revenge, set in the context of confessional conflict and religious change, are at the very centre of the action. I think it is profitable, as I have argued above, to see *Titus* as a first stab at this topic, and *Hamlet* as a second go-round, written at a different point in the Elizabethan *fin de siècle*, using a plot with some of the same characteristics and narrative tropes, differently arranged and assembled to address what were recognizably the same set of topics.

Neither play resolves those issues. Nor should we expect them to. These, after all, were plays – not treatises or sermons or pamphlets. They were designed to engage the interests and anxieties of their audiences, and thus to put 'bums on seats' and turn an honest penny – not to convert viewers and readers to one or other of the available sets of ideological responses either to their own circumstances or to the current religio-political conjuncture. Since the ideological questions at stake remained controversial – indeed, decidedly dangerous to discuss in public in all but the most anodyne ways – we should not expect any play (and especially not one by the notoriously elusive William Shakespeare) directly to address or resolve them in anything but the most conventional way. Hence the bog-standard Tudor myth-making with which one of Shakespeare's earlier treatments of some of those issues, *Richard III*, at least appears to conclude.[11]

But more importantly, the questions at issue here – When does (or even could) revenge become resistance, that is to say cease being an essentially private act and become a public doing of justice, directed at the protection of those ultimately public entities, the commonweal or true religion? How could contemporaries negotiate the religious conflicts and changes through which they were living with both their bodies and souls intact? How could the irreparable rent in the social and moral fabric created either by tyranny or resistance be mended? Could those doing the mending, i.e. the perpetrators of revenge, or even of resistance, hope to go to heaven? – were all, in some sense, if not irresolvable, then subject, in debates conducted both between and among Protestants and Catholics, to such contest and controversy as not to be susceptible of any stable or consensual answer. And, of course, neither of these plays answers them. Rather, they stage various versions of these questions in ways that invite (one might almost say require) the reader or viewer, in responding to the action of the play, to provide an answer for him or herself. Thence, from the emotional and intellectual energies thus released, I would argue, proceeds their continuing hold over modern audiences.

For we are dealing here with a play, not a treatise or a piece of polemic; and it is perfectly possible to read, watch, produce or perform this play without knowing or caring about any of the issues dealt with, or any of the arguments advanced in this book. Plays do things in performance that are not always apparent on the page, and one reason why I have taken obsessively to watching every and any performance of an early modern play that I can attend is that one regularly sees things in performance that I, at least, do not get from any number of readings of the text.

Hamlet and *Titus* are not puzzles to be solved, but plays to be imaginatively inhabited, watched, performed and enjoyed. And it must be admitted that my first intention in writing this book has not been to further any of those purposes, but rather to use the plays to think about the period in which they were first produced. This has been intended primarily as a work of history. But having said that, an attempt to explicate the contemporary concerns, the modes of thought and feeling in and out of which a play was first written and performed might reveal something about the sources of the emotional energy, the suspense and fascination that it has been able, over the centuries, to elicit from a range of very different audiences and performers.

Notes

Introduction

1. For the translation and printing of Senecan tragedy, see Jessica Winston, 'Early "English Seneca": From "coterie" translation to the popular stage', in Eric Dodson-Robinson (ed.), *Brill's Companion to the Reception of Senecan Tragedy: Scholarly, theatrical and literary reception*, Leiden and Boston, 2016, pp. 174–202.

2. There has long been debate among scholars about the Senecan origin of the revenge tragedy and, in particular, of Shakespeare's versions thereof. For a recent summary, see Patrick Gray, 'Shakespeare versus Seneca: Competing visions of human dignity', in Dodson-Robinson (ed.), *Brill's Companion to the Reception of Senecan Tragedy*, pp. 203–30. Also see Dodson-Robinson, ' "By a brother's hand": Betrayal and brotherhood in Shakespeare's *Hamlet* and Senecan tragedy', in Kristina Mendicino and Betiel Wasihun (eds), *Playing False: Representations of betrayal*, Bern, 2013, pp. 81–102; the main purport of both of these articles is that, while Seneca was a pagan Roman stoic, Shakespeare was some sort of Elizabethan Christian. Also see Gordon Braden, 'Senecan tragedy and the Renaissance', *Illinois Classical Studies*, 9 (1984), pp. 277–92; Curtis Perry, 'Seneca and the modernity of *Hamlet*', *Illinois Classical Studies*, 40 (2015), pp. 407–29.

3. I stress this relation to the murder pamphlets, rather than, say, to certain central strands in Senecan tragedy, not because I wish to advance the pamphlets as sources for the plays in any conventional sense of the term, but because, as a ubiquitous presence among the cheap print of the day, the pamphlets give us a certain access to the narrative expectations and interpretative assumptions of the play's first audiences. This is not because the pamphlets alone would have inculcated such expectations in the audience, but rather because the pamphlets themselves were refracting, appropriating and applying established proverbial wisdom, 'common knowledge', of a sort that dated back at least to the high middle ages. The murder pamphlets, then, were scarcely original: they reflected and organized an existing body of assumption and conventional wisdom. For instance, the saw that 'murder will out' was of medieval provenance and can be found twice in Chaucer. However, in at least some examples of the genre, the providential, and even at times predestinarian, aspects of the pamphlets had been given new meaning and significance by the religious changes of the Reformation and the reformed doxa of the day. The pamphlets provided Shakespeare's first audiences, not to mention Shakespeare and us, with a compressed template of the assumptions surrounding murder, and both the legal and religious proceedings that ought to attend and effect its detection and punishment. Those assumptions – in particular the linked spheres of activity of the minister and the magistrate (that is to say, of the relevant secular and spiritual authorities) in setting the world to rights and bringing the felon to light, to justice and to repentance – provide a crucial context for the play. More specifically, they provide one of the main sets of narrative expectation which the play was at once eliciting, toying with and (ultimately) satisfying.

4. On Shakespeare's plays as, at times, a site of confrontation or exchange between a pagan *Romanitas* and Christianity, see Patrick Gray, 'Choosing between shame and guilt: *Macbeth, Othello, Hamlet*

and *King Lear*', in A.D. Cousins and Daniel Derrin (eds), *Shakespeare and the Soliloquy in Early Modern English Drama*, Cambridge, 2018, pp. 105–18, and Dodson-Robinson, '"By a brother's hand"'. Also see Patrick Gray, *Shakespeare and the Fall of the Roman Republic: Selfhood, stoicism and civil war*, Edinburgh, 2019, especially the Introduction. On issues of providence and predestination, see Robert G. Armstrong, *Shakespeare and the Mysteries of God's Judgment*, Athens, GA, 1976, and now Timothy Rosendale, *Theology and Agency in Early Modern Literature*, Cambridge, 2018. Both books are outstanding, but remarkably Armstrong's has fallen so far down the memory hole as not to earn so much as a mention in Rosendale's text or bibliography.

5. Michael Neill, 'The designs of *Titus Andronicus*', in M. Neill and D. Schalwyk (eds), *The Oxford Handbook of Shakespearean Tragedy*, Oxford, 2016, pp. 339–57, quotation at p. 341.

6. Colin Burrow, *Shakespeare and Classical Antiquity*, Oxford, 2013, pp. 113, 114.

7. See Brian Vickers, *Shakespeare, Co-author: A historical study of five collaborative plays*, Oxford, 2002. For an extended discussion of the authorship question, in the light of Vickers' and others' work, see Jonathan Bate's revised Arden edition of *Titus Andronicus* (London, 2018), pp. 123–39. Given the avidity with which Shakespeare cannibalized, appropriated and adapted existing plays in the repertoire while writing his own, the issue of collaboration, even of a sort of co-authorship, might be thought to pertain to plays other than those where a specific co-author can be identified. Perhaps the best extant example is *King John*, where the extent of Shakespeare's reliance on a former play on the same subject, *The Troublesome Reign of King John* – a play now thought to be almost certainly by his former collaborator, Peele – is so extreme that Peele might almost be thought to be a 'co-author' of Shakespeare's version. In his revised Arden edition of *Titus*, Jonathan Bate goes so far as to suggest that, using the *King John* material as a model, *Titus*, as it has come down to us, may well have been 'Shakespeare's reworking of an earlier play (either complete or incomplete) by Peele' (Bate, *Revised Arden edition*, 2018, p. 133).

8. See Lisa Parmelee, *Good Newes from Fraunce: French anti-league propaganda in late Elizabethan England*, Rochester, NY, 1996.

9. On this, see Peter Lake, *Bad Queen Bess? Libels, secret histories and the politics of publicity in the reign of Queen Elizabeth I*, Oxford, 2016, p. 478.

10. John Bossy, *Christianity in the West, 1400–1800*, Oxford, 1985; for a worked example of these forces operating in one place and time, see Keith Brown, *The Bloodfeud in Scotland, 1573–1625: Violence, justice and politics in an early modern society*, Edinburgh, 1986.

11. John Bossy (ed.), *Disputes and Settlements: Law and human relations in the west*, Cambridge, 1983; Bossy, *Christianity in the West*; Brown, *Bloodfeud in Scotland*; Mervyn James, *Society, Politics and Culture: Studies in early modern England*, Cambridge, 1986; Lawrence Stone, *The Crisis of the Aristocracy, 1558–1641*, Oxford, 1965. Out of a vast literature, for the earlier period see Paul Hyams, *Rancor and Reconciliation in Medieval England*, Ithaca, NY, 2003.

12. Peter Lake and Michael Questier, *The Antichrist's Lewd Hat: Protestants, papists and players in post-Reformation England*, London, 2002, chapters 1–3; Malcolm Gaskill, *Crime and Mentalities in Early Modern England*, Cambridge, 2000.

13. Natalie Zemon Davies, 'The rites of violence', reprinted in her *Society and Culture in Early Modern France: Eight essays*, Stanford, CA, 1975. Also see Stuart Carroll, 'The rights of violence' and the other essays collected in G. Murdoch, P. Roberts and A. Spicer (eds), *Ritual and Violence: Natalie Zemon Davies and early modern France*, Oxford, 2012.

14. Susan Doran and Paulina Kewes (eds), *Doubtful and Dangerous: The question of succession in late Elizabethan England*, Manchester, 2014.

15. Lake and Questier, *The Antichrist's Lewd Hat*, chapter 7.

16. The strongest statements of this view of the queen are to be found in William Allen, *An Admonition to the Nobility and People of England* (1588) and Nicholas Sander, *De origine ac progressu Schismatis Anglicani* (1585).

17. Helen Gardner, 'The historical approach to *Hamlet*', in J. Jump (ed.), *Shakespeare: Hamlet, a casebook*, London, 1968, p. 138. Also see Stuart M. Kurland, '*Hamlet* and the Scottish succession', *Studies in English Literature 1500–1900*, 34 (1994), p. 282.

18. For such a view of resistance, see George Buchanan's *De iure regni apud Scotos* and Robert Parsons' *Conference about the Next Succession*, which both make this point, the first using the rhetoric of 'the people', the second that of 'the commonwealth'. On this, see my article, 'The king (the queen) and

the Jesuit: James Stuart's *True law of free monarchies* in context / s', *Transactions of the Royal Historical Society* 6th series, 14 (2004), pp. 243–60.

19. This is the argument of the second half of his tract of 1584, *A True Sincere and Modest Defence of English Catholics*, reprinted with William Cecil's *The Execution of Justice in England*, to which it is a reply in an edition by Robert M. Kingdon, published by Cornel University Press for the Folger Shakespeare Library in 1965.

20. See Lake, *Bad Queen Bess?*, chapter 10, esp. pp. 241–45. Also see *Martin Mar-Sixtus* (1591).

21. Such, for instance, is the logic of James VI's *The True Law of Free Monarchies*, which argues that tyrants will almost inevitably come to a bad end in this world, as well as the next, but which also affirms that any form of resistance to a regnant monarch is an extremely grave sin.

22. Winston, 'Early "English Seneca"', pp. 183–87; Lake, *Bad Queen Bess?*, pp. 19, 29–30.

23. Linda Woodbridge, *English Revenge Drama: Money, resistance, equality*, Cambridge, 2010, pp. 161, 163, 131. For a more balanced assessment, see Perry Curtis, 'Seneca and English political culture', in Malcolm Smuts (ed.), *The Oxford Handbook of the Age of Shakespeare*, Oxford, 2016, pp. 306–21. Also see Perry, 'Seneca and the modernity of *Hamlet*'.

24. Cf. Paulina Kewes, '"I ask your voice and your suffrages": The bogus Rome of Peele and Shakespeare's *Titus Andronicus*', *Review of Politics*, 78 (2016), pp. 551–70.

Chapter 1

1. Heather James, *Shakespeare's Troy*, Cambridge, 1997, chapter 2. Recently Peter Culhane has emphasized the origins of many of the play's central themes in Livy. See his 'Livy and *Titus Andronicus*', *English*, 55 (2006), pp. 1–13.

2. T.J.B. Spencer, 'Shakespeare and the Elizabethan Romans', *Shakespeare Survey*, 10 (1957), pp. 27–38, quotes at p. 32.

3. James, *Society, politics and culture*.

4. J.E. Neale, 'Peter Wentworth', *English Historical Review*, 39 (1924), pp. 36–54, 175–205; 'Peter Wentworth', *Oxford Dictionary of National Biography* (*ODNB*); Patrick Collinson, 'The monarchical republic of Queen Elizabeth I', in his *Elizabethan Essays*, London, 1994, pp. 31–57; Patrick Collinson, 'The Elizabethan exclusion crisis', in his *This England: Essays on the English nation and commonwealth in the sixteenth century*, Manchester, 2011. Now see Paulina Kewes, 'The puritan, the Jesuit and the Jacobean succession', in Doran and Kewes (eds), *Doubtful and Dangerous*, chapter 3.

5. Collinson, 'Monarchical republic', 'Elizabethan exclusion crisis'. Now see Lake, *Bad Queen Bess?*

6. For a reading of *Titus* against the Elizabethan succession problem, see Barbara L. Parker, *Plato's Republic and Shakespeare's Rome*, Newark, NJ, 2004, pp. 111–16.

7. Christopher Crosbie, 'Fixing moderation: *Titus Andronicus* and the Aristotelian determination of value', *Shakespeare Quarterly*, 58 (2007), pp. 147–73, quote at p. 157.

8. Megan Elizabeth Allen, '"Titus unkind": Shakespeare's revision of Virgil's Aeneas in *Titus Andronicus*', in P. Holland (ed.), *Shakespeare Survey 70: Creating Shakespeare*, Cambridge, 2017, pp. 228–39, quotations at pp. 233, 236.

9. Hence Megan Elizabeth Allen is surely wrong when she claims that Titus acts out of 'vengeance' brought on by 'grief' (Allen, '"Titus unkind"', pp. 238, 236) for in Shakespeare's play Titus sacrifices Alarbus with a formal *pietas*, as the discharge of an obligation owed to the shades of his dead sons, not as a passion-fuelled act of vengeance of the sort ascribed to Aeneas by Virgil's poem.

10. Parker, *Plato's Republic and Shakespeare's Rome*, pp. 117–18.

11. Danielle St Hilaire, 'Allusion and sacrifice in *Titus Andronicus*', *Studies in English Literature 1500–1900*, 49 (2009), pp. 311–31.

12. For which see Lake and Questier, *The Antichrist's Lewd Hat*, chapter 7.

13. For an extended discussion, see James, *Shakespeare's Troy*, pp. 64–69.

14. Eugene Waith, 'The metamorphosis of violence in *Titus Andronicus*', *Shakespeare Survey*, 10 (1957), pp. 39–49, quote at p. 47.

15. John Klause, 'Politics, heresy and martyrdom in Shakespeare's sonnet 124 and *Titus Andronicus*', in James Schiffer (ed.), *Shakespeare's Sonnets: Critical essays*, New York, 1999, pp. 219–40, quotes at

pp. 232–33. To take the point, we do not have to assert that Shakespeare must have read Southwell's verses – although as Klause wants to argue, he may well have done – merely that the works of both authors partake directly of the same linguistic and affective universe. Andreas Hofele makes the association between the horrific violence portrayed in the play and the real events played out on the scaffold. He also makes an explicit link between the style of dehumanizing violence found in the play and martyrdom, but the form of martyrdom he chooses to discuss is that of Protestants, or rather proto-Protestants – his main example is John Hus – by Catholics, as recounted by John Foxe. He makes no mention of the far more obvious and directly contemporary referent, the martyrdom of Catholics by the Protestant Elizabethan regime, which, with its dismemberment and disembowelling of the victim's body and the subsequent boiling and public display of the resulting body parts, fits rather more closely both with the events staged and the imagery deployed in the play and with Hofele's concern with cannibalism as a way of figuring the dehumanizing effects of extreme violence. See his *Stage, Stake and Scaffold*, Oxford, 2011, esp. chapter 4, 'Cannibal-Animal: Figurations of the (in)human in Montaigne, Foxe and Shakespearean revenge tragedy'.

16. Klause, 'Politics, heresy and martyrdom', p. 225.
17. Lorna Hutson, 'Rethinking the "Spectacle of the Scaffold": Juridical epistemologies and English revenge tragedy', *Representations*, 89 (2005), pp. 30–58. As will become clear, the following discussion is much indebted to this article.
18. Klause, 'Politics, heresy and martyrdom', pp. 219–40.
19. As Klause and Barbara Parker both observe, if the name Pius was Virgilian, it was also papal. Pius V was the pope who excommunicated Elizabeth. Klause, 'Politics, heresy and martyrdom', p. 234; Parker, *Plato's Republic and Shakespeare's Rome*, pp. 116–17.
20. See, Vernon Guy Dickson, ' "A pattern, precedent and lively warrant": Emulation, rhetoric and cruel propriety in *Titus Andronicus*', *Renaissance Quarterly*, 62 (2009), pp. 376–409.
21. Hutson, 'Rethinking the "Spectacle of the Scaffold" '.
22. Through a series of verbal echoes between Southwell's *Humble Supplication* and Shakespeare's sonnet 124, many of which seem to me to be anything but conclusive, Klause makes the case that Shakespeare knew this book. He also establishes another set of what seem to me rather closer verbal echoes between another of Southwell's tracts, *An Epistle of Comfort* (printed on a secret Catholic press in 1587), and Marcus' speech on discovering the mutilated Lavinia in 2.4. He concludes that 'the effect of Southwell's writings in *Titus* is of such extent and quality . . . that one must imagine Shakespeare deliberately seeking them out for inspiration'. However that may be, these were precisely the sorts of text to be found in the Catholic loyalist circles around the earl of Southampton, whose patronage Shakespeare seems to have been seeking and enjoying in the early 1590s. See Klause, 'Politics, heresy and martyrdom', pp. 232–33.
23. Francis Yates, *Astraea: The imperial theme in the sixteenth century*, London, 1977, pp. 29–87, 'Queen Elizabeth I as Astraea'.
24. Jonathan Bate (ed.), *Titus Andronicus*, The Arden Shakespeare, London, 1995, p. 21.

Chapter 2

1. The account of the Catholic tracts is based on my *Bad Queen Bess?* For the analysis of the *Henry VI* plays on which these remarks are based, see Peter Lake, *How Shakespeare Put Politics on the Stage: Power and succession in the history plays*, London and New Haven, 2016, parts II and III.
2. William Allen, *Admonition to the Nobility and People of England* (1588).
3. Carol Levine, *'The Heart and Stomach of a King': Elizabeth I and the politics of sex and power*, Philadelphia, PA, 2013.
4. On this see the *ODNB* article on Walsingham.
5. This strand of Catholic commentary and critique is expounded at considerable length in my *Bad Queen Bess?*
6. James, *Shakespeare's Troy*, pp. 48, 57–58. This chapter owes a great deal to a number of discussions with Professor James.
7. Coppelia Kahn, *Roman Shakespeare: Warriors, wounds and women*, London, 1997, p. 55.
8. Ibid., p. 104.

9. Indeed, Christopher Crosbie has gone so far as to claim that 'from the outset, his reaction to the crimes against his family – for all its intensity – represents an almost organic sense of proportionality and an Aristotelian temperance of anger, preparing for his revenge to appear as a redefined moderation within extreme circumstances'. Under the most extreme of provocations, Titus displays neither an 'excessive passivity that never rises to anger', nor a propensity to seek revenge at the first provocation. And when he does move to secure his revenge, as Crosbie observes, his actions are based on a 'substructure of moderation beneath the grotesque appearance of Titus's revenge', a finely judged 'proportionality and Aristotelian temperance of anger' (Crosbie, 'Fixing moderation', pp. 163, 170). For a very different view, see Gary Kuchar, 'Decorum and the politics of ceremony', in A. Marotti and K. Jackson (eds), *Shakespeare and Religion*, South Bend, IN, 2011, pp. 46–78, p. 75, n. 16, who cites Titus' slaughter of Lavinia to argue that rather than 'advocating an Aristotelian ethics, the play performs a *reductio ad absurdum* of it'. One might conclude that even if Crosbie is right and there is an element of considered moderation in Titus' revenge, under such circumstances, even moderation can only produce the most cruel and extreme of outcomes.

10. Crosbie, 'Fixing moderation', p. 170.

11. Kahn, *Roman Shakespeare*, p. 71. There seems no reason to follow Kahn in her attempt to associate the former, political plot exclusively with Lucius, and the latter, private revenge plot exclusively with Titus. It is true that Titus kills Tamora while Lucius dispatches Saturninus, but they do so in a scenario entirely scripted by Titus. We are surely dealing here with a coordinated political manoeuvre comprised of Titus' domestic conspiracy and Lucius' invasion from abroad.

Chapter 3

1. Lake, *How Shakespeare Put Politics on the Stage*, chapters 6 and 7.

2. Hutson, 'Rethinking the "Spectacle of the Scaffold"'.

3. *The Most Cruel and Bloody Murder Committed by an Innkeeper's Wife Called Annis Dell and Her Son, George Dell* (London, 1606) and *The Horrible Murder of a Young Boy of Three Years of Age* (London, 1606). For discussion of these tracts, see Lake and Questier, *The Antichrist's Lewd Hat*, pp. 16–7, 29.

4. St Hilaire, 'Allusion and sacrifice'.

5. See Lake and Questier, *The Antichrist's Lewd Hat*, pp. 41–64.

6. Thus, it is surely not an accident that in Timothy Rosendale's brilliant account – *Theology and Agency in Early Modern Literature* – chapter 3 (on revenge tragedy) leapfrogs from a discussion of *The Spanish Tragedy* to one of *Hamlet*. *Titus* is nowhere to be seen.

7. Not only that, but to the genuinely informed viewer or reader the play announces as much. For, as Culhane points out, the ode of Horace appended, with such menace, to Titus' gift of arrows to Chiron and Demetrius has what he calls a 'third meaning', because in the ode itself 'the naïve stoic sentiment that just men are protected in this life is gently mocked'. Titus, then, is not waiting for providence to rescue him, but is rather now taking matters into his own hands. Culhane, 'Livy and *Titus Andronicus*', p. 10.

8. Felicity Heal, 'What can King Lucius do for you? The Reformation and the Early British Church', *English Historical Review*, 120 (2005), pp. 593–614; Felicity Heal, 'Appropriating history: Catholic and Protestant polemics and the national past', *Huntington Library Quarterly*, 68 (2005), pp. 109–32.

9. Cf. Crosbie, 'Fixing moderation', pp. 161–62.

10. See, for instance, James, *Shakespeare's Troy*, chapter 3; St Hilaire, 'Allusion and sacrifice'; Culhane, 'Livy and *Titus Andronicus*'; Dickson, '"A pattern, precedent and lively warrant"'.

11. St Hilaire, 'Allusion and sacrifice', pp. 315–16.

12. Ibid., p. 316; Dickson, '"A pattern, precedent and lively warrant"'.

13. St Hilaire, 'Allusion and sacrifice', pp. 318–19.

14. Culhane, 'Livy and *Titus Andronicus*', p. 6.

15. Culhane observes that 'the revulsion that Shakespeare's Livian hero inspires when he most vigorously pursues Roman honour' presents 'a challenge to the broader desire in early modern England to adopt Roman literature in the service of Christian instruction' and both Culhane and Dickson have argued that one of the things at stake here is a critique of *Romanitas* as a fit source of moral and political wisdom for a Christian age (Culhane, 'Livy and *Titus Andronicus*', p. 11). Given

what I take to be the play's association of the Andronici not only with pagan *Romanitas*, but also with Roman Catholicism, the warnings inscribed in the play go to the heart of the religious, as well as the cultural, politics of the day.

16. While I do not agree with all of his conclusions, the following reading of the significance of Christianity for the argument of the play and of the play's address of immediately contemporary Christian concerns and politics is deeply indebted to Nicholas Moschovakis, ' "Irreligious piety" and Christian history: Persecution as pagan anachronism in *Titus Andronicus*', *Shakespeare Quarterly*, 53 (2002), pp. 460–86. Indeed, Nick played a crucial role in persuading me that *Titus Andronicus* was central to my wider interpretative purposes.

17. An iron age figured and framed by pagan *Romanitas*, but also, on the argument being pursued here, through the association of the Andronici with Catholicism and of their persecutors with the Elizabethan regime, directly transferable to the horrors of post-Reformation England.

18. St Hilaire, 'Allusion and sacrifice', p. 325.

19. John Jewel, *The Works of John Jewel*, ed. John Ayre, Cambridge, The Parker Society, 1847, vol. 2, p. 452.

20. Peter Lake, 'Anti-popery: The structure of prejudice', in Richard Cust and Ann Hughes (eds), *Conflict in Early Stuart England*, Basingstoke, 1987, and Glyn Parry, *A Protestant Vision: William Harrison and the Reformation of Elizabethan England*, Cambridge, 1987.

21. Parker, *Plato's Republic and Shakespeare's Rome*, pp. 118–19.

22. Crosbie, 'Fixing moderation'. Crosbie systematically fails to take such issues into consideration, and consequently tends simply to endorse the justice and moderation of the Andronici. This seems mistaken. For while critics who simply take against Titus do indeed fail to recognize that he is doing a sort of justice, and that his actions are in some sense 'moderate' accommodations to the most extreme of circumstances, it can scarcely be said that the play wants us simply to endorse his actions as, in any straightforward sense, virtuous or pious. Rather it takes a great deal of its energies from the difficulties it imposes upon us in trying to reach or sustain such a verdict. The audience is surely supposed to be horrified by Titus' actions, even as they thrill to the appalling violence being staged before them, acknowledge the retributory symmetries that constitute the play's ending and accept the necessity and justice of the violent overthrow of the tyranny of Saturninus, Tamora and Aaron. To quote Megan Elizabeth Allen, the play 'repeatedly portrays a character insistently associated with *pietas* performing impious acts in the name of piety' (Allen, ' "Titus unkind" ', p. 234).

23. Moschovakis, ' "Irreligious piety" '.

24. See, for instance, Jeffrey Knapp, *Shakespeare's Tribe: Church, nation and theater in renaissance England*, Chicago, IL, 2002. Also see David Kastan, *Will to Believe: Shakespeare and religion*, Oxford, 2014.

25. Ethan Shagan, *The Rule of Moderation*, Cambridge, 2012.

26. Crosbie, 'Fixing moderation', p. 148.

Chapter 4

1. Magreta de Grazia, *Hamlet without Hamlet*, Cambridge, 2007, p. 51.

2. Ibid., pp. 59, 60.

3. For a pioneering reading of the play in terms of issues of succession and the right to resist, see Andrew Hadfield, 'The power and rights of the crown in *Hamlet* and *King Lear*: "The King – the King's to blame" ', *Review of English Studies*, 54 (2003), pp. 566–86, esp. pp. 566–77. Hadfield's *locus classicus* for arguments about resistance is the *Vindiciae contra tyrannos* and his conclusion is somewhat downbeat: while *Hamlet* 'demands to be read in terms of the political anxieties of (very) late Elizabethan England', it 'provides no obvious answers to the variety of political questions it raises' (pp. 576–77).

4. See, for instance, James Shapiro, *1599: A year in the life of William Shakespeare*, London, 2005; Kurland, '*Hamlet* and the Scottish succession', pp. 279–300; Lake, 'The king (the queen) and the Jesuit'; Helen Stafford, *James VI of Scotland and the Throne of England*, New York, 1940.

5. For which see Lake, *Bad Queen Bess?*, chapter 5.

6. Gardner, 'The historical approach to *Hamlet*', p.138; Kurland, '*Hamlet* and the Scottish succession', p. 282.

7. Behind these pressingly contemporary resonances there lurked the tragic history of the House of Stuart, which had seen James' mother marry the murderer of his father with a haste so indecent that it had precipitated her own removal from the Scottish throne – a removal accompanied, indeed to an extent legitimated, by appeals to James, the rightful successor, to avenge the death of his father. On this, see Roland Mushat Frye, *The Renaissance Hamlet*, Princeton, NJ, 1984, pp. 29–37. You do not have to agree with Lillian Winstanley who, in her *Hamlet and the Scottish Succession*, Cambridge, 1921, reads the play as an elaborate allegory based on these events, or even to view them as a 'source' for the play, in order to appreciate how such parallels might have lent it an immediate political resonance. To quote Frye, 'they do provide some pertinent guidance to us in our search for Elizabethan responses to the kinds of conflicts and problems' dramatized in the play (p. 37). Also see the discussion in Robin Headlam Wells, *Shakespeare on Masculinity*, Cambridge, 2000, pp. 62–63, which draws heavily on Frye.

8. For a brilliant account of *Hamlet* in this context, and a necessarily speculative argument that Q2 represents a rewritten version of the play produced for court performance under James I, see Richard Dutton, '*Hamlet* and succession', in Doran and Kewes (eds), *Doubtful and Dangerous*, pp. 173–91.

9. de Grazia, *Hamlet without Hamlet*, p. 51, citing Daniel Woolf, *The Idea of History in Tudor and Stuart England*, Toronto, 1990, pp. 16–17.

10. de Grazia, *Hamlet without Hamlet*.

11. Ibid., pp. 72–73.

12. Rosendale, *Theology and Agency*, p. 127.

13. Rhodri Lewis, *Hamlet and the Vision of Darkness*, Princeton, NJ, 2017, chapter 2, 'Hamlet, hunting and the nature of things'.

14. For an account of Polonius as the quintessential bad counsellor, figured as both an 'ineffective humanist' and, as it turns out, an equally ineffectual 'Machiavellian' flatterer, see Joanne Paul, 'The best counsellors are the dead: Counsel and Shakespeare's *Hamlet*', *Renaissance Studies*, 30 (2015), pp. 646–65.

15. For an account of the narrative structure of the murder pamphlets – and indeed of the criminal, judicial and punitive proceedings they described – see Lake and Questier, *The Antichrist's Lewd Hat*, section I, esp. chapter I.

16. On the link between 'punishing the usurper and protecting the state' and thus on Hamlet's public role as revenger, see the important article by Grace Tiffany, 'Hamlet, reconciliation and the just state', *Renascence*, 58 (2005), pp. 111–33.

17. Robert Weimann, *Shakespeare and the Popular Tradition in the Theater*, Baltimore, MD, 1978, pp. 217–18.

18. See Peter Lake and Michael Questier, *All Hail to the Archpriest: Confessional conflict, toleration, and the politics of publicity in post-Reformation England*, Oxford, 2019.

19. See the excellent discussion of contemporary, both Catholic and Protestant, attitudes to ghosts in Eleanor Prosser, *Hamlet and Revenge*, Stanford, CA, 1971, chapters iv and v. Prosser's analysis is somewhat vitiated by what may be her excessive certainty that contemporaries would have regarded the ghost as a devil. (For a perhaps overly aggressive critique along these lines, see P. Mercer, *Hamlet and the Acting of Revenge*, Basingstoke, 1987, pp. 132–33, 136–37.) What I think Prosser shows is the range of contemporary opinions which the play uses to stage a series of questions, of which one of the least important becomes the precise status of the ghost. To be fair, Prosser at times acknowledges as much: 'given the perspective of the entire play, we can discern probabilities; but in the fleeting perspective of the dramatic moment we find only questions. If we could unequivocally pronounce the Ghost a demon and its command a damnable temptation, the tragedy would be destroyed. We cannot and as a result are caught up in Hamlet's dilemma. The warnings have not made us pull back and condemn his vow to take revenge; they have made us aware of the intolerable alternatives he faces' (p. 143). My point is that at least some of the questions a contemporary audience would have been left with were confessional, and therefore, in the broadest sense, also political issues, raised by the ghost's self-proclaimed pedigree as a soul on night release from purgatory.

20. Stuart Clark, *Vanities of the Eye: Vision in early modern European culture*, Oxford, 2009, p. 211, quoting Ludwig Lavater, *Of Ghostes*, p. 140.

21. Clark, *Vanities of the Eye*, p. 211, quoting Adam Tanner, *Disputatio de angelis*, in his *Diversi tractatus*, p. 76.

22. Ibid., p. 217.

23. K.V. Thomas, *Religion and the Decline of Magic*, London, 1973, p. 704.

24. Ibid.; Peter Marshall, *Beliefs and the Dead in Reformation England*, Oxford, 2002, p. 261.

25. Malcolm Gaskill, *Crime and Mentalities in Early Modern England*, Cambridge, 2000, pp. 217–19, 231–34.

26. Marshall, *Beliefs and the Dead*, pp. 257–58.

27. Prosser, *Hamlet and Revenge*, p. 105.

28. Thomas, *Religion and the Decline of Magic*, p. 703.

29. Clark, *Vanities of the Eye*, pp. 59, 143, citing Samuel Harsnet, *A Declaration of Egregious Popish Impostures* (1603) in F.W. Brownlow, *Shakespeare, Harsnet and the Devils of Denham*, London, 1993, p. 304.

30. Timothy Bright, *A Treatise of Melancholy*, London, 1586, p. 192.

31. See, for instance, the comments of Mercer (*Hamlet and the Acting of Revenge*, p. 205) that 'the performance of revenge is used to combine a crafty silence about the thing that really matters with a covert expression of the passion it arouses' and de Grazia (*Hamlet without Hamlet*, p. 89), 'the persona he assumes licenses him to express his resentment, not openly but in the "wild and whirling worlds" (I, v, 139) of the Antic, the madman who even in the court of law is not held accountable for the meaning of his words'.

32. On the subject of religious melancholy in the post-Reformation period, see especially Jeremy Schmidt, *Melancholy and the Care of the Soul: Religion, moral philosophy and madness in early modern England*, Aldershot, 2007, and Angus Gowland, *The Worlds of Renaissance Melancholy*, Cambridge, 2006, esp. chapter 3.

33. Rosendale, *Theology and Agency*, p. 131.

Chapter 5

1. John Lee, *Shakespeare's Hamlet and the Controversies of Self*, Oxford, 2000, p. 206.

2. Lewis, *Hamlet and the Vision of Darkness*.

3. See, for example, L.B. Campbell, 'Theories of revenge in Renaissance England', *Modern Philology*, 28 (1931); Fredson Bowers, 'The audience and the revenger of Elizabethan England', *Studies in Philology*, 31 (1934); Prosser, *Hamlet and Revenge*; Mercer, *Hamlet and the Acting of Revenge*.

4. As de Grazia summarizes the situation, in revenge tragedies, 'once the command to revenge was issued . . . it was only a matter of time before it was satisfied . . . the challenge for the dramatist was to find some way to fill the interval' (de Grazia, *Hamlet without Hamlet*, p. 174).

5. William Empson, *Essays on Shakespeare*, Cambridge, 1986, pp. 82, 92. Cf. the remarks of Graham Bradshaw in his *Shakespeare's Skepticism*, Ithaca, NY, 1987: 'when Hamlet begins to protest against the role he is being forced to play, what I have called the "Pirandellian effect" would be accentuated by memories of the old play: this overwhelmingly original prince had been grafted onto, and is indeed trapped within, a framework provided by what had been "Hamlet without the prince"' (p. 112). In an analysis of *Hamlet* set entirely within the framework of the 'revenge tragedy' (*Hamlet and the Acting of Revenge*), Peter Mercer demonstrates the extent to which *Hamlet* was in fact no such thing, remarking at one point on 'the persistent failure of the structure of revenge to impose its archaic reality upon the world of the play' (p. 204).

6. See Lake and Questier, *The Antichrist's Lewd Hat*, section I.

7. I owe this point to the kindness of András Kiséry.

8. See Lake and Questier, *The Antichrist's Lewd Hat*, section I, esp. chapter 5.

9. On this, see Patrick Collinson, ' "A magazine of religious patterns": An Erasmian topic transposed in English Protestantism', in his *Godly People*, London, 1983, pp. 499–525.

10. Edward Dering, *Certain Godly and Very Comfortable Letters*, Middelburg, 1590, and then included in M. Dering's works (London, 1597); Thomas Wilcox, *A Discourse Touching the Doctrine of Doubting*, Cambridge, 1598. For a brief discussion of Dering's activities as a doctor of the soul, see Patrick Collinson, 'Godly Master Dering', in his *Godly People*, pp. 289–324.

11. For an expansion of this point and an account of the sort of puritan practical divinity being preached and also circulating in manuscript in the 1580s and 1590s, see P. Lake, *Moderate Puritans and the Elizabethan Church*, Cambridge, 1982, chapter 7, 'Puritan practical divinity'; an account based, for the most part, on various manuscript sermon notes and the commonplace book of Abdias Ashton. For Greenham, see Eric Carlson and Kenneth Parker, *'Practical Divinity': The works and life of Reverend Richard Greenham*, Aldershot, 1998. For Perkins, see Ian Breward (ed.), *The Works of William Perkins*, Abingdon, 1970. As Breward points out, Perkins' works, many of them, if not pointed towards the bottom end of the market, then certainly proclaiming themselves intended for the edification of 'the ignorant', started to appear in print during his own lifetime in the 1590s. See, among other titles, his *A Case of Conscience, the greatest that ever was, how a man may know whether he be a son of God or no*, first published in Edinburgh by the puritan printer William Waldegrave in 1592, and then in London in 1592 and in Cambridge in 1595; *A Golden Chain, or the description of theology containing the order of the causes of salvation and damnation, according to God's word*, first printed in London in 1591 and then in Cambridge in 1592, 1595 and 1597; *A Grain of Mustard Seed, or the least measure of grace that is or can be effectual to salvation*, London, 1597; *A Treatise Tending unto a Declaration whether a man be in the estate of damnation or in the estate of grace, and, if he be in the first, how he may in time come out of it; if he be in the second, how he may discern it and persevere in the same, to the end*, printed in London in 1590, 1591 and 1595.

12. For Wilcox see the *ODNB* article by Patrick Collinson. For the practical divinity of Cartwright, see his *A Commentary upon the Epistle of Saint Paul Written to the Colossians. Preached by Thomas Cartwright, and now published for the further use of the Church of God*, London, 1612.

13. For Foxe as a doctor of the soul and an exorcist, see Thomas Freeman, 'Demons, deviance and defiance: John Darrell and the politics of exorcism in late Elizabethan England', in Peter Lake and Michael Questier (eds), *Conformity and Orthodoxy in the English Church, c.1560–1660*, Woodbridge, 2000, pp. 34–63.

14. Lake, *Moderate Puritans*, chapter 7.

15. M. Questier, *Conversion, Politics and Religion in England, 1580–1625*, Cambridge, 1996.

16. Michael MacDonald, ' "The fearefull estate of Francis Spira": Narrative, identity, and emotion in early modern England', *Journal of British Studies*, 31 (1992), pp. 32–61.

17. Alison Chapman, 'Ophelia's "Old Lauds": Madness and hagiography in *Hamlet*', *Medieval and Renaissance Drama in England*, 20 (2007), pp. 111–35, quotation at pp. 128–29. Chapman is citing Harold Jenkins' Arden edition of *Hamlet*, p. 377, nn. 10–20, and Frye, *The Renaissance Hamlet*, p. 363, n. 15.

18. MacDonald, ' "The fearefull estate of Francis Spira" '.

19. Bright, *A Treatise of Melancholy*, pp. 225, 227–28.

20. Ibid., p. 237.

21. Ibid., pp. 187, 190; epistle dedicatory, sig. *iii r.-v.

22. Ibid., epistle dedicatory, sig. *iii r.-v. and p. 190.

23. Ibid., p. 235.

24. See Gowland, *The Worlds of Renaissance Melancholy*, pp. 175–76, and more generally Schmidt, *Melancholy and the Care of the Soul*, chapter 3, 'Melancholy in Calvinist England'.

25. Schmidt, *Melancholy and the Care of the Soul*, p. 48.

26. As Bright pointed out, Satan could only act as God's agent or scourge: 'the devil hath power, where God permitteth him, over the minds and judgement and wills of the reprobate and wicked and may also in such sort tempt the faithful servants of God' (*Treatise of Melancholy*, p. 229).

27. Schmidt, quoting Greenham (*Melancholy and the Care of the Soul*, pp. 64–65).

28. Robert Weimann, 'Mimesis in Hamlet', in Patricia Parker and Geoffrey Hartman (eds), *Shakespeare and the Question of Theory*, New York, 1985, pp. 275–91. Also see J. Cox, *The Devil and the Sacred in English Drama, 1350–1640*, Cambridge, 2000.

29. Out of a voluminous literature, see Brad Gregory, 'The "true and zealouse service of God": Robert Parsons, Edmund Bunny, and *The first booke of the Christian exercise*', *Journal of Ecclesiastical History*, 45 (1994), pp. 238–68; P. Lake and M. Questier, *The Trials of Margaret Clitherow*, London, 2011, pp. 67–76; Victor Houliston, 'Why Robert Persons would not be pacified: Edmund Bunny's theft of *The Book of Resolution*', in Thomas M. McCoog (ed.), *The Reckoned Expense: Edmund Campion and the early English Jesuits*, Woodbridge, 1996, pp. 159–77.

Chapter 6

1. Shapiro, *1599*, pp. 325–26: 'It's one of the keys to understanding what makes Hamlet so distinctive: even as he paints over an earlier work of art, Shakespeare allows traces of what's been whitewashed to remain visible.'
2. Jonathan Bate, *How the Classics Made Shakespeare*, Princeton, NJ, 2019, p. 143.
3. As Jonathan Bate points out, the image of Pyrrhus standing over Priam with his sword raised is picked up in the play, in the scene in which Hamlet stands over Claudius and considers whether to kill him. Hamlet, of course, relents on Christian premises, but scarcely for Christian purposes. Bate, *How the Classics Made Shakespeare*, pp. 141–43.
4. Richard Halpern, 'The classical inheritance', in Neill and Schalkwyk (eds), *The Oxford Handbook of Shakespearean Tragedy*, pp. 19–34, quotation at p. 26.
5. Burrow, *Shakespeare and Classical Antiquity*, p. 183.
6. Halpern, 'The classical inheritance', p. 25.
7. Burrow, *Shakespeare and Classical Antiquity*, pp. 174,175. As Dodson-Robinson observes, *Hamlet* shows its hero refusing to allow what he terms 'the revenge tragedy tradition to saturate agency or determine identity' (Dodson-Robinson, ' "By a brother's hand" ', p. 97).
8. Burrow, *Shakespeare and Classical Antiquity*, p. 175.
9. Lewis, *Hamlet and the Vision of Darkness*, p. 21.
10. On Perkins on false faith, see R.T. Kendall, *Calvin and English Calvinism to 1649*, Oxford, 1980, chapter 5, 'William Perkins' doctrine of temporary faith'; Michael Winship, 'Weak Christians, backsliders, and carnal gospelers: Assurance of salvation and the pastoral origins of Puritan practical divinity in the 1580s', *Church History*, 70 (2001), pp. 462–81.

Chapter 7

1. Out of a large literature, see the seminal article by Michael Hunter, 'The problem of atheism in early modern England', *Transactions of the Royal Historical Society*, 5th series, 35 (1985), pp. 135–77.
2. *Pace* Patrick Gray, I fail to see anything coherently 'epicurean' about any of this. After all, while Hamlet wants to escape from the world of the court and from the role that fate, or perhaps his father's ghost, or God's providence, has now thrust upon him, he is tempted by the despair and self-immolation of the atheist, the apostate and the reprobate, rather than by the decorous retirement of the Epicurean. And various verbal echoes from Montaigne will not prove otherwise. See Gray's article, ' "HIDE THY SELFE": Montaigne, Hamlet and Epicurean ethics', in Patrick Gray and John Cox (eds), *Shakespeare and Renaissance Ethics*, Cambridge, 2014, pp. 213–36.
3. Thus, it seems to me simply not true that, as Rhodri Lewis claims, Hamlet 'is only paying lip service to the immortality of the soul in moments of mortal crisis' (Lewis, *Hamlet and the Vision of Darkness*, p. 264). This seems mistaken; the immortality of the soul, and therefore questions of salvation and damnation, appear in the play as an emergent concern, and then increasingly as a recurrent obsession, of Hamlet's. This is expressed both in a number of the play's most famous speeches, delivered by both Hamlet and Claudius, and – surely at least as important – in Hamlet's actions. And then there is the increasingly providential language on display in the latter stages of the play. For the play's first audiences, this would surely have placed questions about the ultimate destination of Hamlet's soul (and indeed of other souls) at the very centre of the action. That has not been true of all too many of the play's determinedly secular-minded modern critics.
4. Rosendale, *Theology and Agency*, p. 134.
5. Alison Thorne's claims that 'in lieu of the expected confession from Claudius, the play and its dumbshow succeed in eliciting only varying degrees of bafflement' and that Hamlet is 'still left unsure of the king's culpability and his own moral bearings' seem almost entirely off beam. Similarly wrong-headed is Rhodri Lewis' argument that since 'only Hamlet views it as indicative of guilt', Claudius' reaction 'to the play is ambiguous'. Here Lewis' logic chops his way around Horatio, taking his relative reticence as a sign of scepticism. This seems a basic mis-reading. As John Gillies remarks, throughout 'neither toady nor conspirator', Horatio necessarily 'walks a fine line' (Gillies, 'The question of

original sin in *Hamlet*', *Shakespeare Quarterly*, 64 (2013), pp. 396–424, at p. 420). Their previous conversation makes the stakes quite clear. There they agree to 'rivet' their eyes on Claudius' face during the performance and Horatio undertakes that if 'a steal aught the while this play is playing / And scape detected, I will pay the theft' [Q2, III, ii, 84–85]. If anything, Q1 is even more explicit, for there Horatio proclaims that 'mine eyes shall still be on his face / And not the smallest alteration in him but I shall note it' [Q1, 9, 6–7]. After that, the exchange between Horatio and Hamlet – 'Didst perceive?' 'Very well my lord' / 'Upon the talk of poisoning' / 'I did very well note him' [Q2, III, ii, 280–282; F, III, ii, 279–280] – leaves precious little room for ambiguity or interpretation. It seems to me that we are meant to assume that Horatio clearly shares Hamlet's perception of Claudius' guilt – as, of course, by this point does the audience, who in the first scene of act III have already been alerted by Claudius himself to his consciousness of his own guilt. Claudius' ejaculation then – 'How smart a lash that speech doth give my conscience' [Q2, III, i, 29; F, III, i, 49–50] – very deliberately removes any doubt that the audience might have felt to this point about Claudius' identity as a murderer, or indeed about the susceptibility of his conscience to guilt and remorse about his crime; and while Claudius' response to *The Mousetrap* remains opaque to all of the other characters in the play (who have been party neither to the testimony of the ghost nor to Claudius' soliloquy), neither Hamlet nor the audience is, by this point, left in any doubt at all of the king's culpability. (The fact that these crucial lines do not figure in Q1 might be taken to imply that, since there was a version of the play without them, their inclusion in other texts was deliberately designed to gloss the effects of the play within a play in the way suggested here.) Certainly, by this stage of the action, neither the question of Claudius' guilt nor the effectiveness of the play in revealing it is called into the least question by the diverse responses of the rest of the court, whose reaction to the play has never been the point. It was, after all, on *Claudius'* face that the attention of Hamlet and Horatio had been concentrated. It is true, of course, that, despite his ecstatic reaction to the effects of the play, Hamlet's new certainty concerning Claudius' guilt does not, and, as it turns out, cannot, confer a similar certainty about any of the other (really crucial) questions of conscience that still confront him; none of which, *pace* Thorne, concerns issues of visual perspective (Alison Thorne, *Vision and Rhetoric in Shakespeare: Looking through language*, Basingstoke, 2000, p. 129). Similarly misguided is the reasoning of William Hamlin, who cites a recent RSC production as suggesting that the play within a play has 'not so much exposed Claudius as that Claudius has exposed Hamlet, obtaining conclusive evidence of his hostility', which, of course, he has. But since that would only be the case if Claudius recognized his own murder of old Hamlet in the murder just played out before him, for both Hamlet and the audience this is a distinction without a difference (William Hamlin, *Montaigne's English Journey*, Oxford, 2016, p. 122). Moreover, despite the fact that, as Lewis observes, 'Hamlet has betrayed himself and his intentions to Claudius' and that 'Claudius now knows that Hamlet suspects him of murder', the king's response is not (yet) to arrange Hamlet's death, but rather to kneel in prayer, in a desperate attempt to repent for his crying sins, which the play within the play has brought home to him in such a crushing fashion. It is only *after* this attempt at repentance has conclusively failed that Claudius seeks to secure his own political future by doing away definitively with Hamlet. All of which can only confirm the audience in its conviction that the play within the play has indeed activated Claudius' guilty conscience, in ways that definitively signal his guilt to those – like themselves and Hamlet – already in the know, albeit not to any of the other courtiers, or to Gertrude, who, having no knowledge of the ghost, or of the real circumstances of old Hamlet's death, have no reason whatsoever to suspect Claudius of murder. To all this can be added the virtual impossibility of playing this scene in a way that does not register Claudius' guilt – a point made by Michael Dobson in his brilliant review of Lewis' book (*London Review of Books*, vol. 40, no. 17, 13 September 2018, pp. 7–9). Since we are, after all, dealing here with a play, not a treatise, such considerations might be thought to matter.

6. Margreta de Grazia observes that 'Hamlet's desire in the prayer scene to damn a soul to eternal pain is the most extreme form of evil imaginable in a society that gave even its most heinous felons the opportunity to repent before execution', although she does *not* go on to note that that is precisely the opportunity, which, despite his own best/worst intentions, Hamlet confers upon Claudius. Hamlet does so first, by staging *The Murder of Gonzago*, and then by refusing to dispatch Claudius while he is at prayer (de Grazia, *Hamlet without Hamlet*, p. 188). In neither case is he intending to offer Claudius the chance of a saving repentance, but as Claudius' reaction shows, that is precisely what Hamlet is doing.

7. On this, see Armstrong, *Shakespeare and the Mysteries of God's Judgment*: 'The motives that prevent Hamlet's committing a damnable act are themselves damnable. Hamlet's goodness and nobility . . . do not stop him murdering a man at prayer. His evil and ignobility do, and when we see human evil result in good, we may justifiably suspect that we are being shown an example of providence at work' (p. 113).

8. On this, see Jesse Lander, *Inventing Polemic*, Cambridge, 2006, p. 142. Thus, it is simply not true that 'after working his way through the soteriological implications of his predicament, Claudius opts to disregard them' (Lewis, *Hamlet and the Vision of Darkness*, p. 264). Rather he finds himself unable effectually to act upon them.

9. To quote Armstrong again, 'Hamlet's determination to damn Claudius is thus ironically employed to permit his enemy to seek salvation'. 'The Mousetrap presents Claudius with alternatives – the Christian and the Machiavellian. He proves incapable of the Christian', but 'superbly capable of the Machiavellian' (*Shakespeare and the Mysteries of God's Judgment*, pp. 114–15). Hamlet, however, eschews – indeed, does not even notice – the Machiavellian imperatives that might shape his behaviour, if he were a different person, but rather continues to pursue a distinctively religious, indeed a bracingly evangelical, agenda towards his mother; albeit one riven with error, false zeal and potentially damning misapprehension.

10. Gillies, 'The question of original sin in *Hamlet*', pp. 410–11.

11. Cf. Mercer, *Hamlet and the Acting of Revenge*, p. 217, where he observes of this scene that 'Hamlet's struggle is to change not himself but his mother. It is not he that must be, like Atreus, "replete with monster more" but she that must be brought to a knowledge of herself. And it is impossible not to feel that for him this is the only performance, the only setting-up of a glass, that really matters.' Also see p. 222, 'Hamlet turns now upon his mother with all the fierce conviction of a castigating preacher determined to keep the squirming sinner firmly impaled upon the hook of his reproach.'

12. For an insightful discussion of Gertrude's spiritual status, see Gillies, 'The question of original sin in Hamlet', pp. 411–12.

13. Bright, *Treatise of Melancholy*, p. 216. It was with the fate of such people in mind that some of the more evangelically minded of the murder pamphlets portrayed those murderers whose crimes were discovered and who were therefore forced – in prison and indeed on the gallows – to confront their desperate spiritual condition and, thus enabled, to achieve a true saving repentance, not only (or even mainly) as victims of God's justice, but rather as beneficiaries of his mercy. They were certainly far better off than averagely sinful professors who died in their own beds, blissfully unaware of the extent and nature of their sins and consequently of their urgent need for a soul-shattering repentance and true conversion, if they were to be saved. As one (un)fortunate felon was told by one of the ministers attending him on the scaffold, it was better by far to go to heaven from the gallows than to hell from a feather bed.

14. In Q1, many of the characters have different names from those ascribed to essentially the same character functions in Q2 and the Folio. I refer here to 'Gertrede' in Q1 to distinguish her from the character 'Gertrude' in Q2 and the Folio.

15. For the crucial acknowledgement that, despite his intentions, Hamlet's actions open up the possibility of a potentially saving repentance for Claudius, see Tiffany, 'Hamlet, reconciliation and the just state', p. 115. Rather bizarrely, Tiffany attributes these effects to the potential beneficence of the ghost. Thus, while I am in entire agreement with Russell M. Hillier that Hamlet is in some sense seeking to convert a range of characters, Gertrude among them, by confronting them with an image of their own corruption, I cannot agree that 'Gertrude is Hamlet's one success at conversion'. In order to make that case, he has to argue that, in her repeated declarations to Claudius 'that Hamlet is as mad as the contending sea and wind', Gertrude might conceivably not be betraying, but rather honouring, Hamlet's request that she preserve the rumour that 'he is "essentially" mad and not "mad in craft"' – a reading which I find even less persuasive than Hillier (with his tell-tale recourse to the weasel word 'conceivably') does himself. See Russell M. Hillier, 'Hamlet the rough-hewer: Moral agency and the consolations of Reformation thought', in Gray and Cox (eds), *Shakespeare and Renaissance Ethics*, pp. 159–85, quotation at pp. 171, 172. In fact, all of Hamlet's 'evangelical efforts' in this regard are a bust.

16. Margreta de Grazia has commented upon the remarkable extent to which commentary on the play is dominated by the question of 'Hamlet's delay'. Indeed, she goes so far as to assert that the acceptance

of that 'single question', 'from one generation to the next', as '*the* question to ask of the play is a unique phenomenon in the history of criticism'. 'Even among today's most theoretically sophisticated literary critics,' she writes, 'it is hard to find a reading that does not propose or imply a solution.' Indeed, de Grazia suggests that the prominence of the problem of delay has been the reason for the play's extraordinary capacity to attract or elicit new modes of analysis. 'There is now a long tradition in which critics identify Hamlet's delay as the play's problem and propose a new disorder to account for it, often drawing upon the latest theories in philosophy, psychology, and psychoanalysis, discrediting the proposals of their predecessors by showing how more and different aspects of Hamlet's behaviour can be explained by their diagnosis of the problem . . . Through this question, *Hamlet* is continually reopened to yield a different problem which can in turn account differently for varying textual details. When organized around it, the play lends itself to infinite reprogramming: any theory of what makes a subject, however construed, tick (or stop ticking) can be fed into the machinery of the play to set in motion some measure of its inexhaustible verbal energies' (de Grazia, *Hamlet without Hamlet*, pp. 158, 170). De Grazia is here drawing on the work of Empson (*Essays on Shakespeare*, esp. pp. 80–81).

17. Rosendale, *Theology and Agency*, p. 136.

18. de Grazia, *Hamlet without Hamlet*, pp. 164–65. Also see Weimann, *Shakespeare and the Popular Tradition in the Theater*, pp. 116–60. For one example among many, see, for instance, Andrew Gurr, *Hamlet and the Distracted Globe*, Edinburgh, 1978, p. 52: 'He does not pause out of doubt, nor from a vicious desire to damn Claudius as totally as he can, which is what he tells himself is his reason for hesitating. Rather he pauses because to kill Claudius at this point would be a furtive and trivial act . . . It would not acknowledge the stature of Claudius' misdeed nor the proper immensity of the struggle the two adversaries have started on.' Similarly, Rhodri Lewis is certain – because otherwise his own argument makes no sense – that Hamlet's 'words comprise a post-factum justification for failing to do that which he, at some level, already knows to be beyond him' (Lewis, *Hamlet and the Vision of Darkness*, p. 264).

19. Gray, '"HIDE THY SELFE"', p. 223.

20. See de Grazia, *Hamlet without Hamlet*, pp. 193–94, for the claim that the 'prayer-scene' represents a 'conspicuous forestalling of the climactic action'.

21. It is worth noting that in having Horatio give a much-abbreviated account of Hamlet's ship-board adventures, Q1 in effect downplays the role of providence in bringing about Hamlet's return to Denmark. Having been told by Horatio that Hamlet 'had his father's seal' 'by great chance', Gertrede's comment that 'thanks be to heaven for blessing of the Prince!' together with Claudius' later expostulation 'Hamlet from England! Is it possible?', *might* just be thought to gesture in a providential direction; but if so, the gesture is an extremely weak one [Q1, 14, 29, 31; 15, 1].

22. Cf. Alan Sinfield, 'Hamlet's special providence', *Shakespeare Survey*, 33 (1980), pp. 89–97; also see Fredson Bowers, 'The moment of final suspense in *Hamlet*: "We defy augury"', in his *Hamlet as Minister and Scourge*, Charlottesville, VA, 1989, pp. 114–22. For a very different take, see Mercer, *Hamlet and the Acting of Revenge*, which consistently discusses this aspect of the plot under the heading of 'fortune', 'chance' or 'fate' – noting, for instance, of Hamlet's refusal to kill Claudius at prayer, 'that this moment of ironic frustration marks the beginning of the process whereby he [Shakespeare] employs, again and again, the chances of Fortune to rescue his hero from the annihilating necessities of revenge, to preserve him for some far more resonant end' (p. 216). Or again on p. 224, where he observes that 'as a revenger Hamlet was weighed down with the burden of an intolerable responsibility, but now, as the victim of another's plot he is free to engage with the chances of Fate'. Or again at p. 237, he describes Hamlet's rescue by the pirate ship as 'this new movement of Fortune'. 'Shakespeare . . . makes the escape of his hero as fortuitous as possible. The pirate ship comes out of nowhere but his own desire, like a device in a romance. As we have noted already, chance in tragedy is usually fatal, not in the least obliging . . . But here chance brings a ship full of "thieves of mercy" from over the horizon to pluck the hero from his doom.' Similarly, see Lewis' remark that 'for all the heat with which Hamlet protests the providential integrity of his behavior after the murder of Polonius, the vocabulary and assumptions with which he does so are incontestably in the domain of Fortuna' (Lewis, *Hamlet and the Vision of Darkness*, p. 293). This seems mistaken; or at least there seems small enough textual warrant for such a consistent emphasis on fortune or chance or fate rather than on providence. There is nothing innocent or inadvertent

about Mercer's choice of key terms here; rather it underpins what remains, for all its acuity, the consistently 'secular' or a-religious tenor of his analysis. Not, of course, that an analysis of such events in terms of 'fortune' was unavailable to Shakespeare, to his protagonist, Hamlet, or indeed to the play's first audiences. It is just that the play itself does nothing to induce such a reading of events and Hamlet himself seems entirely free from any such hermeneutic tendency or temptation. Lewis' remark that 'it takes a special kind of credulity to discern the workings of providence . . . through the interstices of the Danish court' betrays a complete lack of understanding of how contemporaries tended to discern the workings of providence in precisely the tergiversations of political change, confessional conflict and events and outcomes that we would attribute to mere contingency. See, among many others, Thomas, *Religion and the Decline of Magic*, chapter 4, and more recently, Alexandra Walsham, *Providence in Early Modern England*, Oxford, 1999, passim.

23. Prosser, *Hamlet and Revenge*, p. 221, fn. 9.
24. Michael Bristol, *Carnival and Theatre*, London, 1985, p. 187.
25. de Grazia, *Hamlet without Hamlet*, p. 139.
26. B. Gellert, 'The iconography of melancholy in the graveyard scene of *Hamlet*', *Studies in Philology*, 67 (1970), pp. 57–66.
27. See Prosser, *Hamlet and Revenge*, pp. 221–26.
28. de Grazia, *Hamlet without Hamlet*, p. 138.
29. Cf. Hillier, 'Hamlet the rough-hewer', p. 179.
30. Given the ambiguities surrounding Hamlet's madness, it is by no means clear that Armstrong is right to state baldly that 'this [apology] is a lie' (*Shakespeare and the Mysteries of God's Judgment*, p. 120).
31. See, for instance, the comments of Mercer, *Hamlet and the Acting of Revenge*: 'the real shape of Hamlet's action is almost a reverse image of that of the heroes of the more conventional tragedies. Othello and Anthony are taken by their experiences not merely from prosperity to misery but from a unity and certainty of self, a heroic integrity, to an intolerable forfeiture of those things. But Hamlet's loss of himself, his reduction from that epitome of noble youth . . . was almost complete at his play's beginning.' All this ensures that 'he has moved in the end not from heroic coherence to tragic dissolution but in the exactly opposite direction'. On this basis, Mercer feels able to conclude that 'not only is Hamlet not a revenge tragedy; it is hardly a tragedy at all' (pp. 245–46).
32. Perry, 'Seneca and the modernity of *Hamlet*'.
33. See Shapiro, *1599*, pp. 350–51.
34. Gillies, 'The question of original sin in *Hamlet*', pp. 420–21.
35. As George Walton Williams puts it, Hamlet 'has accomplished the same thing that the Ghost wanted accomplished, but he has done so in his own way and for his own purposes' (Williams, 'Hamlet and the dread command', in John M. Mucciolo (ed.), *Shakespeare's Universe: Renaissance ideas and conventions, essays in honour of W.R. Elton*, Aldershot, 1996, pp. 60–68, quotation at p. 66.
36. Lewis, *Hamlet and the Vision of Darkness*, p. 128.
37. Dodson-Robinson, ' "By a brother's hand" ', pp. 97–98.
38. Cf. Prosser, *Hamlet and Revenge*, pp. 214–15.
39. P.K. Ayers, 'Reading, writing and *Hamlet*', *Shakespeare Quarterly*, 44 (1993), pp. 423–39, quotation at p. 432.
40. Lewis, *Hamlet and the Vision of Darkness*, pp. 152–53.
41. Lander, *Inventing Polemic*, p. 133. See Knapp, *Shakespeare's Tribe*, p. 53.
42. See Knapp, *Shakespeare's Tribe*, p. 53.
43. As Eric Dodson-Robinson observes, 'although Hamlet does eventually kill Claudius . . . it is not clear that he does so to avenge his father, or that his actions have anything to do with the Ghost's command or infernal or divine machinations. Hamlet stabs Claudius only after seeing his own mother murdered by poison and learning that Claudius is to blame in the plot, which has also inflicted on Hamlet a mortal wound' (Dodson-Robinson, ' "By a brother's hand" ', p. 95).
44. The title of a famous pamphlet of 1657, probably by Edward Saxby, urging the legitimacy of assassinating the tyrant and usurper Oliver Cromwell.
45. Peter Ure, *Elizabethan and Jacobean Drama: Critical essays*, ed. J.C. Maxwell, Liverpool, 1974, pp. 40, 42.
46. Dutton, '*Hamlet* and succession', p. 186.

Chapter 8

1. Stephen Greenblatt, *Hamlet in Purgatory*, Princeton, NJ, 2001, pp. 73–76, 84–86.
2. Chapman, 'Ophelia's "Old Lauds"', p. 112.
3. Anthony Low, '*Hamlet* and the ghost of purgatory: Intimations of killing the father', *English Literary Renaissance*, 29 (1999), pp. 443–67, quote at p. 459.
4. Chapman, 'Ophelia's "Old Lauds"', esp. p. 115, where Chapman speculates that 'in effect, the earthly father's physical absence impels her [Ophelia] imaginatively into a bygone world in which the spiritual Father is more physically present' in the mass.
5. However, as Armstrong points out, the question of whether, through his failure to repent, Claudius 'further damns himself' or 'his prior damnation by God is further justified' is left open for the viewer or reader to decide (Armstrong, *Shakespeare and the Mysteries of God's Judgment*, p. 114).
6. Hillier, 'Hamlet the rough-hewer', p. 181.
7. Thus, as Armstrong observes, 'if the God of the play' is conceived in one way, then 'he has foreseen that Claudius will be unable to yield his consent to God's summons, but the failure is of Claudius' will, and God's justice working through Hamlet presents Claudius with this opportunity to exercise his free will. However, this mysterious but comparatively benevolent deity is not insisted upon by the play. It is simultaneously and equally possible to interpret Claudius' failure to repent as evidence that God . . . has willed the reprobation of Claudius, willed his attempt to repent and its failure, withheld from eternity the grace that Claudius vainly seeks' (Armstrong, *Shakespeare and the Mysteries of God's Judgment*, p. 111). I thus do not share Lander's conclusion that, while Q1 is 'conformable to what has been described as a Calvinist consensus', Q2 is not 'susceptible to a Calvinist interpretation'. I think rather that, for any theologically informed contemporary, the play virtually demanded a *predestinarian* reading and that while such a contemporary could have read it in a Calvinist sense, the play, certainly in its Q2 and Folio versions, is rather more readily accommodated within a proto-Arminian version of the theology of grace than a 'Calvinist' one (Lander, *Inventing Polemic*, p. 124).
8. On the 1595/96 disputes, see H.C. Porter, *Reformation and Reaction in Tudor Cambridge*, Cambridge, 1958, chapters 13–17, and Lake, *Moderate Puritans*, chapter 9. On Andrewes, see Nicholas Tyacke, 'Lancelot Andrewes and the myth of Anglicanism', in Lake and Questier (eds), *Conformity and Orthodoxy in the English Church*. Also see P. Lake, 'The Anglican Moment? Hooker and the ideological watershed of the 1590s', in S. Platten (ed.), *Anglicanism and the Western Christian Tradition*, Norwich, 2003, pp. 90–121, esp. pp. 109–10. Cf. Rosendale, *Theology and Agency*, pp. 141–42.
9. While it is true that, as Lewis (*Hamlet and the Vision of Darkness*, p. 287) puts it, 'Hamlet himself has no interest in theological nicety', the same is certainly not true of the play or, very likely, of at least some members of its first audiences, whom the play at the very least enables, if not invites, to think about the theological significance of what they are watching. Hamlet is shown experiencing the existential or emotional consequences of various religious opinions and illusions, and hacking his way through a miasma of despair and doubt, of false zeal and mistaken assurance, to something like, if not certainty, then a settled assurance about the entirely unequal relationship between his own purposes and plans and those of God. The audience is left to make theological sense of that process. In thinking about these issues, it helps to distinguish between Hamlet the character, *Hamlet* the play, Shakespeare the author of the play, and the ways in which said play might be thought to have played upon the interests and circumstances of its first audiences. After all, Hamlet is not a poet, a philosopher or a historian, but rather a character in a play, and Shakespeare an author of plays. The fact that many of Hamlet's observations are commonplace, confused and/or contradictory is a reflection of his situation within the play and of his reactions thereto. They are not best marked out of ten as performances of 'poetry', 'history' or 'philosophy'. To do so rather misses the point of the whole enterprise.
10. Lander, *Inventing Polemic*, chapter 3, quotations at pp. 128 and 139. Lander claims that that topic was 'handled in an oblique fashion' in order to appeal to 'the unperturbed literate gentleman, who can stand above, or rather sit quietly at a remove from, the fray, taking pleasure in speculation and drawing edification from the undermining of dogmatic positions' (p. 139). He is, of course, quite right to point out that plays were not works of theology, and that *Hamlet* was not a piece of religious polemic: '*Hamlet* emerges out of polemical culture, a culture that helps account for the contemporary popularity of and

fascination with *Hamlet*, yet neither the play itself nor its printed versions are polemics' (p. 141). However, I do not see why a theologically informed or engaged contemporary would have seen the play's treatment of these themes as particularly 'oblique' or 'at a remove from' what were, after all, issues of immediate contemporary interest and contest and indeed, on one (prevalent) view of the matter, quite literally questions of spiritual life and death. On the contrary, I think one could argue that the play's treatment of those issues, which (certainly in Q2) are located at the very centre both of the plot and of the characters' consciousness, was remarkably direct and extensive, and that the clown's summary of those issues in act V, which Lander dismisses as 'deliriously confused and confusing' (p.133), was in fact designed directly and rather precisely to advert to that fact.

11. Rosendale, *Theology and Agency*, p. 136.
12. See Dutton, '*Hamlet* and succession'.
13. Rosendale, *Theology and Agency*, p. 137.
14. Lewis notes that Hamlet 'first turns providential immediately after that revenant of medieval Catholicism, the Ghost, finally departs the stage for good'; but for reasons best known to himself, he is convinced that 'the significance of this moment is far from confessional' (Lewis, *Hamlet and the Vision of Darkness*, p. 286).
15. For the anti-puritanism in *Measure for Measure*, see Lake and Questier, *The Antichrist's Lewd Hat*, chapter 15.
16. See Dutton, '*Hamlet* and succession'.
17. Lake, *How Shakespeare Put Politics on the Stage*, part VII.
18. On this *topos*, see Gordon Braden, 'Fame, eternity and Shakespeare's Romans', in Gray and Cox (eds), *Shakespeare and Renaissance Ethics*, pp. 37–55.
19. Cf. Braden, 'Fame, eternity and Shakespeare's Romans'.
20. Maynard Mack, *Everybody's Shakespeare: Reflections chiefly on tragedies*, Lincoln, NE, 1994, p. 125. See the discussion in Hillier, 'Hamlet the rough-hewer', pp. 179–83.
21. Rosendale, *Theology and Agency*, pp. 140–41.
22. Sinfield, 'Hamlet's special providence', p. 95. Sinfield argues that 'commentators have disagreed about Hamlet's attitude to providence because it is confused, but I believe purposefully. Shakespeare is exploiting the contradictions in Stoicism and the embarrassments of Calvinism.' All that may well be true enough. I am merely suggesting that that exploitation had a more coherently and pointedly (anti-puritan and quite possibly anti-Calvinist) polemical thrust than Sinfield's analysis allows. The result, therefore, is not so much 'confused' as perfectly poised between two mutually exclusive positions. The quotes are from Calvin's *Institutes of the Christian Religion*.
23. Armstrong, *Shakespeare and the Mysteries of God's Judgment*, p. 116.
24. Cf. Williams, 'Hamlet and the dread command', where, commenting on V, ii, 64–68, he remarks that 'though in the first of these lines Hamlet mentions the death of the previous monarch . . . in the second he has begun to talk about himself and his readiness to avenge threats to his own proper life. Hamlet's omission of mention of his father at the end of the play contrasts with Laertes' specific reference to his father and Fortinbras' to his ancestors. Hamlet has not remembered his father's Ghost' (p. 66).
25. I use the term 'relative indeterminacy' because while I do think that all of these crucial topics are left equally unresolved by the play, on each of them it leans towards one resolution rather than another: on the current reading, towards a vision of the ghost as a devil, towards a final rupture with the old religion, towards a vision of Hamlet as saved and towards a decidedly proto-Arminian (rather than a high Calvinist) account of predestination, but always with the alternative account available to the viewer or reader inclined to take the opposite view. Hence, *pace* Knapp and Lander, while the play's approach to these issues is anything but straightforwardly partisan, still less polemical, its effects on the more theologically sophisticated or committed members of its first audiences are unlikely to have been anything like unifying, still less 'reconciliatory'.

Conclusion

1. Moschovakis, ' "Irreligious piety" '.
2. Weimann, *Shakespeare and the Popular Tradition in the Theater*, pp. 149–50, 159–60, where Hamlet and Richard of Gloucester are compared as vice figures and Richard of Gloucester is identified as

'pointing the way' towards 'the first great artistic portrait of a nascently tragic figure'. For another discussion of the development of the soliloquy from Richard III through Brutus to Hamlet, see Lee, *Shakespeare's Hamlet and the Controversies of Self*, p. 182.

3. Weimann, *Shakespeare and the Popular Tradition in the Theater*, p. 159.
4. Ibid., p. 150.
5. de Grazia, *Hamlet without Hamlet*, pp. 193–96, quotes at pp. 193, 196.
6. Certainly, the play's gestures towards purgatory, predestination and the divide between Catholicism and Protestantism are rather more clearly discernible where it really matters – that is to say, on the textual and performative surface of the play – than is the allusive mood music so lovingly recuperated by Professor McCullough out of certain passages from various late medieval liturgical and scriptural texts. See Peter McCullough, 'Christmas at Elsinore', *Essays in Criticism*, 58 (2008), pp. 311–32, quotations at p. 311.
7. Lake, *How Shakespeare Put Politics on the Stage*, chapter 24.
8. A case that is, if anything, strengthened by Dutton's informed speculation that Q2 was a version of the play rewritten for court performance in 1603/04. See Dutton, '*Hamlet* and succession'.
9. As Gillies puts it, it is possible to see Hamlet as 'elect in a double sense, as the rightful prince of Denmark and the Pauline athlete whose final deference to providence invites an opportunity for lawful violence that he could never have foreseen if left to his own devices' (Gillies, 'The question of original sin in *Hamlet*', p. 424).
10. Lake, *How Shakespeare Put Politics on the Stage*.
11. For a discussion of the polyvalent nature of the end of *Richard III*, see Lake, *How Shakespeare Put Politics on the Stage*, pp. 166–70.

Further reading

Allen, Megan Elizabeth, ' "Titus unkind": Shakespeare's revision of Virgil's Aeneas in *Titus Andronicus*', in P. Holland (ed.), *Shakespeare Survey 70: Creating Shakespeare*, Cambridge, 2017

Armstrong, Robert G., *Shakespeare and the Mysteries of God's Judgment*, Athens, GA, 1976

Bate, Jonathan, *How the Classics Made Shakespeare*, Princeton, NJ, 2019

Bowers, Fredson, 'The moment of final suspense in *Hamlet*: "we defy augury" ', in Fredson Bowers, *Hamlet as Minister and Scourge*, Charlottesville, VA, 1989

Bradshaw, Graham, *Shakespeare's Skepticism*, Ithaca, NY, 1987

Burrow, Colin, *Shakespeare and Classical Antiquity*, Oxford, 2013

Chapman, Alison, 'Ophelia's "Old Lauds": Madness and hagiography in *Hamlet*', *Medieval and Renaissance Drama in England*, 20 (2007), pp. 111–35

Crosbie, Christopher, 'Fixing moderation: *Titus Andronicus* and the Aristotelian determination of value', *Shakespeare Quarterly*, 58 (2007), pp. 147–73

Culhane, Peter, 'Livy and *Titus Andronicus*', *English*, 55 (2006), pp. 1–13

Curtis, Perry, 'Seneca and the modernity of *Hamlet*', *Illinois Classical Studies*, 40 (2015), pp. 407–29

Curtis, Perry, 'Seneca and English political culture', in Malcolm Smuts (ed.), *The Oxford Handbook of the Age of Shakespeare*, Oxford, 2016

de Grazia, Margreta, *Hamlet without Hamlet*, Cambridge, 2007

Dickson, Vernon Guy, ' "A pattern, precedent and lively warrant": Emulation, rhetoric and cruel propriety in *Titus Andronicus*', *Renaissance Quarterly*, 62 (2009), pp. 376–409

Dodson-Robinson, Eric, ' "By a brother's hand": Betrayal and brotherhood in Shakespeare's *Hamlet* and Senecan tragedy', in Kristina Mendicino and Betiel Wasihun (eds), *Playing False: Representations of betrayal*, Bern, 2013

Dutton, Richard, '*Hamlet* and succession', in S. Doran and P. Kewes (eds), *Doubtful and Dangerous: The question of succession in late Elizabethan England*, Manchester, 2014

Gardner, Helen, 'The historical approach to *Hamlet*', in J. Jump (ed.), *Shakespeare: Hamlet, a casebook*, London, 1968

Gellert, B., 'The iconography of melancholy in the graveyard scene of *Hamlet*', *Studies in Philology*, 67 (1970), pp. 57–66

Gillies, John, 'The question of original sin in *Hamlet*', *Shakespeare Quarterly*, 64 (2013), pp. 396–424

Gray Patrick and John Cox (eds), *Shakespeare and Renaissance Ethics*, Cambridge, 2014

Greenblatt, Stephen, *Hamlet in Purgatory*, Princeton, NJ, 2001

Hadfield, Andrew, 'The power and rights of the crown in *Hamlet* and *King Lear*: "The King – the King's to blame" ', *Review of English Studies*, 54 (2003), pp. 566–86

Hillier, Russell M., 'Hamlet the rough-hewer: Moral agency and the consolations of Reformation thought', in Patrick Gray and John Cox (eds), *Shakespeare and Renaissance Ethics*, Cambridge, 2014

Hofele, Andreas, *Stage, Stake and Scaffold*, Oxford, 2011

Hutson, Lorna, 'Rethinking the "Spectacle of the Scaffold": Juridical epistemologies and English revenge tragedy', *Representations*, 89 (2005), pp. 30–58

FURTHER READING

James, Heather, *Shakespeare's Troy*, Cambridge, 1997

Kahn, Coppelia, *Roman Shakespeare: Warriors, wounds and women*, London, 1997

Kiséry, András, *Hamlet's Moment*, Oxford, 2016

Klause, John, 'Politics, heresy and martyrdom in Shakespeare's sonnet 124 and *Titus Andronicus*', in James Schiffer (ed.), *Shakespeare's Sonnets: Critical essays*, New York, 1999

Kurland, Stuart M., '*Hamlet* and the Scottish succession', *Studies in English Literature 1500–1900*, 34 (1994), pp. 279–300

Lake, Peter, *Moderate Puritans and the Elizabethan Church*, Cambridge, 1982

Lake, Peter, *How Shakespeare Put Politics on the Stage: Power and succession in the history plays*, London and New Haven, 2016

Lander, Jesse, *Inventing Polemic*, Cambridge, 2006

Lewis, Rhodri, *Hamlet and the Vision of Darkness*, Princeton, NJ, 2017

Low, Anthony, '*Hamlet* and the ghost of purgatory: Intimations of killing the father', *English Literary Renaissance*, 29 (1999), pp. 443–67

Marshall, Peter, *Beliefs and the Dead in Reformation England*, Oxford, 2002

McCullough, Peter, 'Christmas at Elsinore', *Essays in Criticism*, 58 (2008), pp. 311–32

Mercer, Peter, *Hamlet and the Acting of Revenge*, Basingstoke, 1987

Moschovakis, Nicholas, ' "Irreligious piety" and Christian history: Persecution as pagan anachronism in *Titus Andronicus*', *Shakespeare Quarterly*, 53 (2002), pp. 460–86

Neill, Michael, 'The designs of *Titus Andronicus*', in M. Neill and D. Schalwyk (eds), *The Oxford Handbook of Shakespearean Tragedy*, Oxford, 2016

Porter, H.C., *Reformation and Reaction in Tudor Cambridge*, Cambridge, 1958, chapters 13–17

Prosser, Eleanor, *Hamlet and Revenge*, Stanford, CA, 1971

Rosendale, Timothy, *Theology and Agency in Early Modern Literature*, Cambridge, 2018

Schmidt, Jeremy, *Melancholy and the Care of the Soul: Religion, moral philosophy and madness in early modern England*, Aldershot, 2007

Shagan, Ethan, *The Rule of Moderation*, Cambridge, 2012

Shapiro, James, *1599: A year in the life of William Shakespeare*, London, 2005

Sinfield, Alan, 'Hamlet's special providence', *Shakespeare Survey*, 33 (1980), pp. 89–97

Spencer, T.J.B., 'Shakespeare and the Elizabethan Romans', *Shakespeare Survey*, 10 (1957), pp. 27–38

St Hilaire, Danielle, 'Allusion and sacrifice in *Titus Andronicus*', *Studies in English Literature 1500–1900*, 49 (2009), pp. 311–31

Thomas, K.V., *Religion and the Decline of Magic*, London, 1973

Tyacke, Nicholas, *Anti-Calvinists: The rise of English Arminianism, c. 1590–1640*, Oxford, 1987

Waith, Eugene, 'The metamorphosis of violence in *Titus Andronicus*', *Shakespeare Survey*, 10 (1957), pp. 39–49

Walsham, Alexandra, *Providence in Early Modern England*, Oxford, 1999

Index